I0800480

IMAGES
of America

ALLAIRE

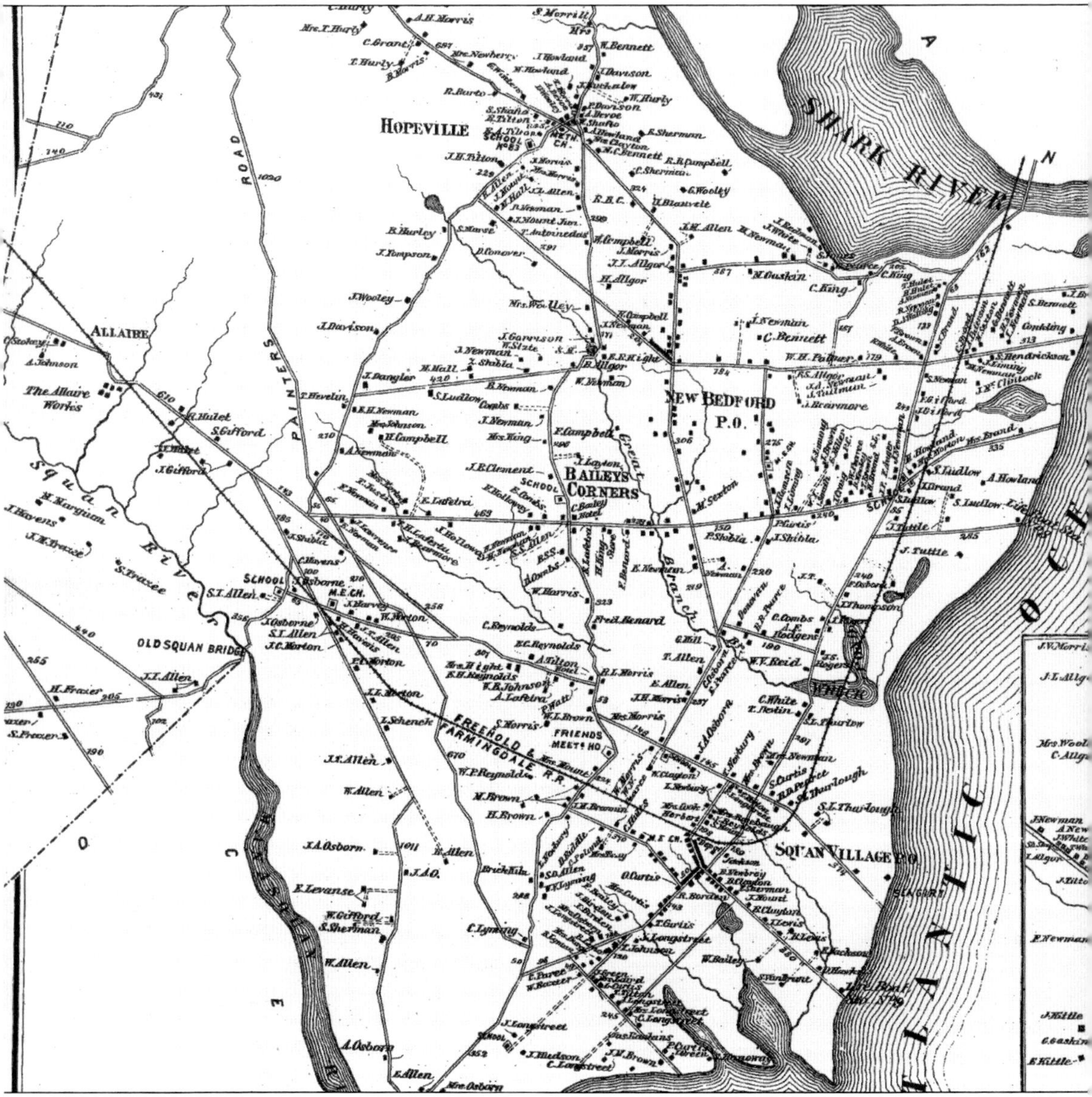

This 1873 Wall Township map was published by Beers, Comstock and Cline of New York City in *Atlas of Monmouth County*. Allaire is located in southern Monmouth County of Wall Township (to the left in this map). "The Pines are of the wildest portion in the state. Except for settlements along the railroad, the forest is broken only by a few lonely roads—abandoned old-time stage routes and lumber tracks; by narrow swift, resinous-colored streams flowing silently through the colonnades of pines, or the gloomy labyrinths of cedar swamps, toward the system of bays to the east or toward Delaware Bay; or by deserted, decaying shanties, grouped around the ruins of the forges which this region harbored in the days long since passed when the manufacture of iron from bog ore was one of the most important industries in the country. The most extensive and picturesque ruins of this kind are Allaire, where the only stack still standing among the Pines may be seen—a pathetic reminder of the spirit of enterprise which created the place and of the activity whose sounds once echoed through the silent forest." —*Jersey Coast Pines*, by Gustav Kobbe, 1889.

IMAGES
of America

ALLAIRE

Hance Morton Sitkus

ARCADIA
PUBLISHING

ISBN 978-0-7385-1083-5

Published by Arcadia Publishing
Charleston, South Carolina

Printed in the United States of America

Library of Congress Catalog Card Number: 2002107832

For all general information contact Arcadia Publishing at:
Telephone 843-853-2070
Fax 843-853-0044
E-mail sales@arcadiapublishing.com
For customer service and orders:
Toll-Free 1-888-313-2665

Visit us on the Internet at www.arcadiapublishing.com

Dedicated to those relatives who have gone before me, those who are with me now, and all those to come. A special dedication to my great-grandmother Mabel Frostick Kessler and grandmother Evelyn Kessler Morton. These two people have meant so much to me and have greatly impacted my life.

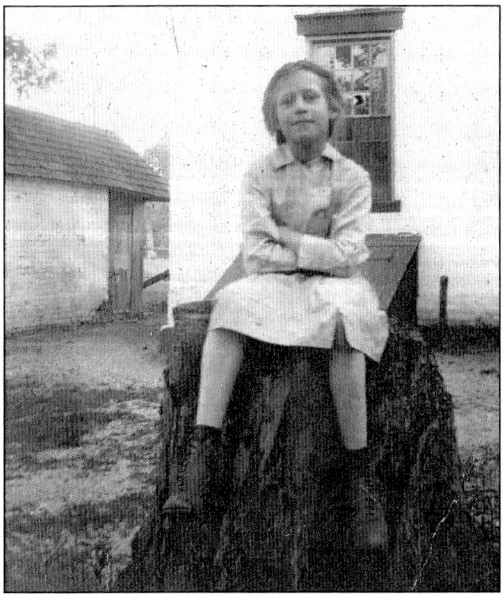

A young Mabel Frostick Kessler sits outside the dormitory at Allaire Village.

Contents

ACKNOWLEDGMENTS

My encouragement to put this book together stemmed from a photography contest I coordinated in the fall of 2000 while serving as the exhibit coordinator at Historic Allaire Village's Enameling Building. Featured were current photographs of the village, blended with photographs from the village's archives and my own collection. At the awards ceremony, an attendee mentioned, "Wouldn't it be great to have this exhibit in a book?" After additional years of research, photograph acquisitions, interviews, and helping hands, I think I have finally completed the task. This book is really a culmination of research and writing since my youth.

It is great to have a family that has lived and worked in the Allaire area since the 1600s. These relatives were great photographers. Most of the relatives who took these photographs have passed away, but their albums have been preserved. I would like to thank my mother, Linda Ann Morton Sitkus, William and Doris Kessler, Lenora Tatum, and especially my grandmother Evelyn Kessler Morton for sharing tons of family information and photographs. These people are living time capsules. My grandmother put me in contact with some great people and even went on fact-finding missions herself. Thanks also to the many photographers and publishers of the postcard views in this book.

I also found that introducing myself as a Morton, Kessler, Frostick, Allen, Gifford, and Sherman relation certainly opens some doors. I would especially like to thank the following people for their willingness and kindness in sharing their knowledge and photography collections: Ed Brown (Monmouth Executive Airport); Louise Thompson King (Thompson Dairy Farm); Inez Smith Tice (Macauley family pictures); James Alexander Jr. (doodlebug pictures); Dick Napoliton; the Furnace Town Foundation Inc.; Friends of the Pennsylvania Railroad Museum; New Jersey Museum of Transportation; Syracuse University (Arthur Brisbane Archival Collection); Bancroft Library, University of California Berkley (William R. Hearst Archival Collection); Allaire Village Inc.; and the Division of Parks and Forestry, New Jersey State Park Service.

I could hardly believe that a real Native American used to live in a lean-to at Allaire Village during the 1930s, let alone hop on a train to sell his wares in neighboring towns. To verify this family story, I found an *Asbury Park Press* article that included an interview with Indian Joe. I repeated similar tasks to ensure accurate captions. Over the years, I have collected many newspaper clippings from the 19th and 20th centuries and have reviewed brochures on the Allaire Inn. I have also collected numerous books on Allaire Village, Arthur Brisbane, iron making, early-19th-century America, James P. Allaire and his empire, W.J. Harrison, Hal Allaire, and the Freehold and Jamesburg Agricultural Railroad. At a young age, my family taught me to appreciate history. In these past couple of months, I found myself rediscovering my collection of research materials and earlier historical writings. Acquiring even more stuff recently, to make this book complete, has been a joy.

Finally, I would like to acknowledge Felicia Martin, Lisa Flick, and Pat Brown for helping to proofread the book. Thanks also go to my coworkers and friends who offered me their support and to my mother, Linda Ann Morton Sitkus, for running my numerous errands so I could get this book done.

INTRODUCTION

"West of the marsh that girds the seashore, lies an immense sandy plain, scarcely broken by any inequalities and originally covered by a pine and scrub oak forest—a great portion of which has been once, and some of it twice, cut over. There are many square miles on which there is not a human inhabitant, and where the deer, foxes, and rabbits are abundant, and the wolf and bear find a lair to protect their race from extinction. But in many places the echo is awakened by the woodsman's axe and the louder din of the forge hammer. The forest glares with the light of furnace or glass house. In this sandy desert there are found veins of generous soil, which yield compensatory crop of corn and rye to the labours of the husbandman." —*A Gazetteer of the State of New Jersey* (1834).

Located in the Wall Township section Monmouth County on the banks of the Manasquan River, the Allaire area was first inhabited by the Leni Lenape Indians, a Delaware Indian tribe of the Algonquin race. Evidence of former Native American campsites can still be found, particularly along the Manasquan River and on the former Gifford and Kessler farms. Materials found at these locations suggest that the local natives traded extensively with tribes from other sections of the country. The men hunted and fished while the women handled most of the farming chores, raising primarily corn, beans, and squash. Shellfish were gathered from the nearby Atlantic Ocean. The Leni Lenapes were a peaceful tribe and welcomed the first Dutch settlers to the area. They traded with the settlers initially and then sold them hunting rights and, finally, the land itself. The last Native American resident in Allaire, Indian Joe, died in the early 1930s after struggling for years to make a living selling handmade Native American relics. He lived near the entrance to what is now Allaire State Park.

Isaac Palmer and Samuel Swain purchased land in Allaire from the East Jersey Proprietors c. 1750 and operated a sawmill. Ironmongers arrived by 1800 to take advantage of the abundant natural resources in and around Allaire to process iron. These resources included bog-iron ore, timber, water, and oyster shells. According to local legend, an iron forge operated during the Revolutionary War. Williamsburg Forge was in operation in Allaire c. 1803, and the Monmouth Furnace was running by 1812. By 1820, William Newbold took ownership of the Monmouth Furnace and, in 1822, leased the ironworks to Benjamin Howell of Philadelphia. In that same year, James P. Allaire, a business acquaintance of Howell, purchased the property. To differentiate it from his Allaire Works in New York City, Allaire called the site Howell Works. During the next 15 years, he intensively developed the ironworks and created a self-sufficient industrial community that boasted more than 300 people during its height in 1836. Today, Historic Allaire Village, named posthumously for its most successful owner and operator, is a memorial to the social thought and planning of the Howell Works era. This village, with its 13 historic structures, has been preserved to educate visitors on the life and times of those who lived and worked at the Howell Works.

The Howell Works ceased iron production in 1846, paralleling the decline of other furnaces that once dotted New Jersey's Pine Barrens. James P. Allaire died in 1858, and the village passed first to his wife, Calicia, and then to his son Hal. A Columbia graduate and architect by trade, Hal Allaire for the most part reveled in his father's ancestral holdings and struggled to preserve his father's estate. He waved aside any redevelopment efforts that ambitious businessmen proposed. In 1872, an extension of the Freehold and Jamesburg Agricultural Railroad had been extended to Manasquan, passing through Allaire on the way. The village slowly succumbed to the forces of Mother Nature and was described by local journalists in the late 1800s as being deserted. To generate income from his landholdings, Hal Allaire rented out various homes in the village, allowed William DeLisle to transform the carpenter shop into a restaurant and inn, and created the Allaire Water Supply and Land Company.

Hal Allaire died in 1901, and the property passed to William Harrison. After paying off its back taxes, Harrison sold the Allaire estate to famed Hearst newspaper editor Arthur Brisbane. From 1907 to 1936, Brisbane built a contemporary country home and created a luxurious country estate at Allaire, once consuming close to 10,000 acres. During the Brisbane era, the focal point of Allaire Village was the Allaire Inn, Brisbane's model farm, and the Boy Scouts' Camp Burton. His caretakers occupied the houses in the village, and other buildings were used by various business enterprises. In 1927, Brisbane began writing to the Allaire family to learn the history of the property. In 1940, some 1,200 acres of land, including the village, was deeded to the people of the state of New Jersey as a gift from the estate of Arthur Brisbane. This gift of land was designated to be used as a "historical center and forest reservation." His widow, Phoebe Brisbane, deeded their home in 1944, and it became the Arthur Brisbane Child Treatment Center. Since then, Allaire State Park has more than tripled in size with acquisitions of land through the Green Acres Program. World War II and a lack of restoration funds deterred any restoration of the village and park developments until 1957.

The outskirts of Allaire Village was best known for farming, which peaked in the early 20th century. In 1917, four brothers began Kessler Farms, the quintessential truck farm in the Garden State. In operation for nearly 70 years, Kessler Farms was perhaps best known for its spinach. Neighboring Kessler Farms was Thompson's Dairy Farm and Spring Meadow Golf Course. The land north of Allaire Village was used by a variety of gravel and sand companies in the 19th and 20th centuries before being developed into an airport in 1937 by Ed Brown, a pioneer in local aviation. A racetrack was later built nearby.

Allaire has been home to many interesting people and thriving enterprises. Today, the farms that once bordered Allaire Village are no more. Much of the forests and former farmland is preserved—spared from commercial and real estate development that has erupted all around—in the 3,500-acre Allaire State Park. Allaire Village, now a state-owned historic site, and the New Jersey Museum of Transportation are the focal points of the park. The Manasquan River Reservoir occupies part of the former Kessler Farms. A bike path traverses the former Freehold and Jamesburg Agricultural Railroad right-of-way. Thompson's Dairy Farm retains some of its former character. Spring Meadow Golf Course and Ed Brown's airport, now called Monmouth Executive Airport, remain thriving enterprises.

This book should not be misconstrued as a complete history of Allaire. Its main purpose is to give everyone a glimpse of the people, sights, and places that make Allaire unique.

One

James P. Allaire and the Howell Works

In 1822, James P. Allaire (1785–1858) bought the village that now bears his name and 5,000 acres in the vicinity for the sum of $19,000. Allaire established the Howell Works on the land, a major center for the production of bog iron. His reasons for buying the property were threefold—its abundance of bog-iron ore, timber, and water, which were necessary for iron making; its proximity to river passage for shipping products to New York City; and its potential to act as a resource for future financial negotiations.

At one time, the New Jersey Pine Barrens were known for their network of bog-iron blast furnaces. These industries dotted the landscape from Colonial times to the 1850s. Although not in the heart of the New Jersey Pine Barrens, Allaire was part of this network. Such blast furnaces used bog iron, a renewable resource that forms naturally along the flood plains and swamps of the Pine Barrens, to make iron. At Allaire, there was an abundance of bog iron along the Manasquan River flood plain, located only a couple of yards from the blast furnace. At the blast furnace, bog iron was smelted into iron using charcoal, flux (oyster shells), and blasts of air pumped in from adjacent air chambers. Allaire used the iron he produced at the Howell Works to make pig-iron and cast-iron products.

Although other ironmongers used the site for iron production prior to James P. Allaire's ownership, Allaire greatly expanded production and developed an integrated industrial village. Between 1827 and 1837, Allaire replaced many of the wooden buildings and mills that had predated his ownership. In their place, he built large and sturdy brick buildings based on the Federal architectural style. In addition, he expanded the buildings directly related to iron production. To overcome the isolation of the village, Allaire created a self-sufficient community, which included a carpenter shop, blacksmith shop, bakery, gristmill, school, church, post office, and apothecary shop. By 1836, during the heyday of the village, more than 300 people lived and worked there. At that time, the Howell Works consisted of about 25 buildings.

To appreciate the life and times of James P. Allaire and his industrial empire, it is important to understand the time period. At the onset of the 19th century, Americans were faced with limitless opportunities. A second war of independence from England had just been won (the War of 1812), and the country had no major political enemies. The land west of the Appalachian Mountains had yet to be explored, measured, and mapped. New natural resources, such as coal and iron, were being discovered in a limitless supply to revolutionize the way people had lived for thousands of years. The Jacksonian Era (1825–1836) is commonly characterized as the beginning of industrialization and mechanization in America. It gave rise to many urban and rural industrial communities. Waves of immigrants were easily absorbed, for the demand for labor to develop the country was endless. Capital markets were being created for investment and spending purposes, and reform movements (such as temperance, antislavery, and free schools) were beginning to surface. James P. Allaire took an active part in this time period of the nation's history. Most notably, he contributed by building and advancing the technology of steamboats.

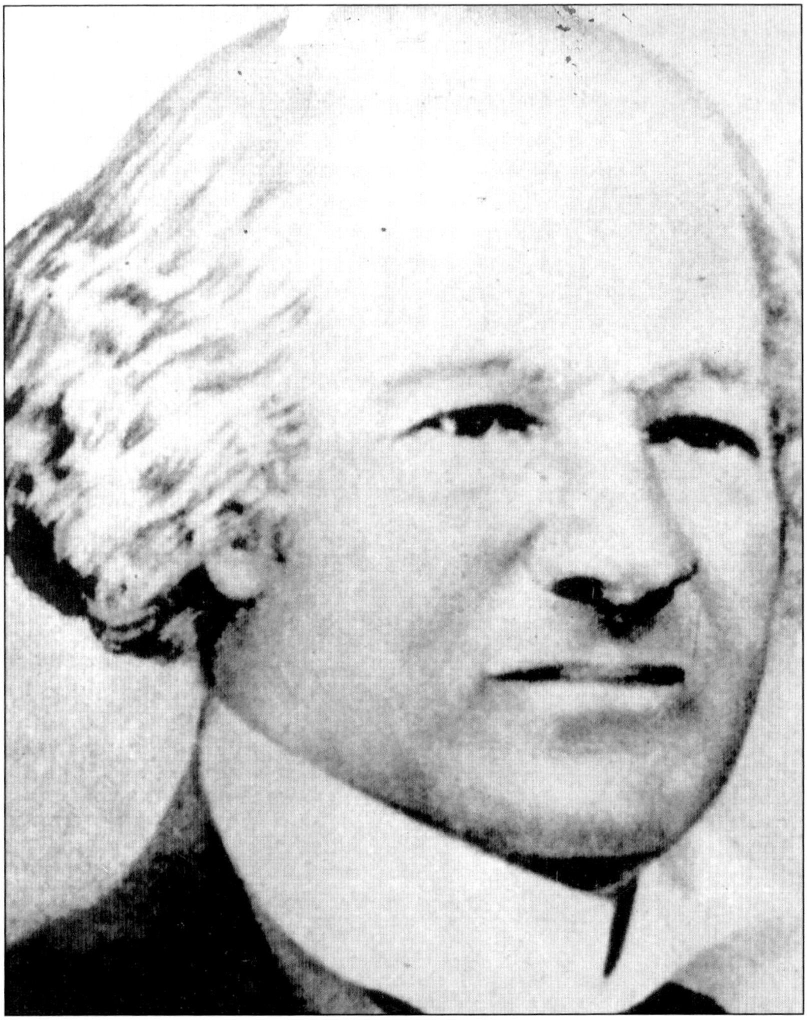

The Allaire family was of French Huguenot origin and helped settle New Rochelle, New York. As Loyalists, they fled to Nova Scotia during the Revolutionary War. James P. Allaire (pictured) was born in Nova Scotia in 1785, and the family immigrated back to the United States soon after. In 1802, Allaire began working for Francis Elsworth, a brass founder in New York City. In 1804, he married Frances Duncan. Together, they had nine children, only five of whom survived to adulthood. In 1806, Allaire bought his own foundry and, just before the War of 1812, received an order from Robert Fulton to make the brassworks for the *Clermont*, the first commercially successful steamboat in the United States. After Fulton's death in 1815, Allaire leased Fulton's Jersey City shop and tools from the estate. He also took as his partner Fulton's chief engineer, Charles Stoudinger. Upon the death of Stoudinger in 1816, Allaire moved the business to Corlear's Hook in lower Manhattan—the site of his main brass foundry, the Allaire Works. Allaire, an inventor, brass founder, marine engineer, and industrialist, worked with Robert Fulton, father of the modern steamboat. Upon Fulton's death in 1815, Allaire became his successor. He designed the first steam frigate and developed the first compound engine for marine use. Allaire's most outstanding achievement, however, was the fulfillment of a dream of a business empire that would be self-sufficient from start to finish and would include an independent community. This dream included the Howell Works (now called Historic Allaire Village). His legacy is perhaps best told today at the industrial community he created—Howell Works.

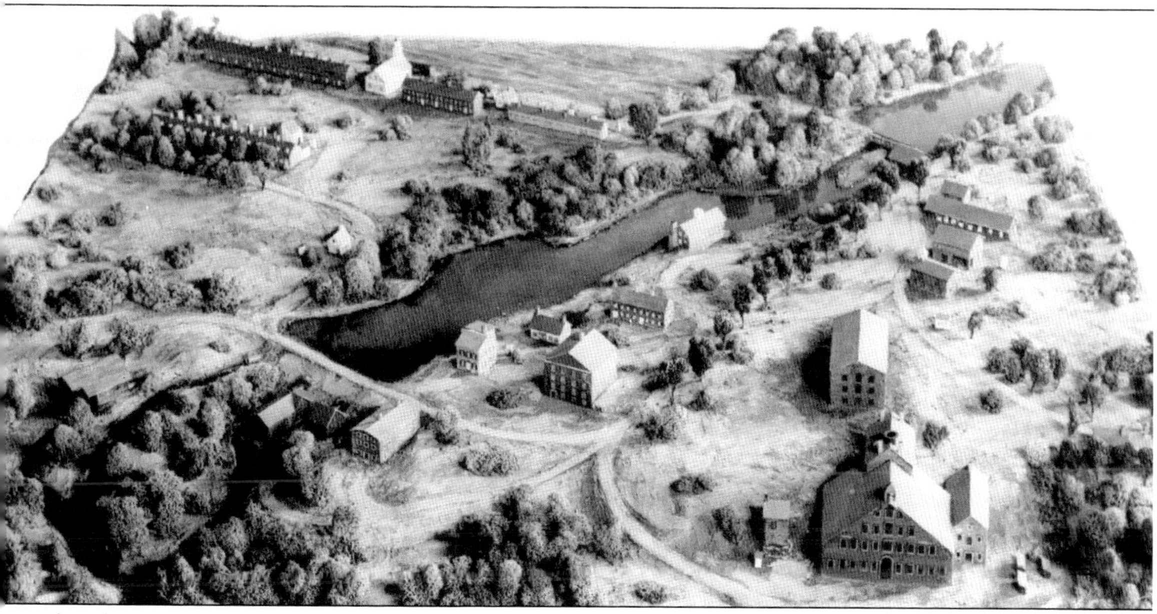

This diorama depicts Allaire Village (then known as the Howell Works) during its height in 1836. Of the 25 buildings shown here, only 13 exist today. During the War of 1812, Allaire found it difficult to secure a source of iron due to the British embargo. Iron was used to make the various steam engine parts and boilers at his Allaire Works in New York City. Moreover, the restrictions placed on the import of iron through the rise of protective tariffs after the war urged Allaire to look for a local supply of iron. He first bought interest in the Aetna Furnace, located in Milton, Delaware. He bought the Howell Works in 1822.

Allaire's attention to detail and high production standards won him the praise of his customers and the admiration of the general public. James P. Allaire gave his personal attention to details and to instructing his subordinates to invariably reject imperfect castings and to permit no piece of machinery to pass their inspection unless it was perfect of its kind. By nature, Allaire was both generous and philanthropic and provided as good a community for his workers as was possible in those days.

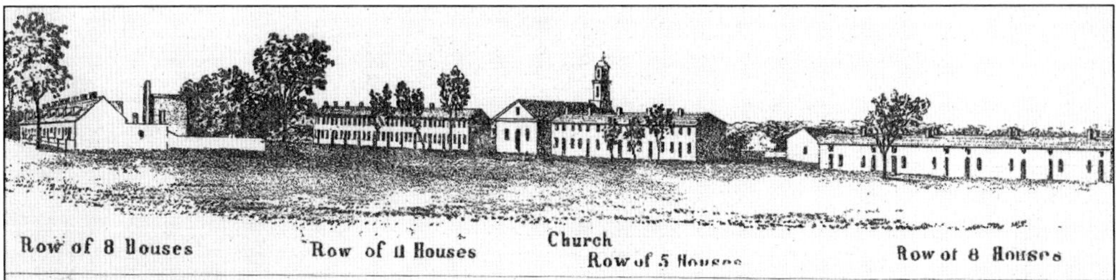

2. A Corner of Allaire, N. J., in 1853. *Published by John R. Allaire, Farmingdale, N. J.*

From left to right are two units of row houses, the church, a unit of five row houses, and a unit of eight row houses. This scene, although printed in 1853, is how the village would have looked during its height in the 1830s. The row houses were principal dwelling places for James P. Allaire's workers. More than 300 people lived and worked at the Howell Works. A great many men and women performing a variety of tasks were needed to keep the operation at Howell Works going. Those who were paid fairly well at the Howell Works included skilled workers, such as colliers, ore raisers, carpenters, fillers, furnace foreman, chief surveyor, master mason, and blacksmiths. Other workers included woodchoppers, firemen, charcoal carters, ware dressers, finishers, teamsters, stage drivers, screw factory workers, brickmakers, store clerks, and gardeners. Many immigrant workers were employed at the Howell Works, mostly of western European descent. The church held Episcopal services on Sunday and served as a school on weekdays. Allaire, ahead of his time, provided for the education of boys and girls. Today, only the church and a unit of row homes (far left) exist.

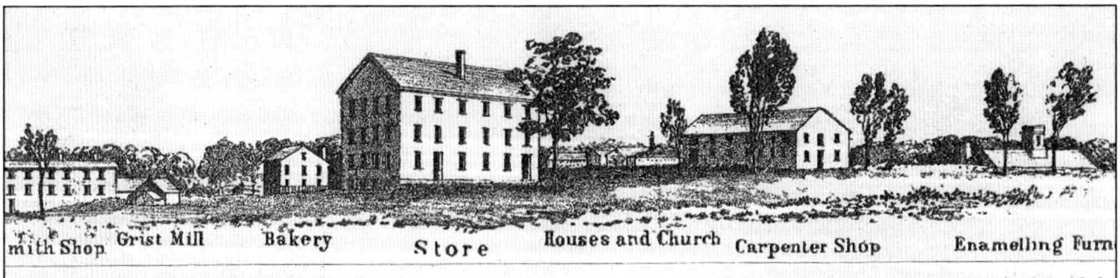

1. A Corner of Allaire, N. J., in 1853. *Published by John R. Allaire, Farmingdale, N. J.*

This view shows the blacksmith shop, gristmill, bakery, general store, carpenter shop, and enameling furnace. These buildings, except for the enameling furnace, helped to make the Howell Works a self-sufficient community. When built in 1835, the general store (often called the company store) was one of the largest stores in the state. This four-story building cost $7,000 to build and sold a variety of merchandise, most of which came from New York City. The carpenter shop employed master craftsmen who produced wooden patterns used for sand molds to make cast-iron products. A wheelwright shop was located in the rear of the carpenter shop. All of these buildings, except for the mills along the millpond, exist today.

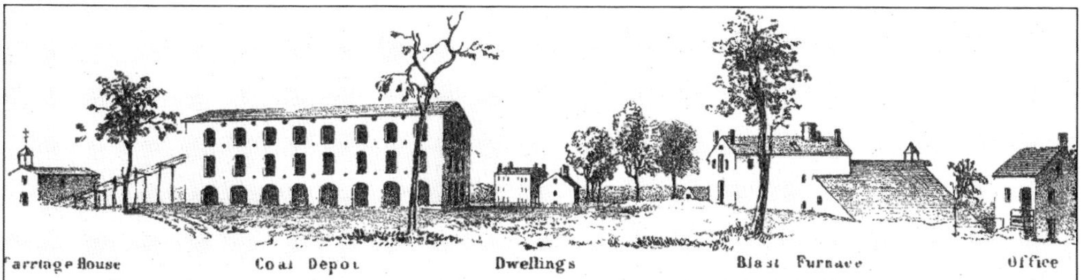

3. **A Corner of Allaire, N. J., in 1853.** *Published by John R. Allaire, Farmingdale, N. J.*

This scene depicts the industrial complex of the Howell Works: the carriage house, charcoal depot, Allaire Big House, dormitory, casting shed, blast furnace, and furnace office. The charcoal depot was where three main ingredients—bog ore, charcoal, and flux—were stored. Today, only the carriage house, Allaire Big House, and blast furnace exist.

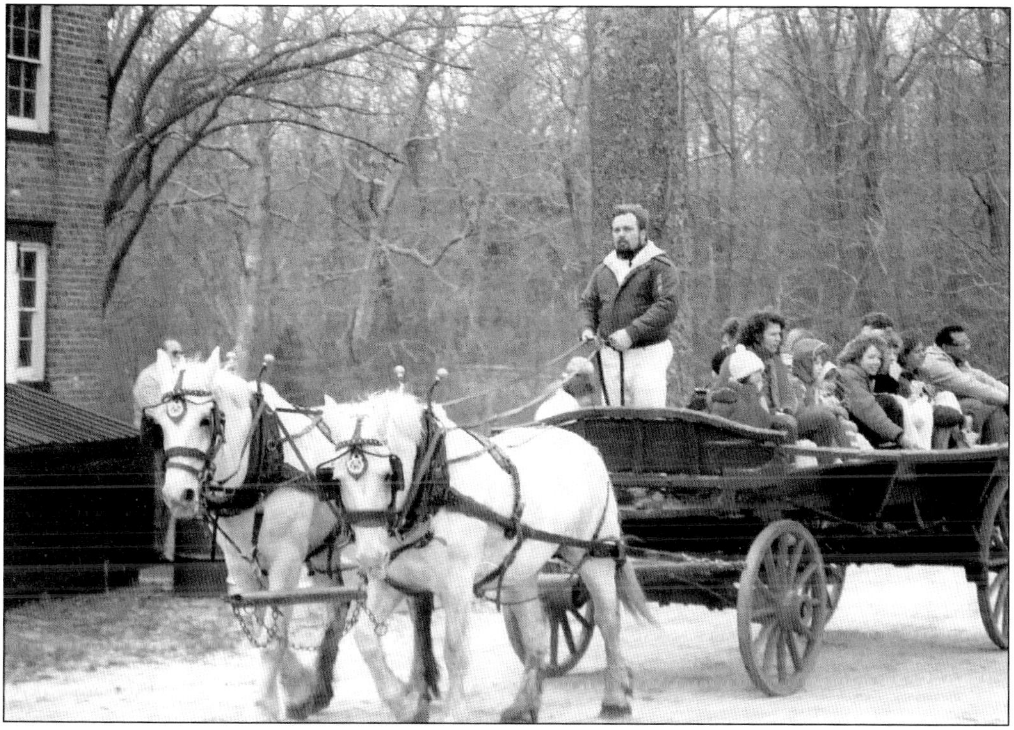

In the early 1800s, the country was rapidly expanding. With this expansion, the transportation system was found inadequate. The 1830s were considered the birth of modern transportation by land and sea. Cast-iron products, pig iron, and farm produce were transported overland via horse and wagon from the Howell Works to docks at Red Bank. At Red Bank, goods were transferred onto Allaire's steamships bound for New York City. In the early years, Allaire may have used the Manasquan River to get his products to New York City. It is rumored that a barge filled with iron products sank not too far from the Allenwood Bridge.

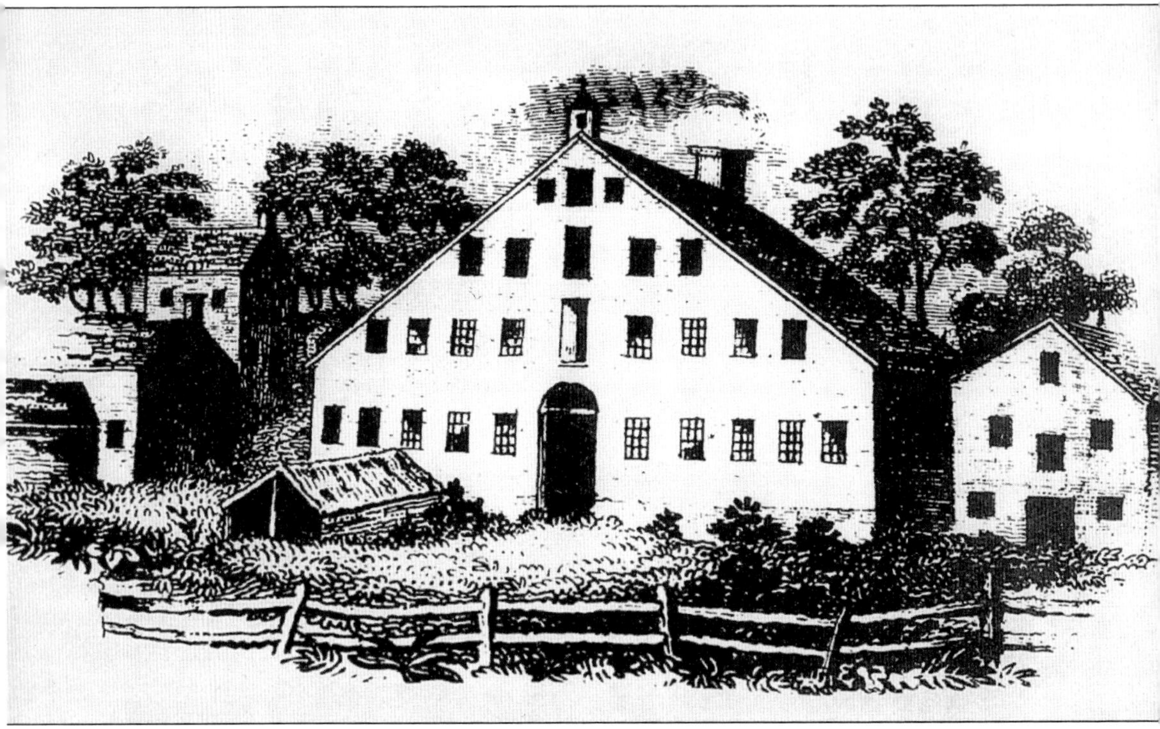

This drawing shows the ironworks as it appeared in 1836. It consisted of the casting shed, bridge house, blast furnace, and wheelhouse (machinery building). The blast furnace was in the middle of the casting shed (as evidenced by the smokestack seen here) and was the heart of this industrial community. At the ironworks, Allaire produced pig-iron and cast-iron products. Pig iron (raw bars or blocks of iron) was the most important product manufactured at the Howell Works. It was shipped from the Howell Works (Allaire Village) to the Allaire Works in New York City, where it was remelted and used to make steam engine parts for steamboats.

To the far right of this picture is the wheelhouse, which housed large air chambers (powered by a waterwheel) for pumping air into the blast furnace. It was not uncommon for the blast furnace to reach a temperature of 2,500 degrees Fahrenheit. Charcoal smelted the ore and was consumed. Impurities in the bog-iron ore united with the flux (oyster shells), forming slag, which was skimmed from the top. About every 12 hours, the furnace was tapped at the base, allowing liquid iron that had accumulated to come pouring out. Because the long trenches on the floor of the casting house and the laterals at right angles looked like a sow suckling her young, the term "pigs and sows" arose for the first run of iron from the smelting process. *Pig iron* is a term still in general use in the trade today.

The smelting process was a continuous one as long as the inside of the furnace could resist the fierce heat. Early furnaces could continue a "blast" for about 16 to 18 weeks, after which time the lining of the furnaces was ruined and the stack had to cool and be rebuilt. Later, as new methods were found, the blast was extended to 7 and 8 months. Hal Allaire claims that the Howell Works furnace operated continuously for 21 months before being taken out of blast in 1838. If this is correct, it is undoubtedly a record for New Jersey furnaces.

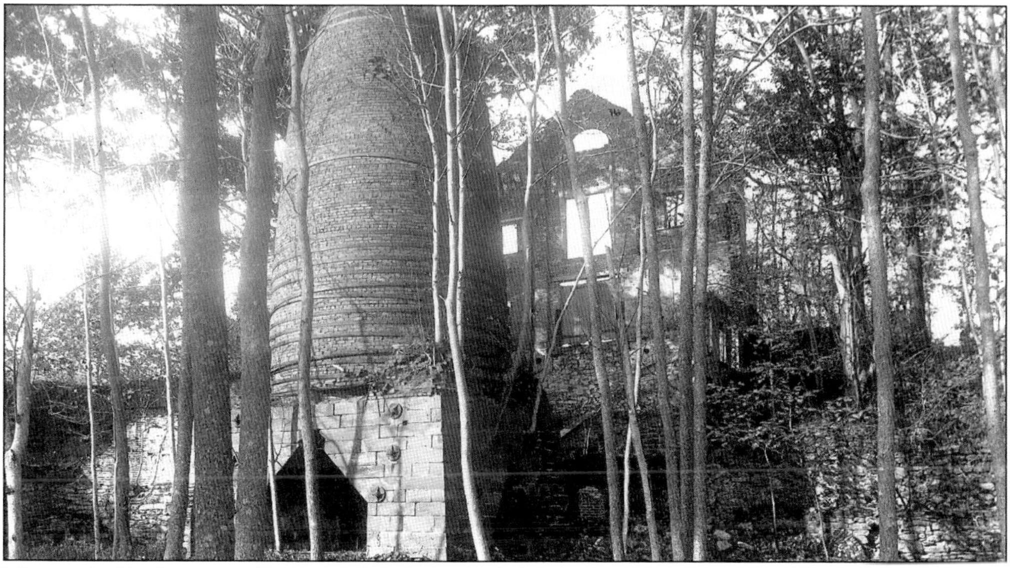

This *c.* 1900 photograph shows the remains of the ironworks. By 1900, only the blast furnace remained. Because the furnace was ideally situated near a bluff, ingredients to make Allaire's iron could be loaded (charged) from an opening near the top, and the end result (iron) could be received at the base. Iron would be channeled into troughs dug out on the floor in order to make pig iron or would be poured into molds to make cast-iron products. This view shows the expanse of the casting shed floor, where trees are now growing, indicating that the roof has long since collapsed.

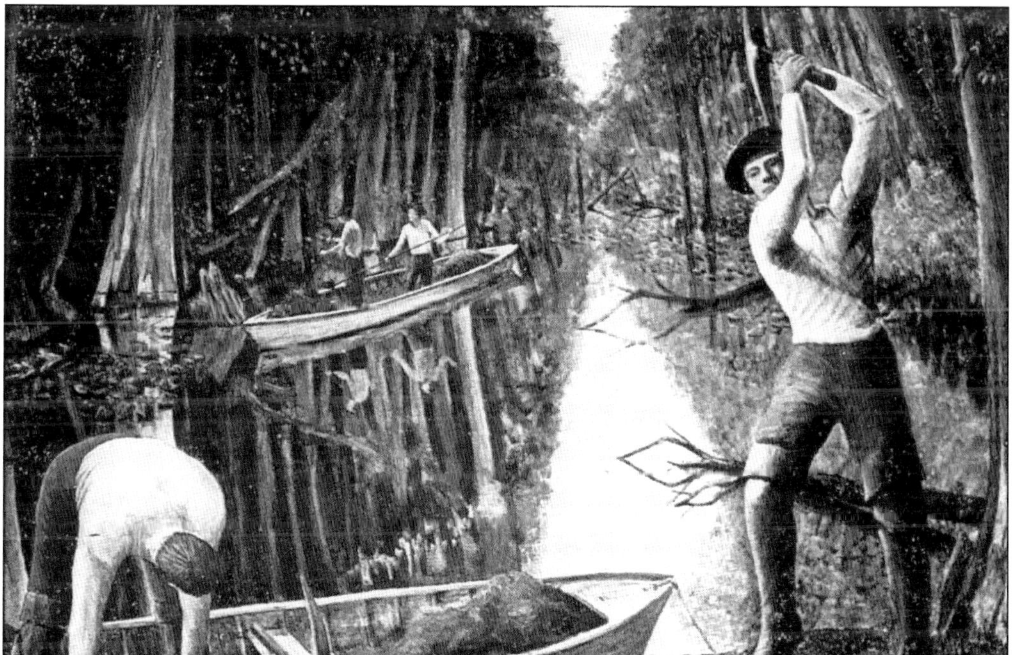

Ore raisers used long-handled scows and flat-bottomed boats to raise iron ore from the bogs. Allaire smelted the iron ore that his ore raisers gathered from the bogs and creeks along the Manasquan River. This painting was done by Cindy Doerzbach. (Courtesy Furnace Town Foundation.)

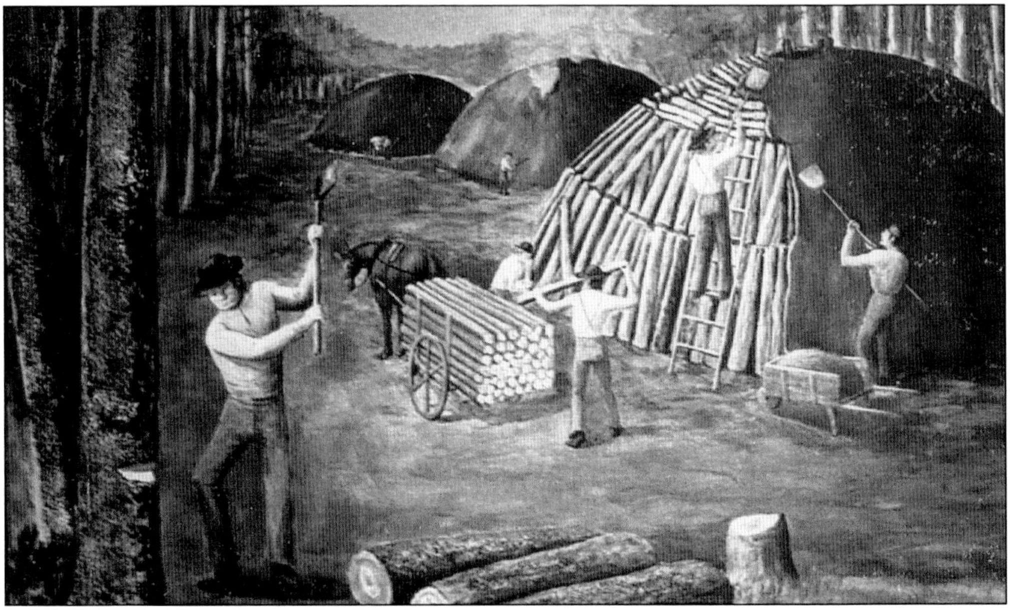

Colliers are shown constructing timber mounds, which will be converted to charcoal. Prior to 1840, charcoal was the nation's most common fuel that generated sufficient heat to smelt iron ore. Charcoal is partially burned wood from which the water, volatile gases, tars, resins, and impurities have been driven off, leaving a residue of practically pure carbon. It was not uncommon for furnaces like Allaire to consume 300 acres of timber a year. This painting was done by Cindy Doerzbach. (Courtesy Furnace Town Foundation.)

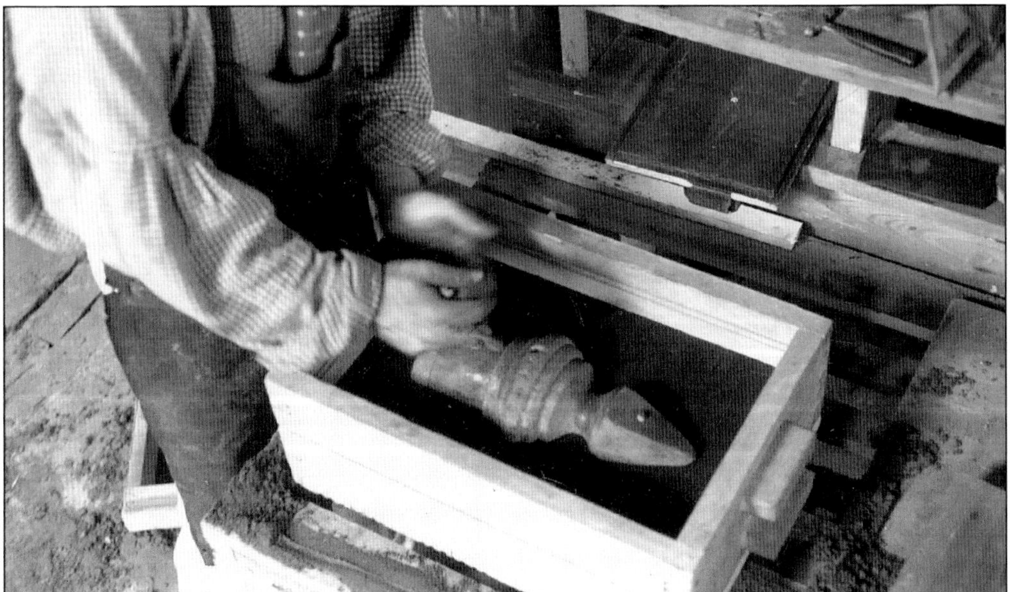

In addition to pig iron, James P. Allaire produced hollowware, stoves, architectural castings, and water pipes. Many patterns and flasks were on hand to make molds for cast-iron products. This image illustrates a molder preparing a flask by packing sand around a wooden pattern. The wooden pattern would then be removed, leaving an impression that would be filled with liquid iron. The iron would harden in the flask to the shape of the pattern.

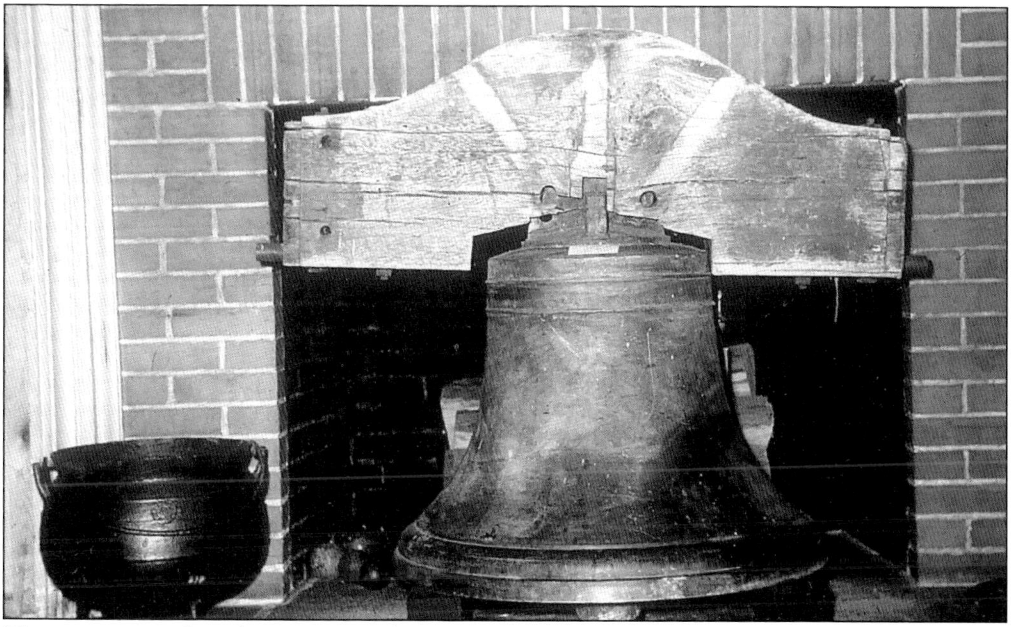

These are examples of cast-iron products made at the Howell Works. To the left is a cast-iron kettle, an example of hollowware, and to the right, a church bell. Allaire Village is reminiscent of the day when furnaces and forges along the waterways of the Pine Barrens and Atlantic coast produced household articles and implements made of native bog iron. Most of the iron lintels over the doors and windows on Allaire Village buildings, including the star truss rods on the facades, were cast at the Howell Works.

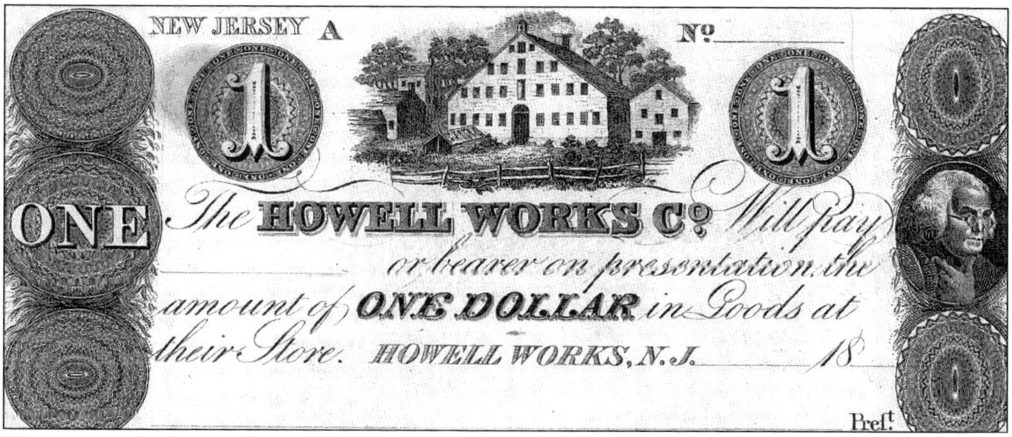

New Jersey had a cash-poor economy until the Civil War. Living in an agricultural state, residents were able to work around this deficiency by the age-old practice of barter. However, at an industrial village such as the Howell Works, this was often not sufficient purchasing power. Allaire issued his own currency in the form of scrip and coins, which could be used at the works and at neighboring businesses. Rawden, Wright and Hatch of New York printed the scrip c. 1832. The scrip was engraved, carrying a picture of the blast furnace, Benjamin Franklin, and the signature of either James P. Allaire (for higher denominations) or the company secretary, Abraham Halsey. The Howell Works scrip and coins were discontinued in 1849 shortly after the ironworks closed.

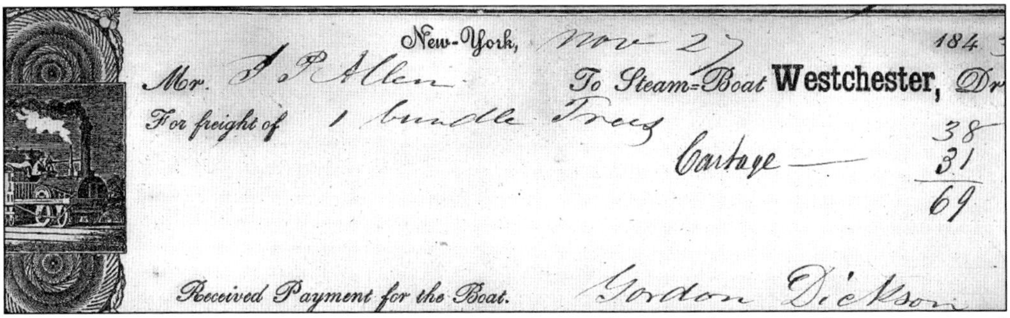

New-York, Nov 27 1843

Mr. J. P. Allen To Steam-Boat Westchester, Dr

For freight of 1 bundle Trees 38

Cartage 31

69

Received Payment for the Boat. Gordon Dickson

Dated November 27, 1843, this receipt for freight on the steamboat *Westchester* was signed by Gordon Dickinson. Allaire was in the forefront of the steamboat industry and built many vessels in the early 1800s. He built the engine and boiler for the *Chancellor Livingston,* the last steamboat designed by Robert Fulton before his death. At a cost of $120,000, this was at one time the largest steamer on the Hudson River. In 1825, Allaire constructed the engines for the steamboat *Henry Eckford*. One writer claims that this was the first compound engine built in this country. As was common for the time, Allaire would take part interest in vessels installed with his engines. In addition to his Southern States Packet Service, Allaire provided steamboat service from Red Bank to New York City with a variety of steamboats, including the *Bellona, Frank, David Brown, Osiris, Iolas,* and *Orus*. With the purchase of the Howell Works in 1822, coupled with Allaire's brass foundry in New York City (the Allaire Works) and steam packet line (delivering finished goods to market), Allaire had the resources to control his business from raw materials to the finished product. He was one of the first industrialists to use vertical integration effectively.

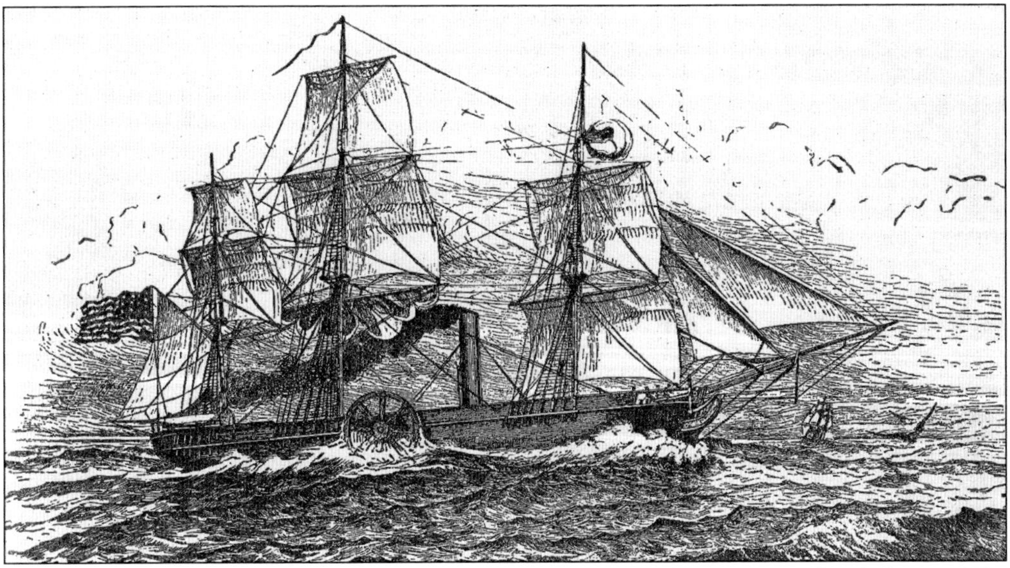

Seen here in a lithograph, the *Savannah* was the first steamship to cross the Atlantic. The cylinders and engine of this vessel were built at the Allaire Works in New York City. During the early 1800s, the Allaire Works was one of the largest marine engine shops in the United States. The Howell Works supplied the iron to make the engines. In 1832, Allaire began the Southern States Packet Service. It conveyed dispatches, mail, passengers and goods to ports between New York City and Charleston, South Carolina.

Two

The Last of the Allaires

The collapse of James P. Allaire's empire occurred slowly over several years. The discovery of anthracite coal near the magnetite rock ore deposits of Pennsylvania and northern New Jersey, coupled with the development of the hot-blast method and the use of anthracite coal to smelt iron, doomed the New Jersey bog-iron industry. This included Allaire's Howell Works (Allaire Village). The New Jersey Pine Barrens furnaces could not compete with the cheaper products of equal and, later, superior quality of Pennsylvania.

The Howell Works ceased operations in 1846. James P. Allaire's chain of vertical integration was lost, for he no longer had a source of iron at his fingertips. By this time, the Allaire Works in New York City was also declining from its peak operations. Allaire suffered financial setbacks beginning with the financial panic of 1837. Steamboats carrying Allaire's products to market sank in storms off the Atlantic coast. Upon losing controlling interest, he was ousted as president of the Allaire Works in 1850. Allaire then declared retirement and spent the remainder of his years at the Howell Works Big House with his second wife, Calicia, and young son Hal. In the early 1850s, Allaire contemplated selling the Howell Works. He commissioned a survey of the property, whitewashed the soot-covered buildings, and undertook various landscaping projects, including the planting of the numerous sycamore trees that still line the roadways. The sale of his 7,000-acre Howell Works never materialized. On Thursday, May 20, 1858, James P. Allaire died.

Allaire left a will that gave rise to a prolonged and bitter litigation between his widow, Calicia, and children of his first wife, Frances, who had died in 1836. Halstead Wainwright, an early Allaire Village historian, recalls, "He saw fit to give the greater part of his estate to his widow and their son Hal, because in the time of his greater prosperity, Allaire had bountifully provided for the children by his first wife." Calicia and Hal finally received rightful ownership in the 1870s, just shortly before Calicia's death.

Most of what we know about Hal Allaire's character and what the village was like during his ownership comes from his obituary columns, both appearing in New York City and Lakewood papers in 1901. One obituary column, titled "Prince Hal's Manor House and Neglected Town," described Allaire Village as follows. "Ivy and mold now cover this dead city and city of the dead. Moss covers the store and gray manor house surrounded by crumbling barns and a charcoal house. The once busy streets are choked with grass, young trees and bushes. Few houses are occupied, the rest stand empty and weather beaten. He let the once flourishing town which bore his name fall into picturesque ruin."

Although ambitious men came and whispered in Hal Allaire's ears of plans for rehabilitating Allaire Village, Allaire waved them aside. He commented to one businessman, "Don't, don't my friend! I couldn't bear to think of this becoming a factory town, dirty and noisy and commonplace. It's just as father left it, only time is mellowing and hallowing it for me." Slowly, village buildings were disappearing, as Hal Allaire had no financial resources to maintain them. "Winter's blast assaulted walls and towers; a crash or two and ruins lay where once men had toiled and sweated," reported the *Lakewood Times*.

Throughout his life, Hal Allaire had limited income. His father's fortune dwindled by the late 1800s and, although an architect by trade, he practiced his trade limitedly. To generate income from his land holdings, Allaire rented out some of the homes. By the 1890s, he had accumulated debt, most notably in the form of unpaid property taxes. His Lakewood friend W.J. Harrison encouraged Allaire to seek more aggressive plans to generate income from Allaire Village. Allaire allowed the carpenter shop to be turned into a roadside inn *c.* 1890. In 1895, he created the Allaire Water Supply and Land Company. These endeavors, however, did not materialize into major sources of income for him.

Hal Allaire died on October 18, 1901, at the age of 51. W.J. Harrison paid off the back taxes on the Allaire property and, after a brief struggle, became the sole owner. Shortly before his own death, Harrison sold the Allaire family estate to famed Hearst newspaper editor Arthur Brisbane in 1907.

It is interesting to note that when the Howell Works closed in 1846, there were 25 buildings still standing at Allaire Village. At the time of Hal's death in 1901, this number dwindled to 16 buildings. The buildings that had once been used for iron production at the village (the casting shed, blast furnace, and charcoal depot) were abandoned in the late 1800s and quickly fell into disrepair. Wooden buildings, especially the mills along the millpond that were completely gone by 1880, fell faster into disrepair than brick buildings did. Brick buildings endured the beating from Mother Nature longer. Poor structural support, lack of maintenance, and abandonment helped contribute to the collapse of many village buildings by 1900. A few lonely souls occupied homes within the village, including the foreman's cottage and row houses. Before 1890, the general store, carpenter shop, and blacksmith shop were most likely unused. Hal Allaire maintained the barns and carriage house and employed a caretaker to tend to the farm animals he kept there—most notably a herd of steer.

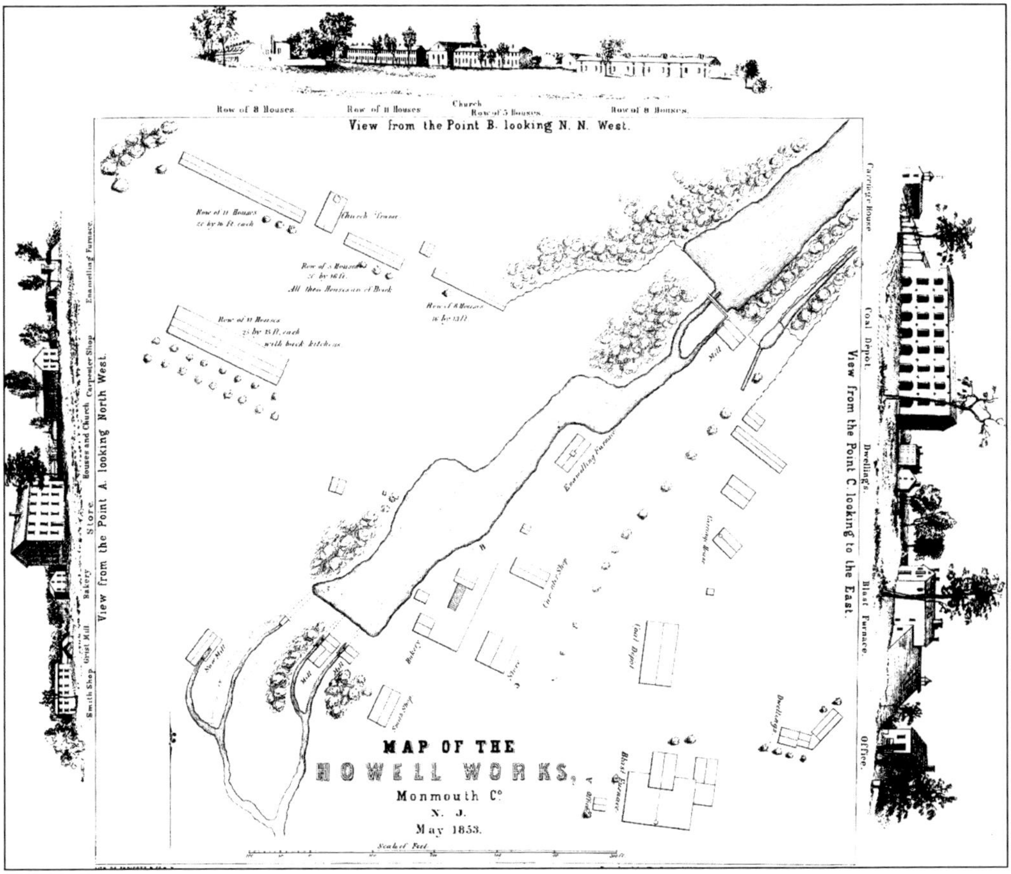

James P. Allaire commissioned this map in 1853, when he contemplated selling the property.

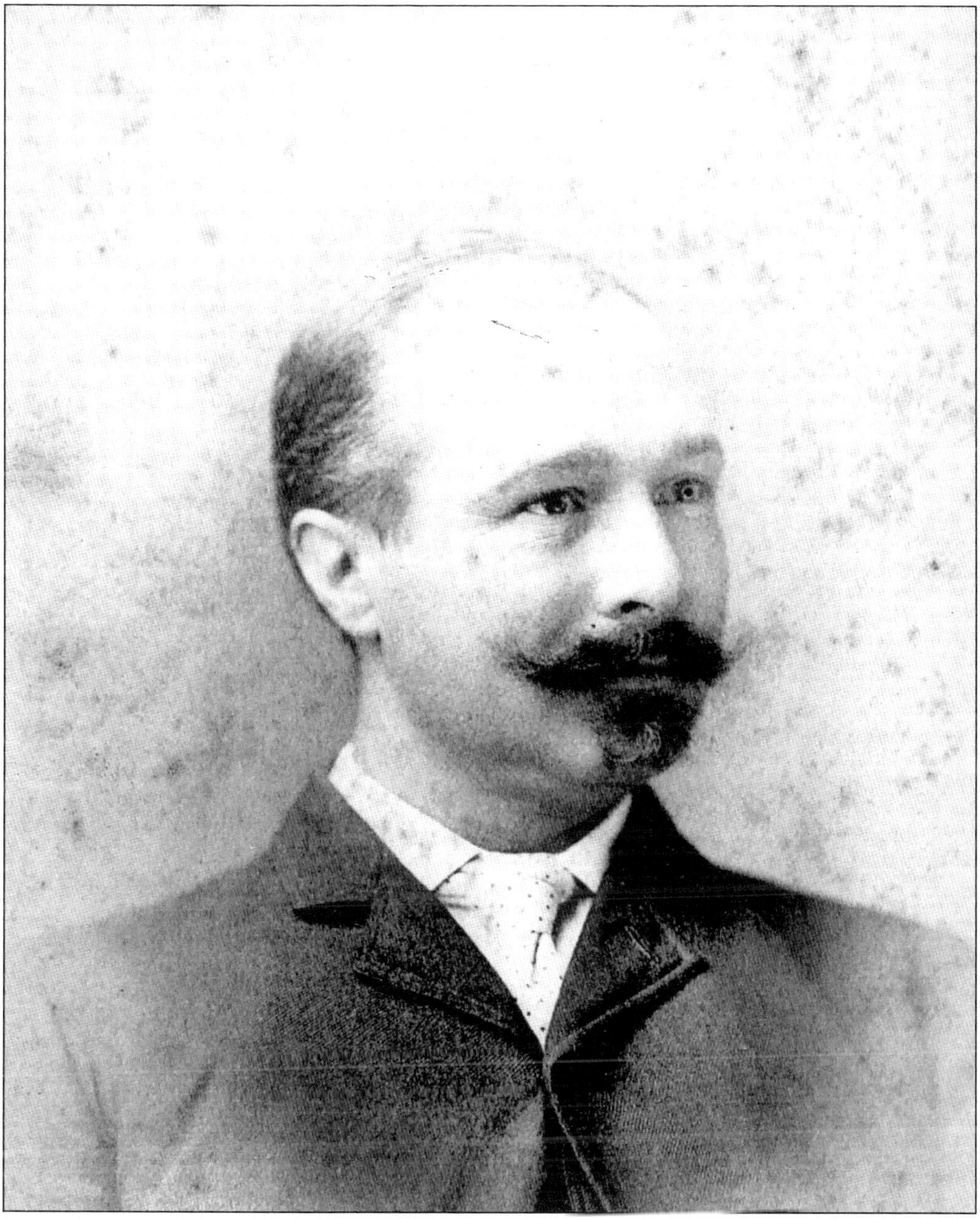

The only child of James P. Allaire and Calicia Tompkins, Hal Allaire (pictured) was born on October 5, 1847, at the Howell Works and grew up in the Allaire Big House. He was only 11 years old when his father died in 1858. Having graduated from Columbia University in 1869 with a degree in architecture, he returned to Allaire Village and lived with his mother. He never married or had any children. Although he was called "Prince Hal" by locals, his professional interests were diverse but not as prolific as his father's were. After his mother's death in 1879, he was described as a recluse. A friend recalled, "Although amiable and popular, he kept busy with his books and drawings, seldom going anywhere. His mother's old housekeeper remained and cared for him devotedly, as did a few men remaining in his employ. He simply grew more and more attached to the old homestead, deserted, decaying, lonely as it was."

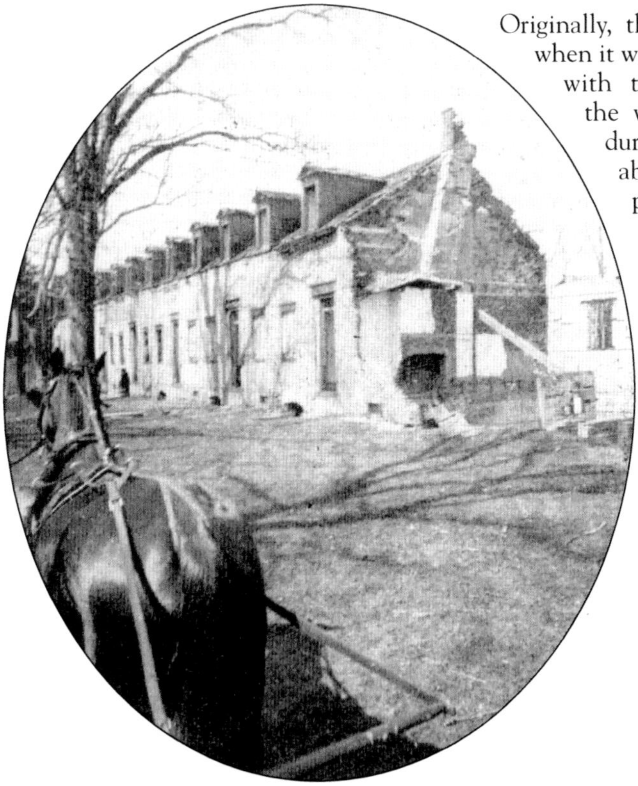

Originally, there were 11 houses in this row when it was built in 1833. These row houses, with their attached kitchens, housed the wealthier residents of the village during the Howell Works era. Only about 8 houses remain in this rare photograph, taken *c.* 1870 from a horse and buggy. A couple of houses may be occupied. All but 2 were reconstructed in 1985 to house the village's modern visitor center.

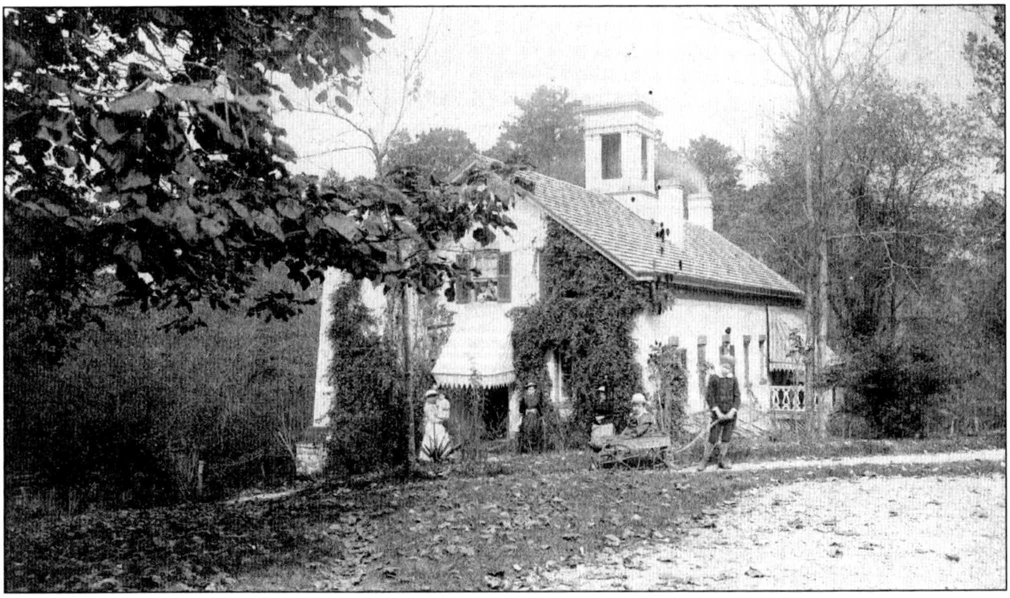

The Enameling Building, built in 1828 and 1834, was used by James P. Allaire to fire an enamel coating onto cookware. By the 1850s, it was known as the Fort and was converted into a private residence. At the time of this *c.* 1880 photograph, the Malcolmsons, good friends of Hal Allaire, were residing there. Hal Allaire rented out other dwellings during his ownership—a primary source of income for him.

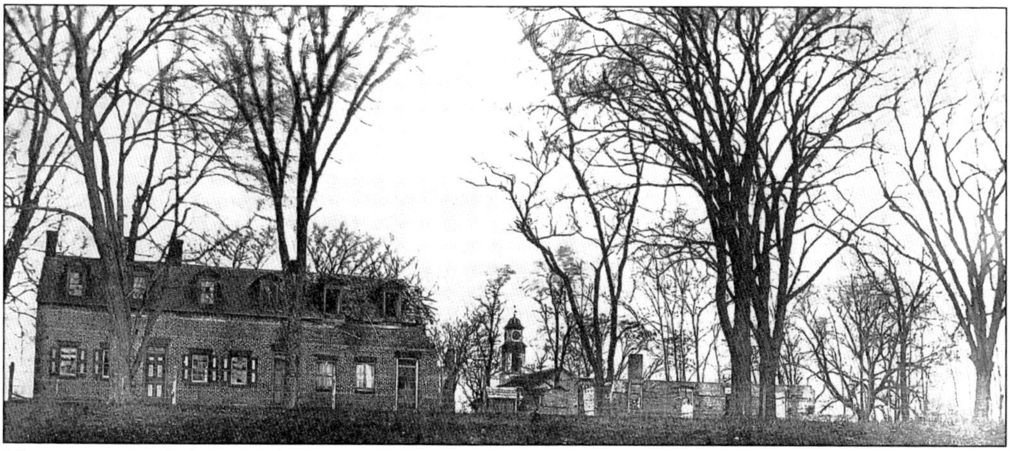

The remains of the row houses are pictured above (*c.* 1890) and below (1900). These two photographs show the same set of row houses as seen in the previous image. The front facades of the row houses are shown. Only 3 of the original 11 homes remain fully intact. Notice the picturesque trees that line the roadway. They were cut down in the 1950s. An interesting perspective of the village can be seen above. You can see ruins of the row houses that have collapsed and the church in the background.

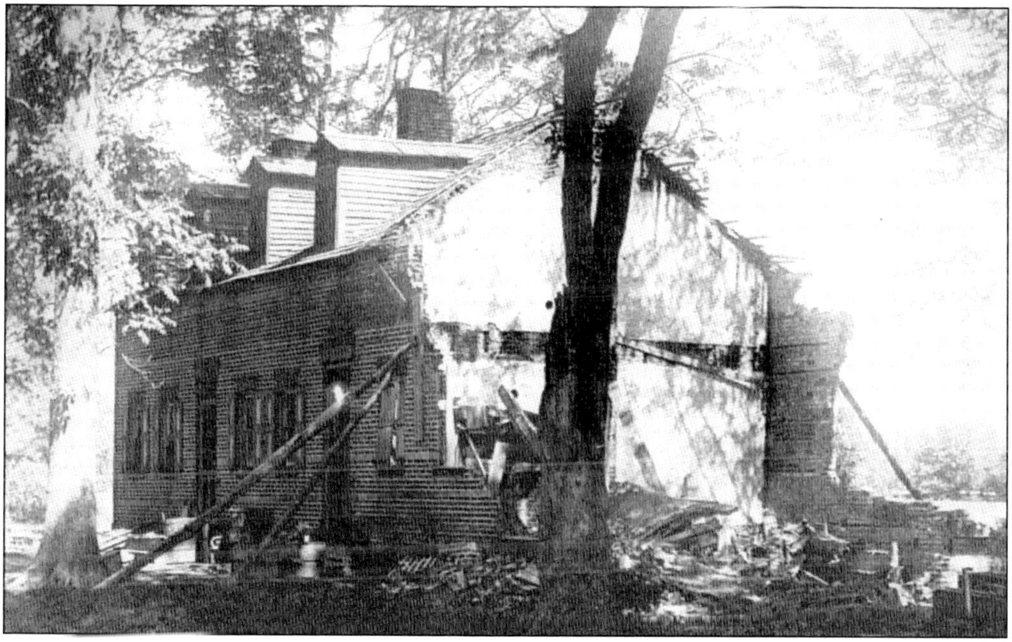

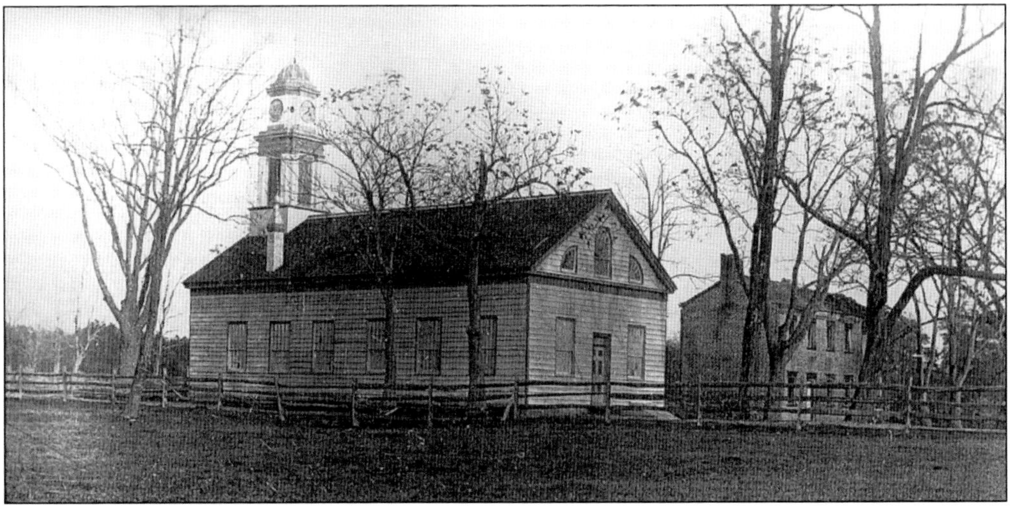

The church and eastern set of row homes are shown *c.* 1890. The church, built in 1832 and 1836, was still being maintained at Hal Allaire's expense at the time this photograph was taken. Like his father, Hal Allaire was deeply interested in educational matters. He was president of the board of education of Wall Township and served as the superintendent of the Sunday school. After church, Allaire would invite churchgoers and their families to a picnic on the village green. To the right are the remains of three row houses, once a row of five built in 1834. There were originally three sets of row homes that flanked the church. All had collapsed by 1907.

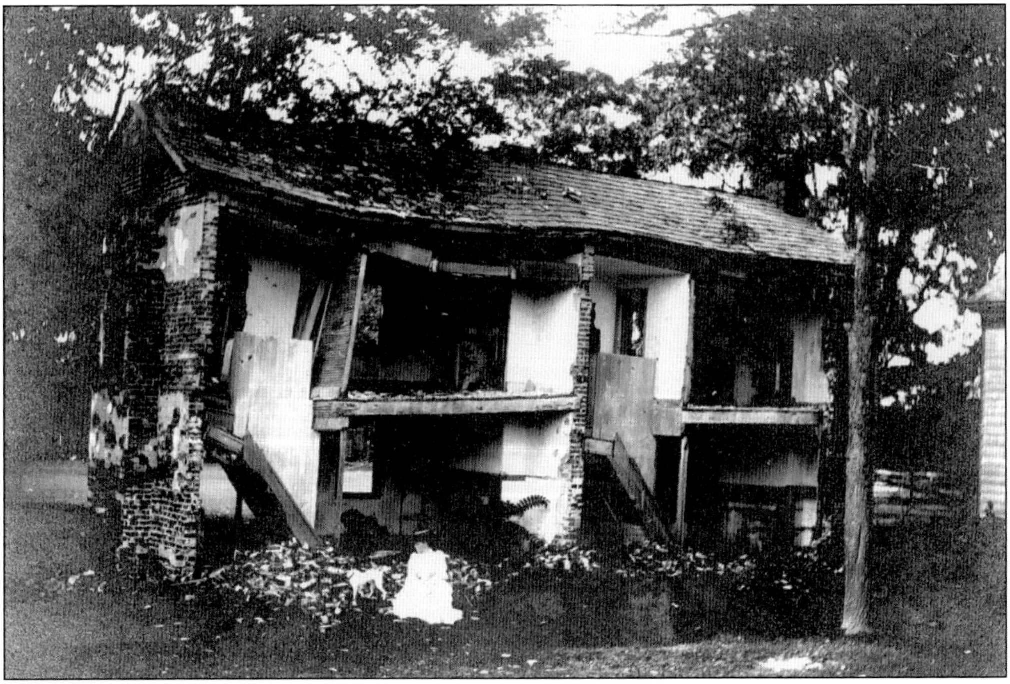

Pictured in 1895 are the same row houses shown in the preceding photograph. Originally, there were five units in this row; only two units remain in this photograph. Each unit consisted of a living space downstairs and sleeping quarters upstairs. Residents could have used a communal kitchen nearby or the bakery.

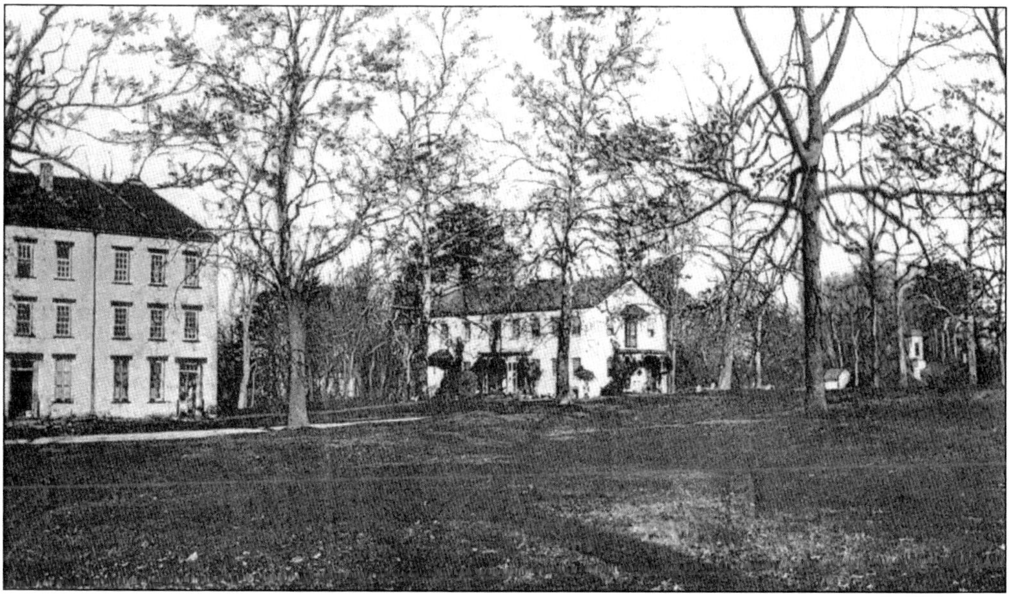

This c. 1890 roadside postcard scene shows the general store and the carpenter shop, both built in 1835. During Hal Allaire's ownership of Allaire Village, it is uncertain as to whether the store was rented to a private enterprise, as was done later. The store has a double roof. A new roof, with a more pronounced pitch, was built c. 1848 over the original roof, which leaked. The carpenter shop produced the wood patterns necessary for making cast-iron products.

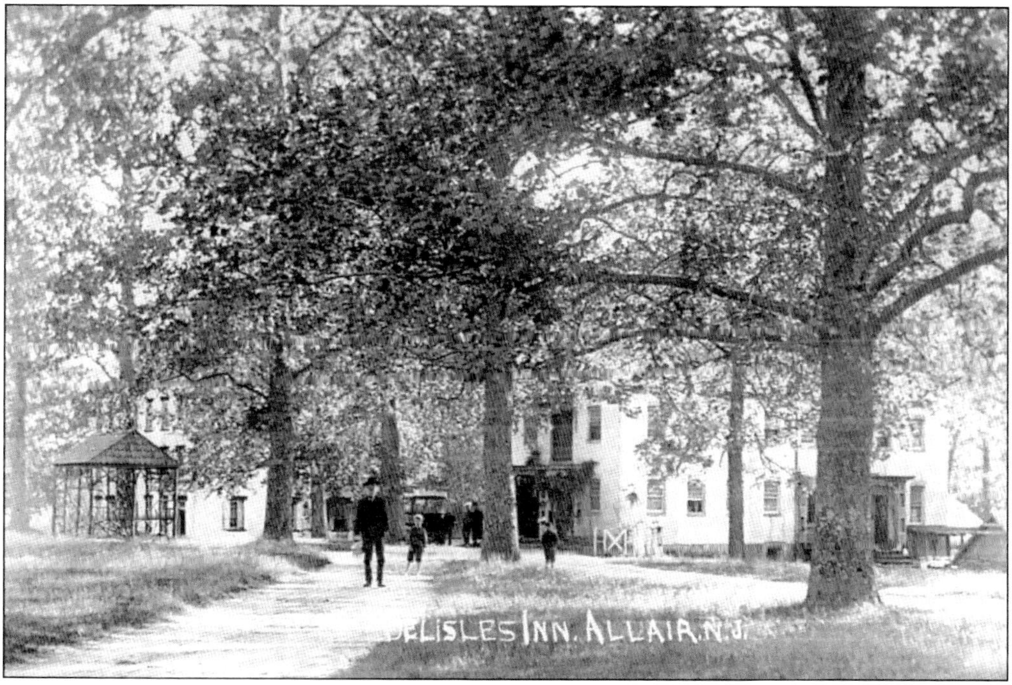

To generate some income, Hal Allaire allowed William DeLisle to transform the interior of the carpenter shop into a French restaurant and inn c. 1892, as seen here. DeLisle was not permitted to alter the exterior appearance of the carpenter shop when Hal Allaire was still living. The general store can be seen in the back on the left.

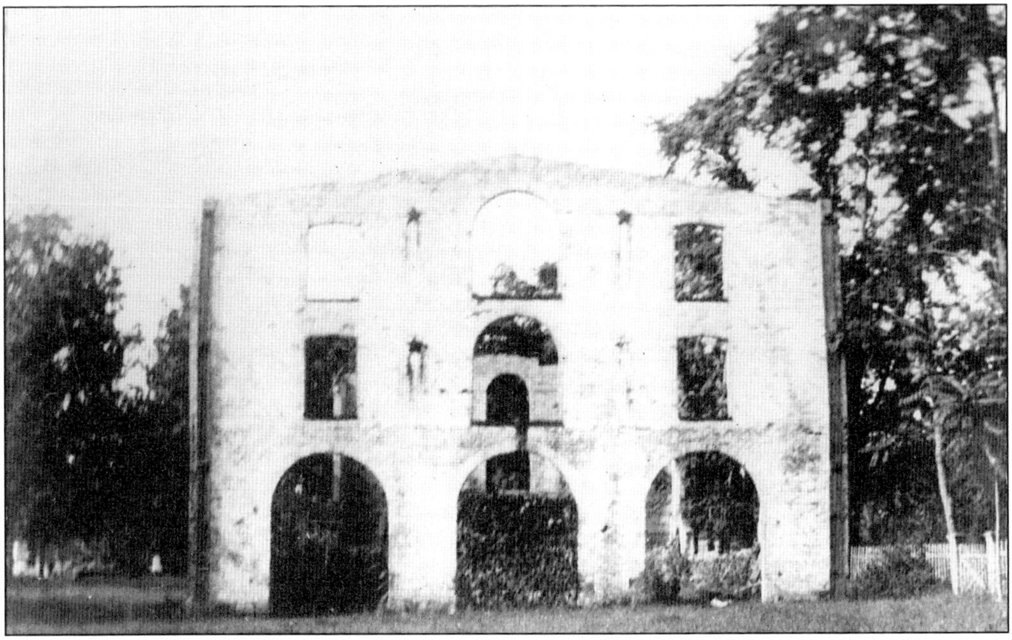

The charcoal depot, as seen here *c.* 1890, was constructed out of brick and was three floors high when it was built in 1832. This building, no longer standing at Allaire, was located between the general store and the Allaire Big House. The charcoal depot was where raw materials (bog ore, charcoal, and seashells) for iron making were stored. The building was known for its large open archways on the first floor so carts could easily be loaded and unloaded. Images like this often led 19th-century journalists to characterize Allaire Village as deserted.

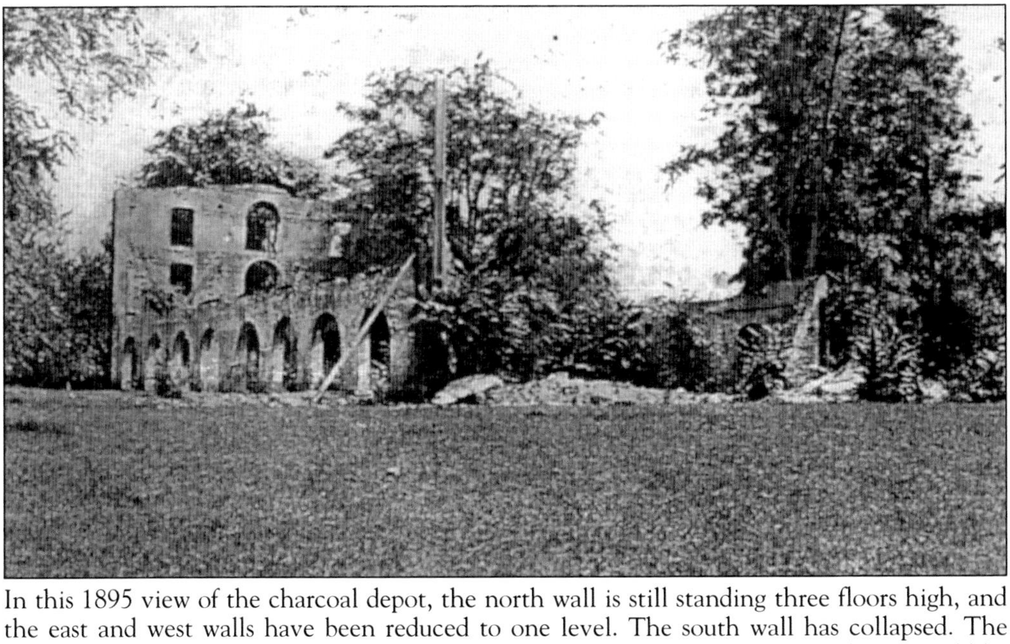

In this 1895 view of the charcoal depot, the north wall is still standing three floors high, and the east and west walls have been reduced to one level. The south wall has collapsed. The remains of the wooden roof are in the middle of the structure. The charcoal depot would be reduced to one floor by 1903. The charcoal depot ruins attracted many sightseers and early automobilists to Allaire.

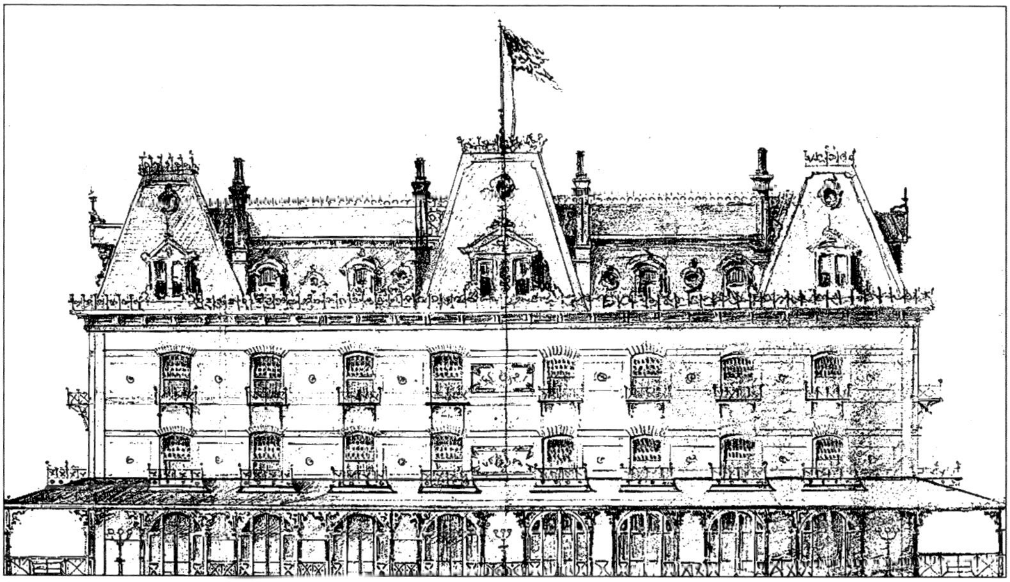

Drawn by Hal Allaire in 1881, this pencil sketch envisions transforming the charcoal depot into an elegant Victorian hotel. Allaire was a notable architect. He designed many Lakewood homes and served as a surveyor. With insufficient financial resources, Allaire never completed this hotel project.

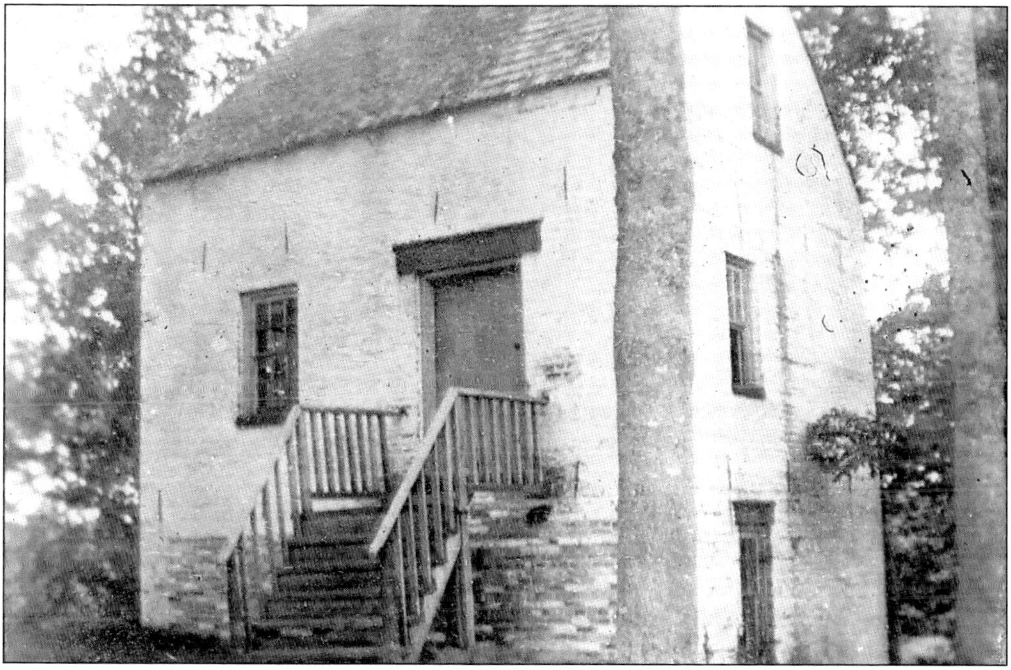

The furnace office, as seen in 1895, had a private office for the superintendent on the top floor, a professional office for the ironworks on the ground floor, and storage space for valuable flasks and wooden patterns (for making cast iron) on the lowest level. The furnace office, built in 1832, collapsed by 1907. There is a false rumor that this building was blown up during the filming of a silent movie. The south wall was built into the bluff, and it is likely that this wall "slipped" down the hill under natural forces, bringing the building down.

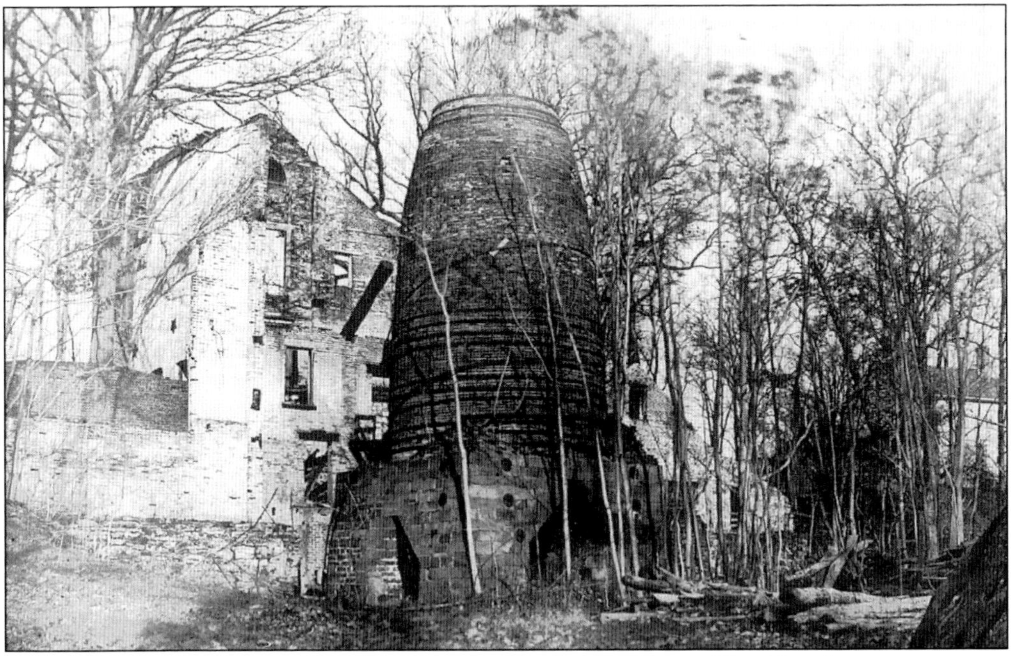

This *c.* 1900 view looks toward the remains of the bridge house. The blast furnace was once surrounded by a larger structure that had fallen down by the time this picture was taken. (See pages 14 and 15 to gain an understanding of this complex.) To the far right are the remains of the wheel house. Note the doorways and window frames.

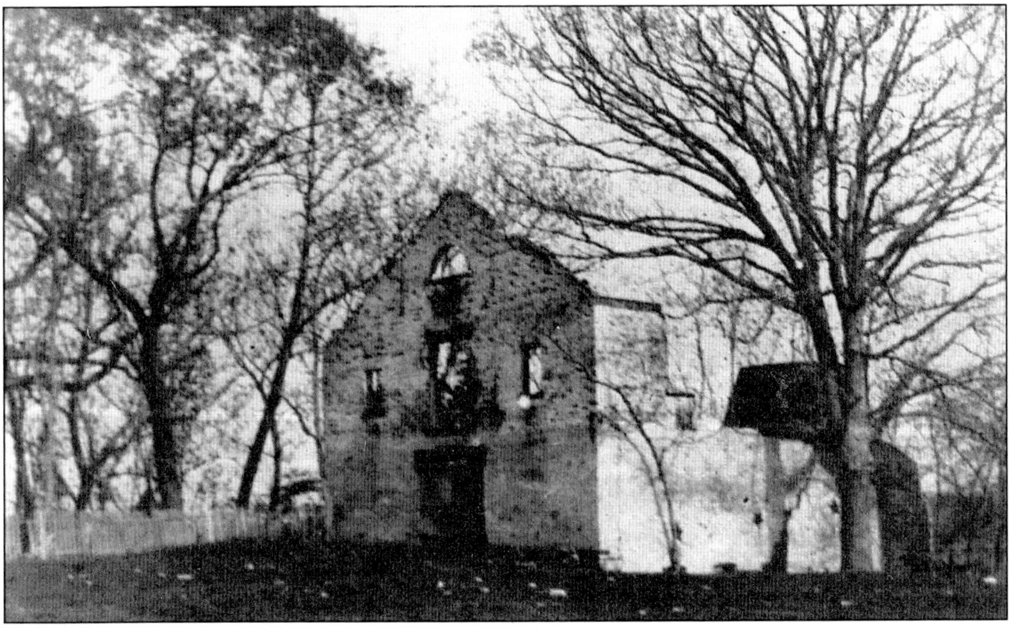

In this *c.* 1890 photograph showing the remains of the bridge house, the blast furnace looms in the background. The picture was taken from the top of the bluff, looking down at the blast furnace. A charging, or loading, ramp would have extended from the bridge house doorways to an opening near the top of the furnace stack. This allowed the fillers to charge the furnace with bog-iron ore, charcoal, and oyster shells to make iron.

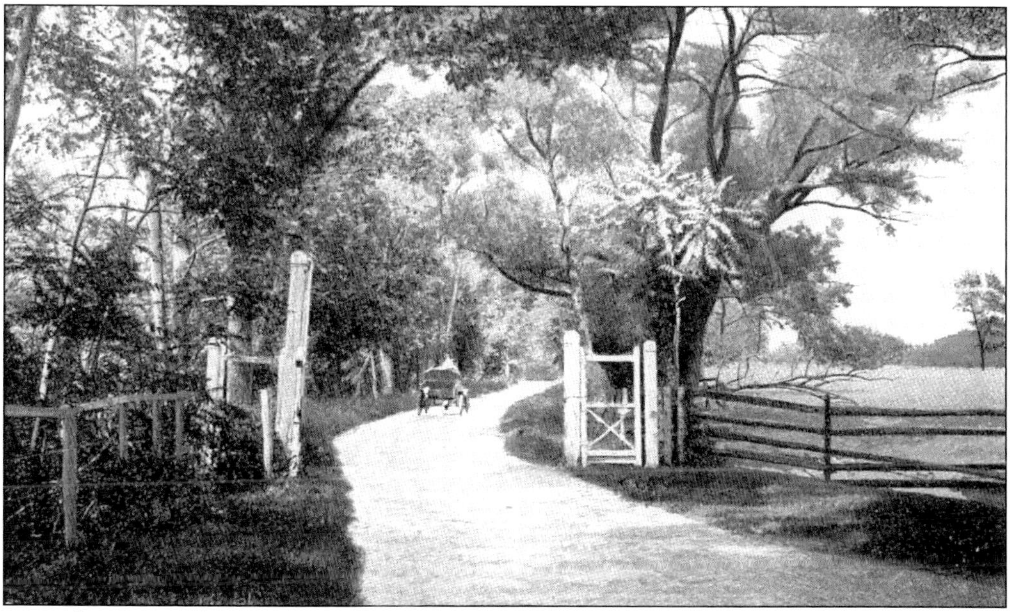

Printed c. 1905, this postcard shows the "Gateway to the deserted Village of Allaire, near Lakewood, NJ," now the east service road entrance to Allaire State Park. Lakewood, a major resort in the early 1900s, was only 10 miles from Allaire and was advertised as a great sightseeing jaunt for early automobilists. Sightseers flocked to see this "deserted village" and to have dinner among the ruins at DeLisle's Inn, which at one time occupied the carpenter shop.

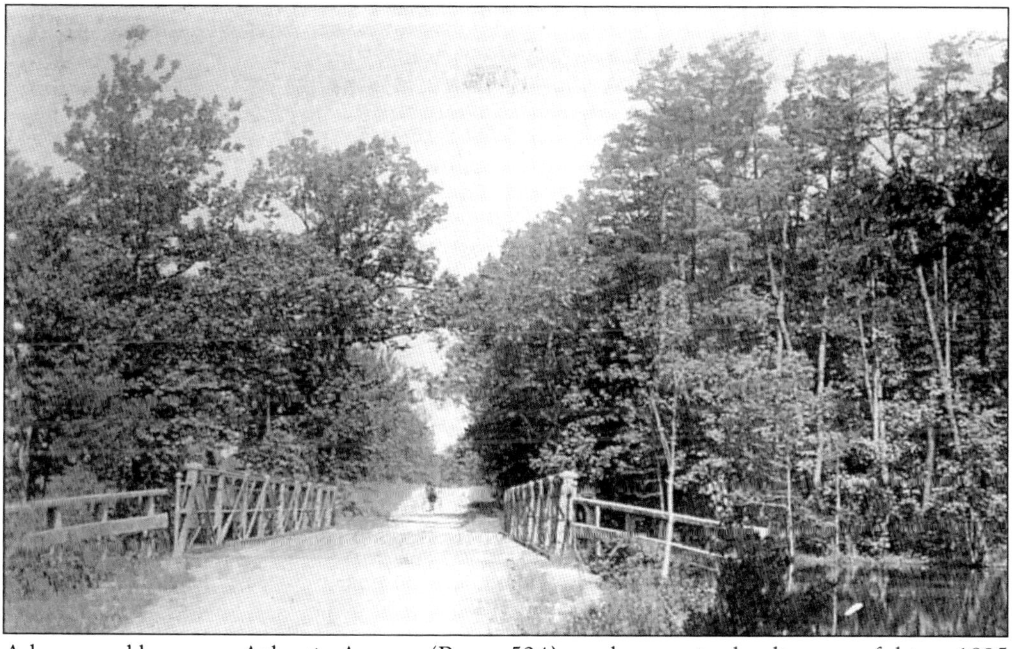

A horse and buggy on Atlantic Avenue (Route 524) can be seen in the distance of this c. 1895 view. Water flowing below this bridge supplied the millpond with water that was harnessed as energy to operate the polishing mill, gristmill, screw factory, sawmill, file mill, and air chambers at the blast furnace. To provide ample water to the millpond, James P. Allaire built a system of lakes and canals to increase the watershed.

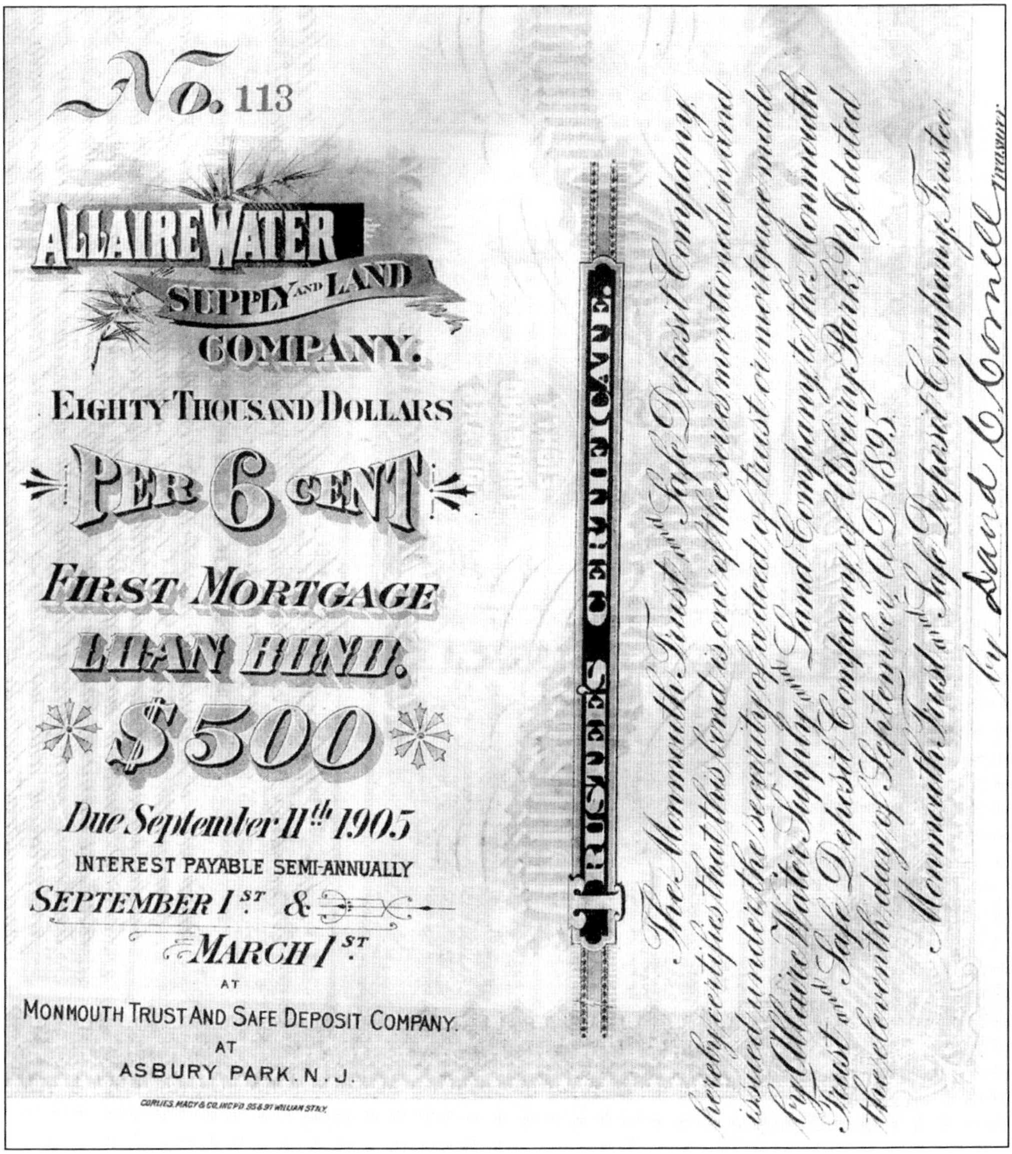

Formed by Hal Allaire in 1895, the Allaire Water Supply and Land Company included the former Howell Works, water rights, and surrounding farmlands. Under the advice of longtime friend W.J. Harrison, Hal Allaire formed the company as a way to create income from his land holdings. This bond is one of a series of 200, issued at either $100 or $500, aggregating to $80,000. The bonds were due on September 11, 1905. The capital of investors was put on deposit at the Monmouth Trust & Safe Deposit Company in Asbury Park.

Hal Allaire served as secretary and treasurer of the Allaire Water Supply and Land Company, and W.J. Harrison was president. Both signed the bond certificates, but only Allaire's signature was on the bond coupons. After Allaire's death in 1901, W.J. Harrison had the arduous task of paying off the back taxes and the bondholders in order to gain full ownership of the Allaire estate.

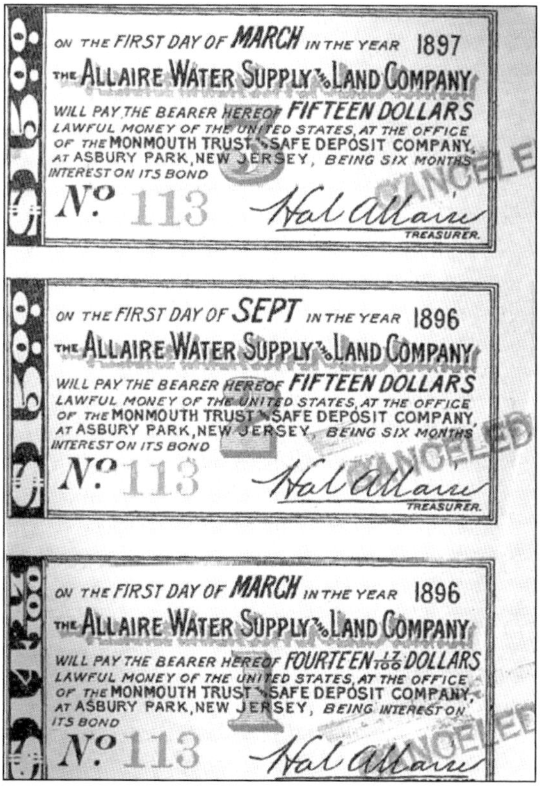

$15.00

ON THE FIRST DAY OF MARCH IN THE YEAR 1897
THE ALLAIRE WATER SUPPLY & LAND COMPANY
WILL PAY THE BEARER HEREOF FIFTEEN DOLLARS
LAWFUL MONEY OF THE UNITED STATES, AT THE OFFICE OF THE MONMOUTH TRUST & SAFE DEPOSIT COMPANY, AT ASBURY PARK, NEW JERSEY, BEING SIX MONTHS INTEREST ON ITS BOND

No 113 Hal Allaire
TREASURER.

CANCELED

$15.00

ON THE FIRST DAY OF SEPT IN THE YEAR 1896
THE ALLAIRE WATER SUPPLY & LAND COMPANY
WILL PAY THE BEARER HEREOF FIFTEEN DOLLARS
LAWFUL MONEY OF THE UNITED STATES, AT THE OFFICE OF THE MONMOUTH TRUST & SAFE DEPOSIT COMPANY, AT ASBURY PARK, NEW JERSEY, BEING SIX MONTHS INTEREST ON ITS BOND

No 113 Hal Allaire
TREASURER.

CANCELED

$14.17

ON THE FIRST DAY OF MARCH IN THE YEAR 1896
THE ALLAIRE WATER SUPPLY & LAND COMPANY
WILL PAY THE BEARER HEREOF FOURTEEN 17/100 DOLLARS
LAWFUL MONEY OF THE UNITED STATES, AT THE OFFICE OF THE MONMOUTH TRUST & SAFE DEPOSIT COMPANY, AT ASBURY PARK, NEW JERSEY, BEING INTEREST ON ITS BOND

No 113 Hal Allaire

CANCELED

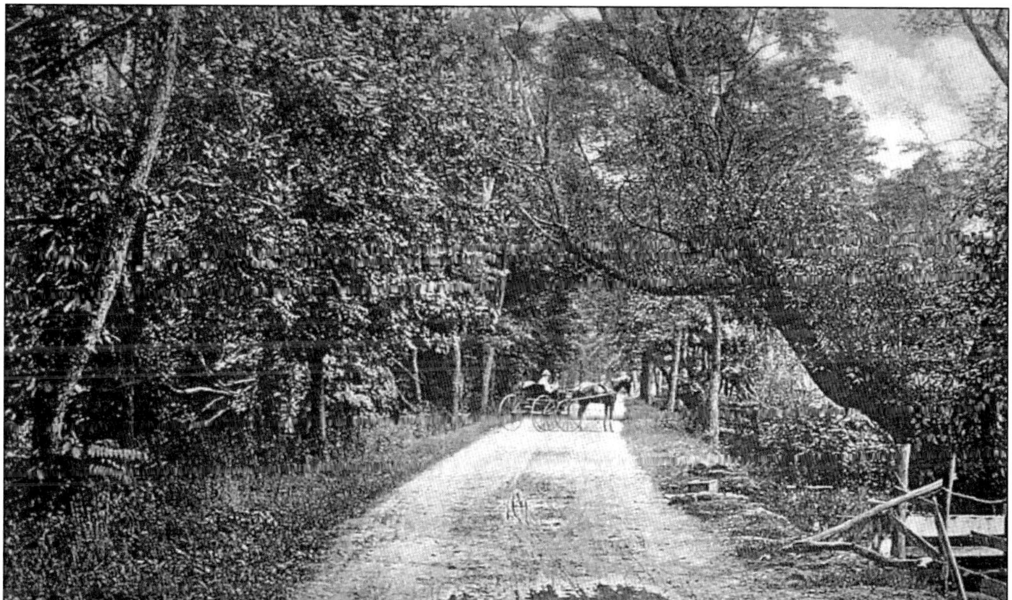

A horse-drawn buggy is shown on the road to Allaire Village c. 1890. Originally, Atlantic Avenue (Route 524) traversed through Allaire Village. The current alignment was built c. 1892, bypassing the village.

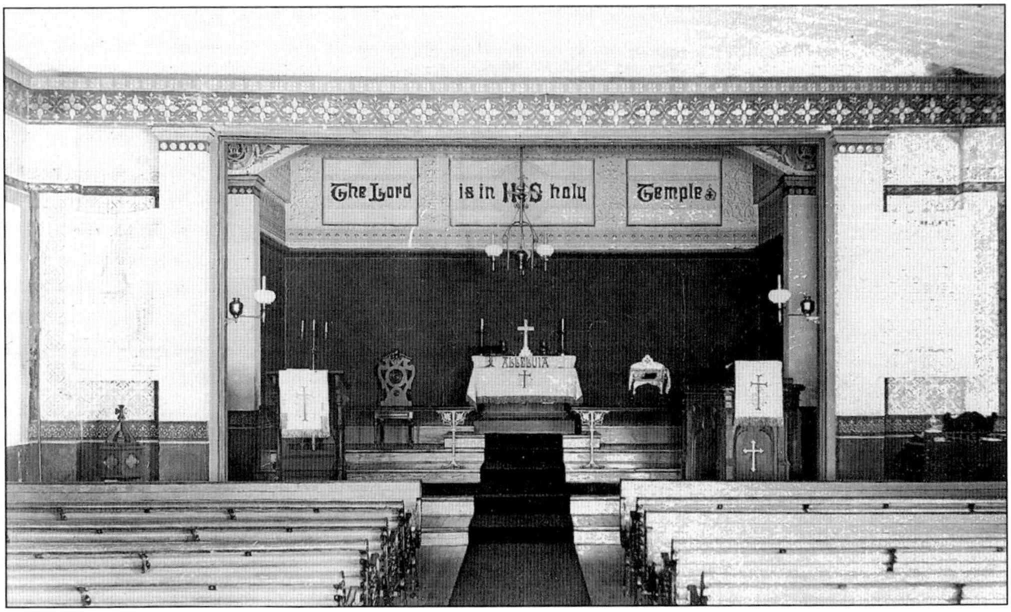

This view shows the church how it probably looked at Hal Allaire's funeral in 1901. Allaire wrote many theatrical plays in his life, and the church was his stage. Many remember the church looking this way in the 1920s and 1930s. The church fell into disrepair after Allaire's death in 1901 but was later restored for local farmers and residents.

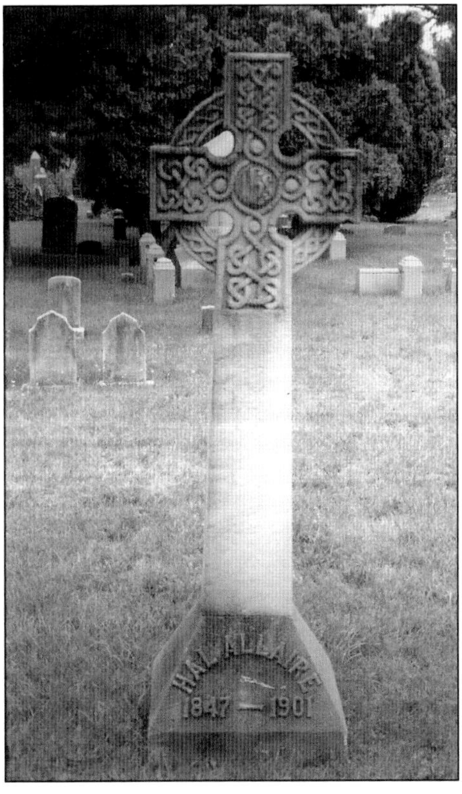

Hal Allaire's burial site, at Atlantic View Cemetery, is pictured here. Allaire died on October 18, 1901, and a funeral service was held at the former Howell Works Church. He was known to some as a "recluse, doing nothing to preserve the town that bore his name" and to others as a "compassionate and humbling caretaker to his father's crumbling ruins—enjoying those who came to see it with him." In his earlier career, Allaire was best known as a cultured, artistic renaissance man. He wrote theatrical plays, drew maps, and painted. Perhaps his greatest contribution was writing a great deal about his father's life and industrial empire. Today, these writings are a primary reference source.

Three

ARTHUR BRISBANE BREATHES NEW LIFE INTO ALLAIRE

In 1907, on a leisurely drive from his Lakewood mansion, Arthur Brisbane bought Allaire Village from W.J. Harrison for the sum of $68,000. His purchase included 6,000 acres of the original Allaire family property, including the Howell Works. Allaire Village, a flourishing bog-iron community in the 1830s, was crumbling and nearly deserted by 1907. During Brisbane's ownership of Allaire, he revitalized it, creating a luxurious country estate for himself, his family, and guests to enjoy.

Those who visit Allaire Village today come to appreciate James P. Allaire and his Howell Works but rarely gain an appreciation of Allaire's other prolific owner, Arthur Brisbane, in the 20th century. Brisbane (1864–1936) was admired as one of the world's greatest editors, journalists, and orators. As a muckraker of the Progressive Era, he initiated crusades for improved public schools, labor laws, and reform for prisons, state hospitals, and drug-addiction centers. As an editor, he initiated crusades against crime, boxing, automobile accidents, capital punishment, and Prohibition. He exposed the election fraud of Tammany Hall, attacked the political bosses of major American cities, and condemned political machines in his writings.

By 1923, Brisbane was the highest-paid journalist in the world—$260,000 a year, equivalent to $2.5 million a year by today's standards. He was considered to be the executive director of William Randolph Hearst's extensive newspaper empire. He played an active role in the expansion of the Universal News Service and the International News Service. Moreover, Brisbane was noted for buying local and national newspapers that were failing, reorganizing them, and then selling them to Hearst. At his death in 1936, the *Daily Times* in Lakewood referred to him as "America's number one all-around newspaperman, for he amuses and instructs more people in a direct relationship than any other man in all of history."

Few realize that Allaire Village would probably have been plowed under or sold for commercial and real estate development if it had not been for Brisbane and his family. The Brisbanes gifted the property that later became the heart of Allaire State Park, including Historic Allaire Village. Through strict land deeds, they set forth the vision of what Allaire is today—a historic center and forest preserve. His Allaire estate once encompassed close to 10,000 acres and included the property that now comprises Allaire Airport. To maintain this acreage, Brisbane had a number of caretakers that included the Frostick, Macauley, Service, and Reynolds families. Of all his real estate holdings, which were quite extensive, Allaire was his favorite. It was here that he liked to vacation and partake in his favorite hobby—horseback riding. It was Allaire that became his final permanent residence.

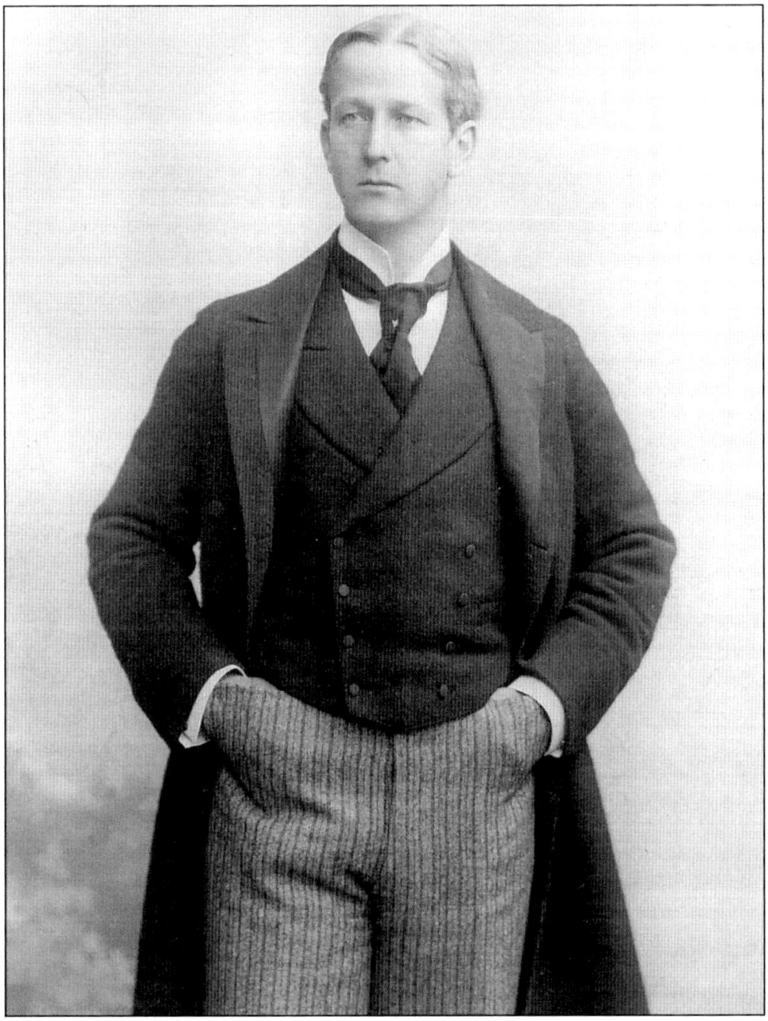

Arthur Brisbane, pictured in his late 20s, was born in Buffalo, New York, in 1864, the son of Sara and Albert Brisbane, founder of many utopian communities. Educated in both the United States and abroad, Brisbane began his journalism career at the age of 19 as a cub reporter for Charles Dana's *New York Sun*. There, he aspired to be the paper's most brilliant news writer by age 20. He served as the paper's London correspondent before assuming command as the evening editor at age 22. Between the ages of 22 and 33, he edited the *Evening Sun* for Charles Dana and the *Evening World* for Joseph Pulitzer. In 1897, at the age of 33, Brisbane gave up a $15,000 annual salary with Pulitzer and accepted an $8,000 salary with William Randolph Hearst. Wanting to try new ideas, he moved over to the Hearst organization and quickly saved Hearst's floundering *New York Evening Journal*. Brisbane made the newspaper appeal to recently arrived immigrants and working people. Reorganizing it to make it different from the morning papers, he employed large type, condensed and illustrated news stories, and took over the editorial page himself. Within four months, circulation of the *Journal* had grown from 40,000 daily copies to a whopping 640,000 daily copies. With that success came a small fortune to Brisbane. For every increase of 10,000 copies in circulation, Brisbane received a $1,000 bonus on top of his $8,000 base salary. Of all the newspapers in the Hearst empire, the *Journal* was the most profitable. Brisbane thought he would only be writing editorials on a temporary basis. However, his union with Hearst and daily editorials lasted until his death in 1936.

Arthur Brisbane is pictured on the telephone in his New York City office in 1917. People who visited the famous Hearst editor could not help to notice all the books, papers, and photographs that occupied his office. Sources for his editorials came from daily events, newspapers, magazines, and books. Brisbane could dictate an editorial in 20 minutes. Once, he dictated 39 editorials in three hours so he could take a vacation for 39 days.

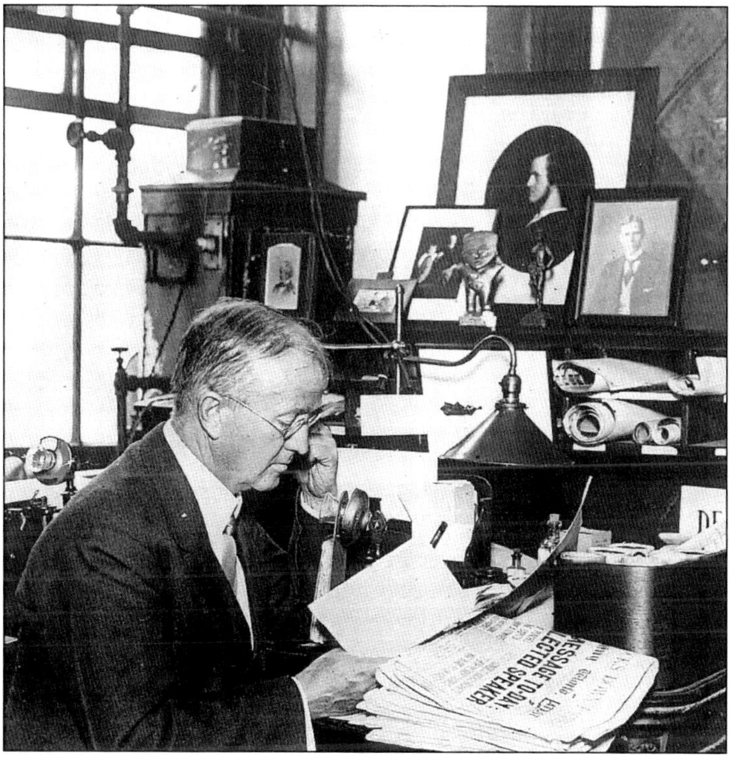

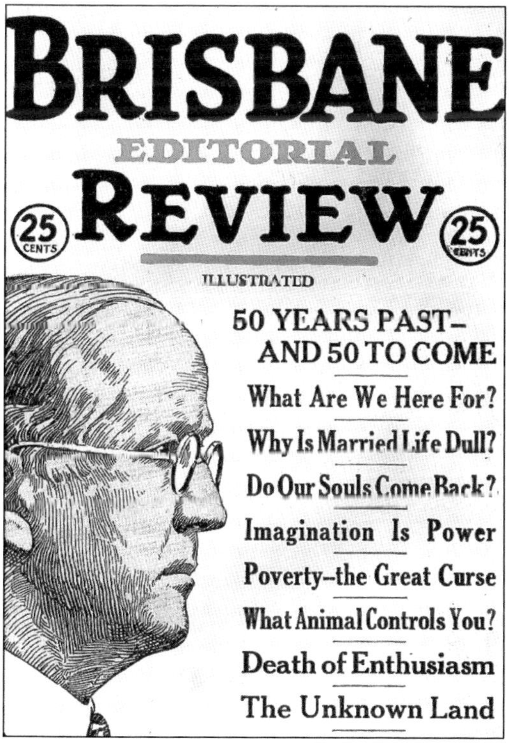

This compilation of Brisbane's most famous editorials was the first of a series to be published in the early 1920s. From the start, the editorials struck a fresh note in journalism and became the feature of many newspapers throughout the world. Instead of the usual run of serious discussions, he wrote of incidents with human interest and drama. He aimed his observations straight at the individual reader. Anyone who could read could understand Arthur Brisbane. Cartoons and illustrations by Hal Coffman enhanced the editorials.

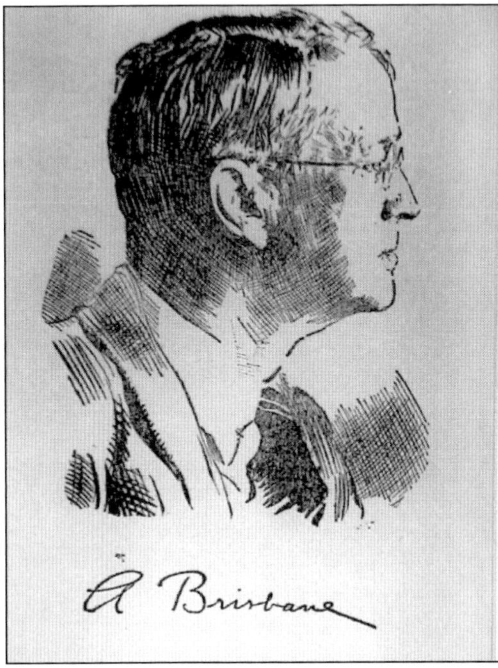

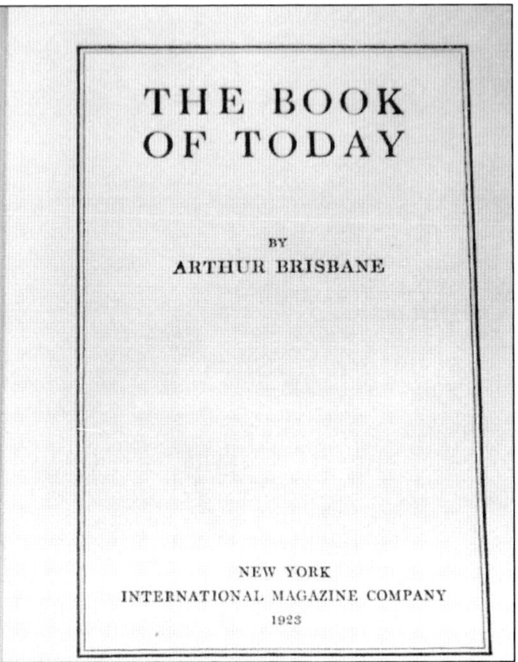
THE BOOK OF TODAY

BY

ARTHUR BRISBANE

NEW YORK
INTERNATIONAL MAGAZINE COMPANY
1923

In 1923, Brisbane published more of his famous editorials in *The Book of Today*. In 1923, *Time* magazine reported that Arthur Brisbane told more things to more people than any other man in the United States. By 1931, it was estimated that more than 40 million people were reading Brisbane's editorials, approximately a third of the world population. His editorial column "Today" was being syndicated to 200 daily papers, and his "This Week" column appeared in 1,200 country weeklies. Four secretaries were constantly on call for Brisbane, and his Edison Dictaphone was usually kept within easy reach.

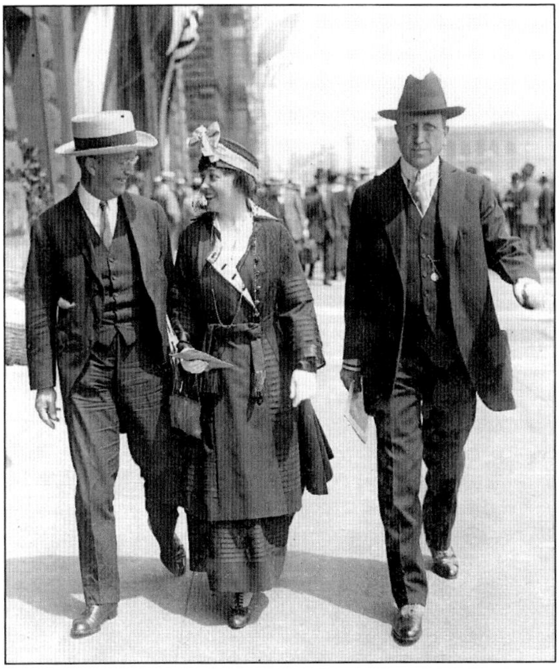

Arthur Brisbane (left) is shown with Mr. and Mrs. William R. Hearst c. 1910. Brisbane and Hearst were a perfect match—both were champions of the working man and craved power, popular success, and above all money. They were dynamos and brilliant newspapermen with a flair for the spectacular and outrageous. Brisbane worked hand-in-hand with Hearst to build his vast newspaper empire. When Hearst invaded Chicago with his *Chicago American* in 1900, Brisbane arrived to edit the first issue, hire and train the staff, and get the paper running. He repeated this task for Hearst in other major American cities. In 1928, Brisbane became the publisher of all Hearst's morning and evening newspapers in New York City.

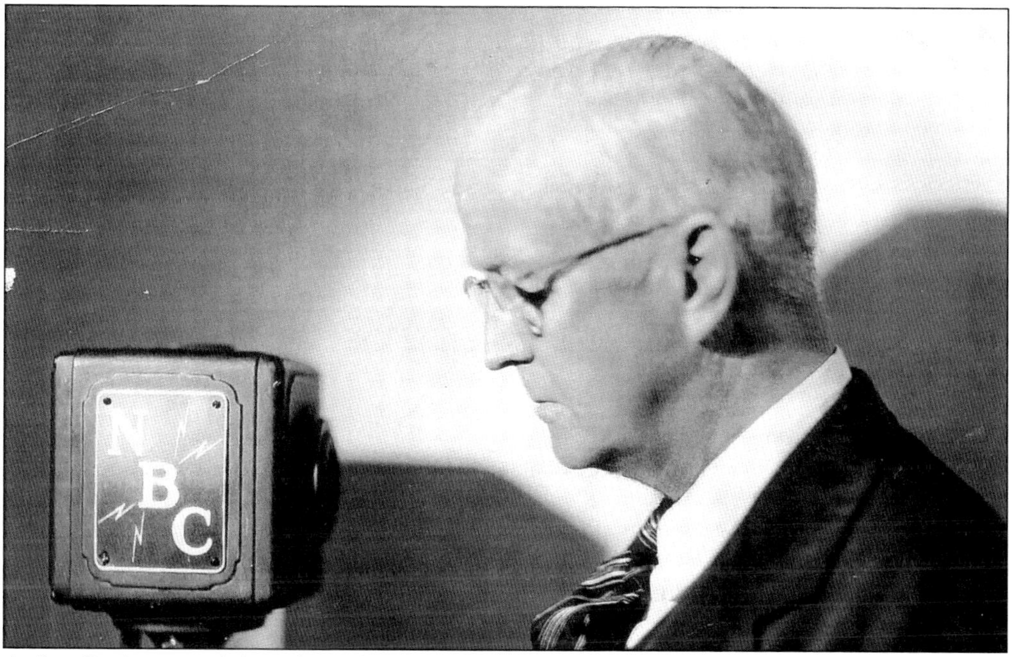

Arthur Brisbane reads his editorial on NBC radio c. 1933. As Brisbane's notoriety expanded, he was called upon to give public speeches, including speeches to college graduates. As an orator, he spoke in a low and clear voice, never hesitating for an answer or grasping once for a word. When he was asked a question, the reply was complete and documented. His notoriety often called him into the field of public relations.

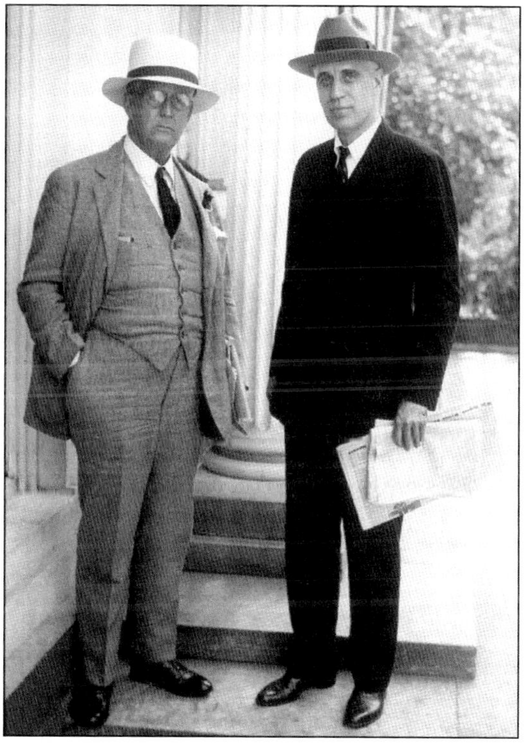

Arthur Brisbane (left) is pictured on the steps of the White House in 1932 with distinguished editorial writer James T. Williams Jr. They have just interviewed Pres. Herbert Hoover. As an editor and columnist, it was only natural for Brisbane to meet and interview most of the U.S. presidents in office during his lifetime. Later, Brisbane was the go-between for Hearst and Franklin Delano Roosevelt as a player in their political game of tit-for-tat. Brisbane served as a consultant and confidant to many politicians and corporate executives. (Courtesy the Bancroft Library.)

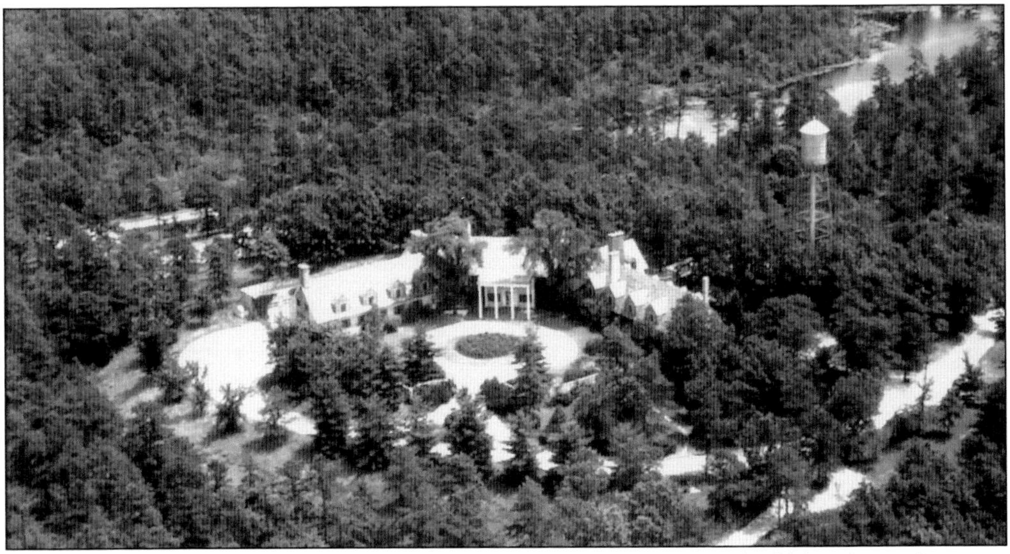

Brisbane married Phoebe Cary in 1912. In the 1920s, he set out to build his dream house at Allaire, as shown here in 1940. It became Brisbane's permanent residence in his later years and was nicknamed the Castle by locals. At first, he used Allaire for vacations, taking in the country fresh air and the outdoor recreational activities offered. Brisbane's first home at Allaire (located along the park's service road) was a poured-concrete home, an architectural design borrowed from Thomas Edison. He boarded his private rail car in Farmingdale and commuted via the Central Railroad of New Jersey to his New York City office.

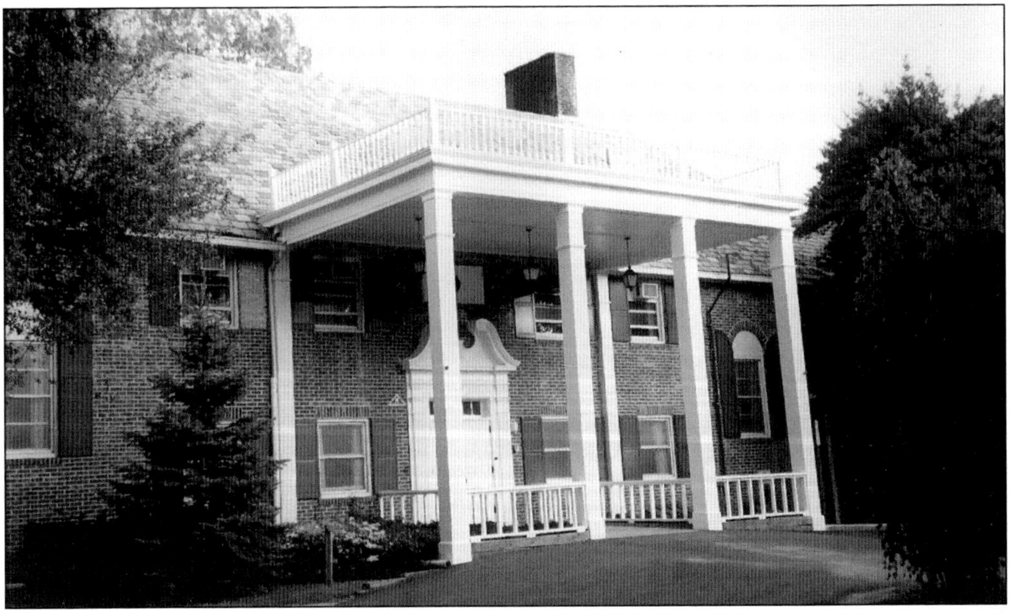

After Brisbane's death in 1936, his wife donated their Allaire mansion (seen in a recent view) to the state for development into the Arthur Brisbane Child Treatment Center, which still exists today. In the 1930s, Brisbane allowed many victims of the Great Depression to take shelter in homes existing at his Allaire estate. During the same time, he financed the erection of steel-frame cottages in New York City that would be sold to workers and paid for out of their income—an investment that ran into the millions.

This Allaire canal scene dates from c. 1910. Brisbane enjoyed acreage, nature, and the ocean. He was a devout nature lover. He developed a part of Allaire into large orchards, farming grounds, and bridle paths.

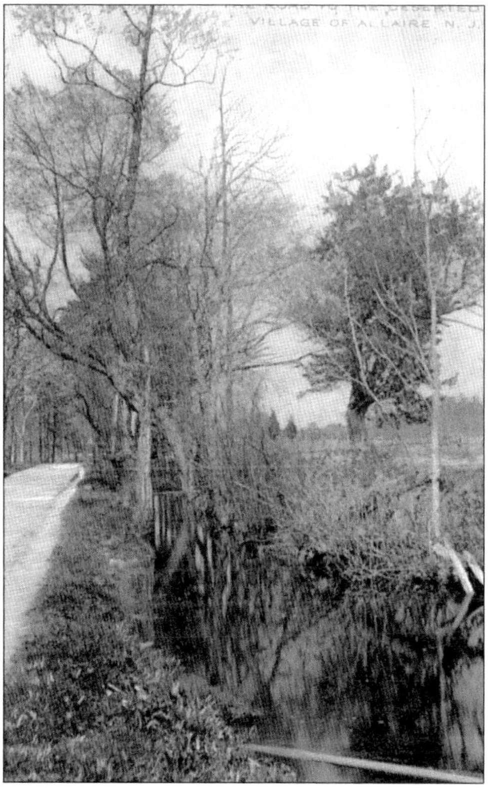

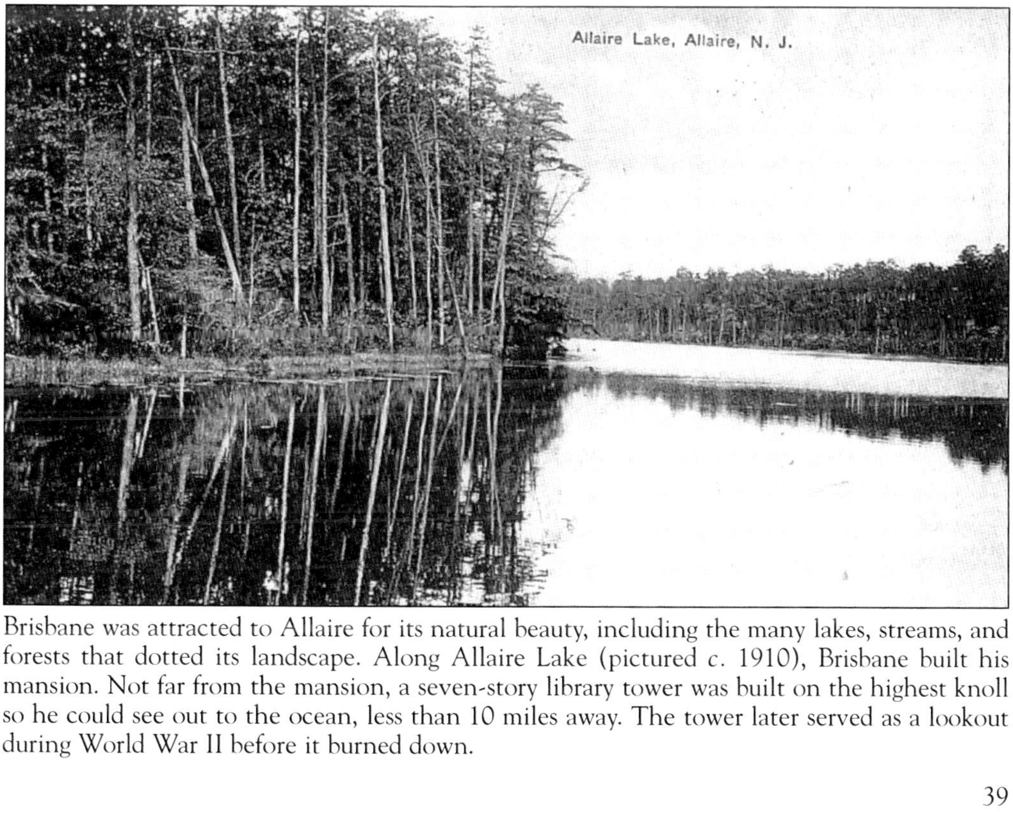

Brisbane was attracted to Allaire for its natural beauty, including the many lakes, streams, and forests that dotted its landscape. Along Allaire Lake (pictured c. 1910), Brisbane built his mansion. Not far from the mansion, a seven-story library tower was built on the highest knoll so he could see out to the ocean, less than 10 miles away. The tower later served as a lookout during World War II before it burned down.

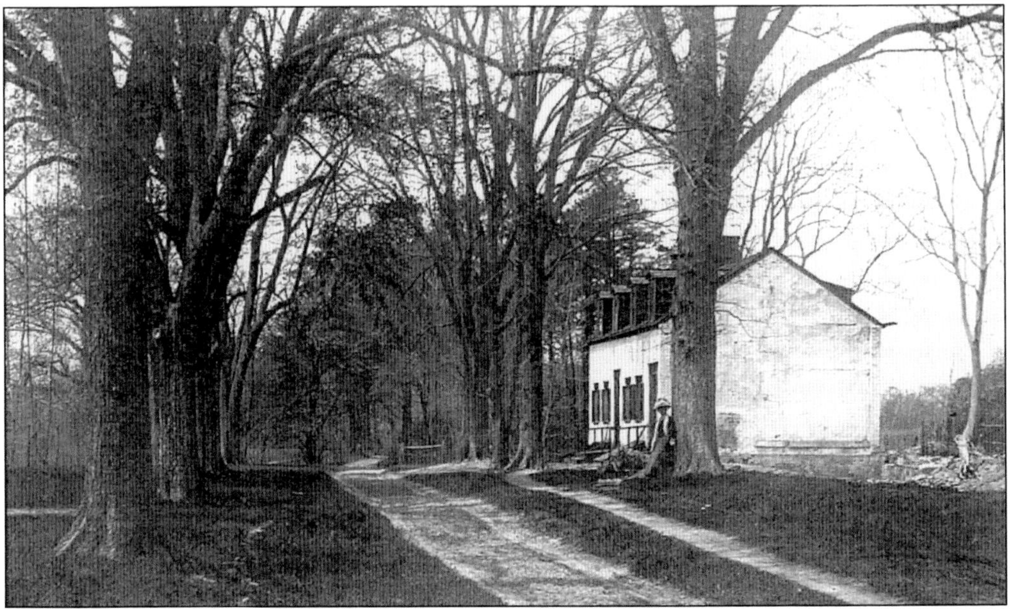

Pictured c. 1915 are the only remaining row houses at Allaire, now part of the visitor center. Brisbane employed a large staff to care for his orchards, farms, and 10,000-acre (at one time) estate. Many of the homes in the village, including the row houses, were renovated to house his employees.

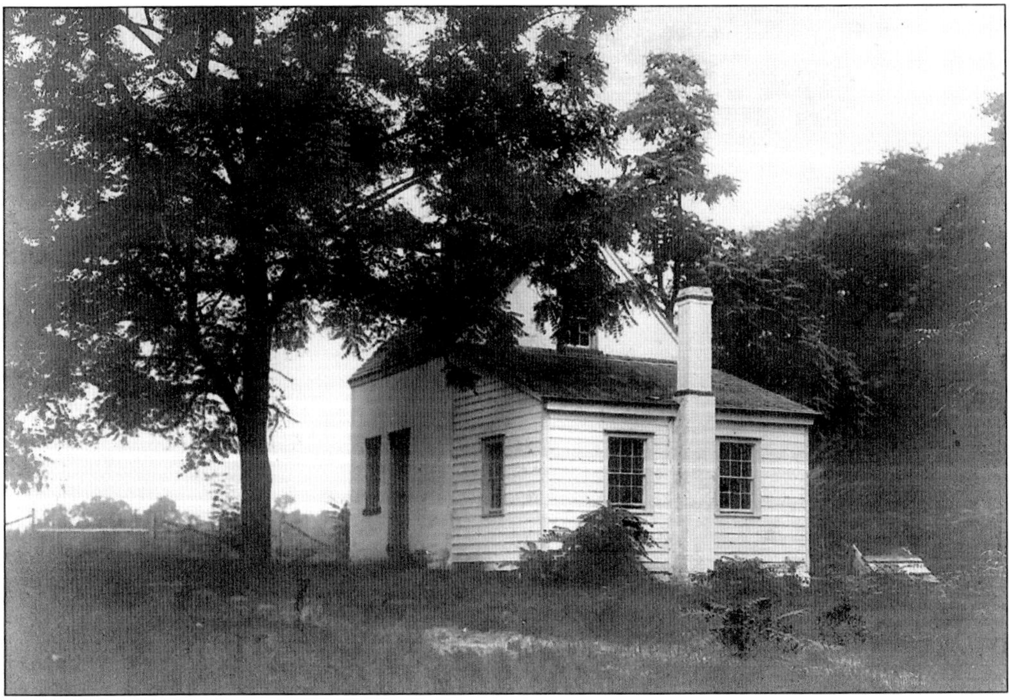

The foreman's cottage, with its southern addition, is shown c. 1915. The southern addition was built onto the home in the late 1800s. It served as a private residence well after James P. Allaire's death in 1858. At the time this photograph was taken, it was probably a residence to one of Brisbane's many caretakers.

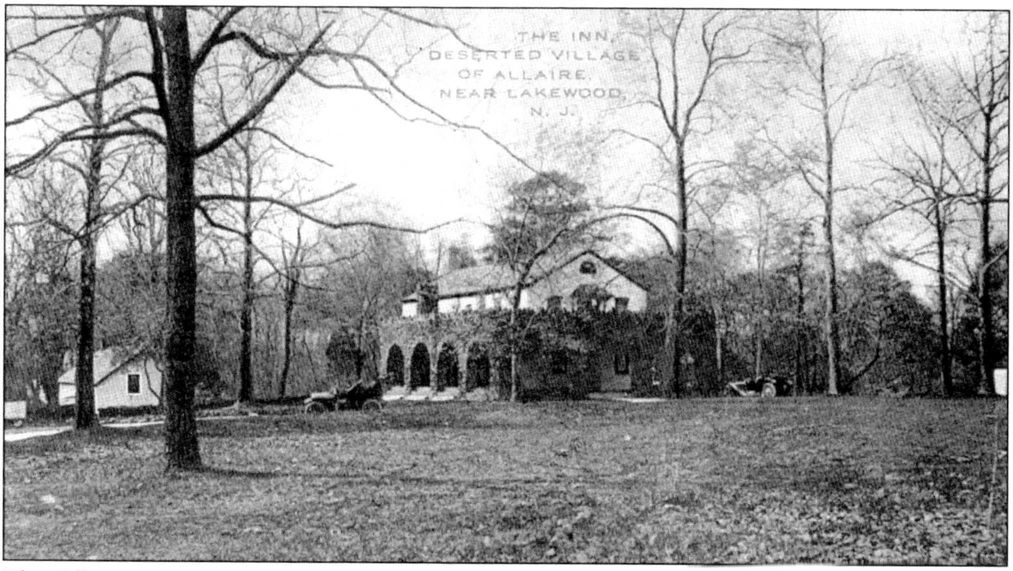

The Allaire Inn, established in the 1890s, occupied the carpenter shop, as seen in this *c.* 1910 view. Brisbane permitted William DeLisle, inn proprietor, to alter the exterior by adding a kitchen wing and large fieldstone porch, where guests could enjoy outside dining and dancing. Guests were allowed to enjoy the amenities and recreational sports that Brisbane's Allaire estate offered.

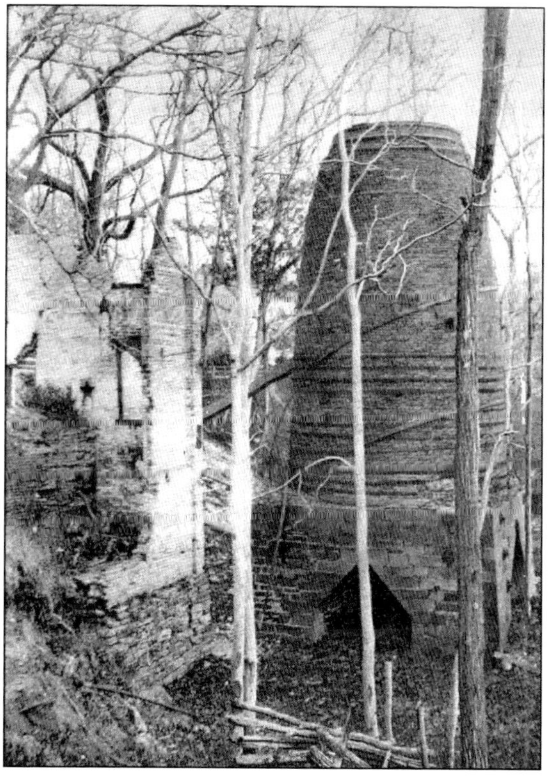

Once the heart of James P. Allaire's Howell Works, the blast furnace was used as a backdrop for sightseers and early automobilists who came to explore the ruins, seen here *c.* 1915. In the 1830s, the furnace operated 24 hours a day, 7 days a week, and about 9 months out of the year. The furnace dumped a considerable amount of soot on the village when it was in operation. Village buildings were whitewashed a few times between 1822 and 1936.

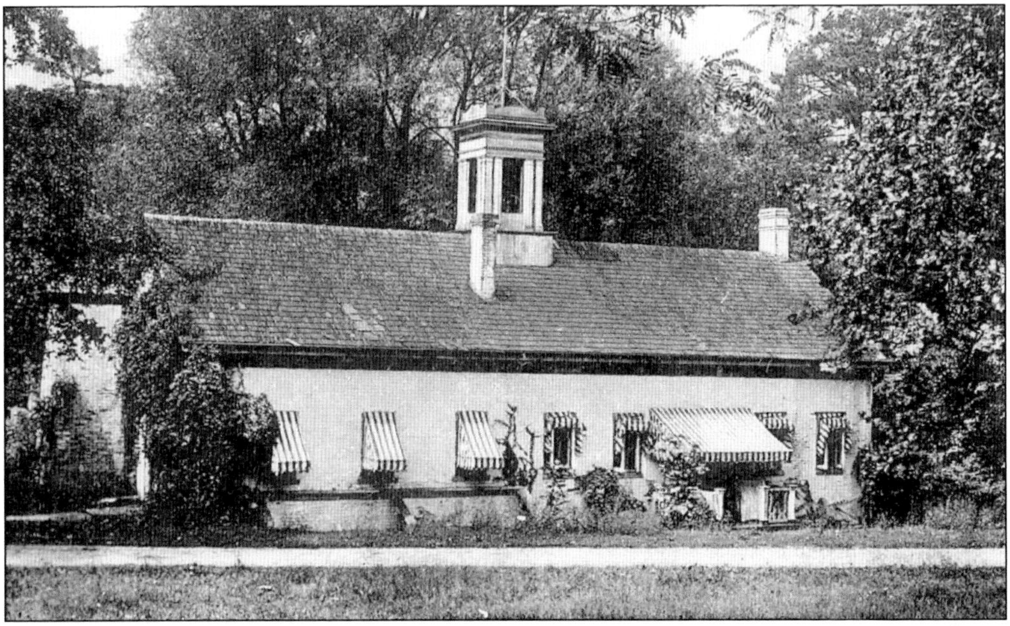

Continuing from the days of Hal Allaire, the Enameling Building (seen in 1909) served as a private residence during Brisbane's ownership and was commonly referred to as the Lakeside House, with its picturesque brook running along the west side of the building. At the time of this photograph, the building was occupied by the Hush family. Village houses that were occupied by James P. Allaire's workers in the 19th century were later occupied by Arthur Brisbane's employees.

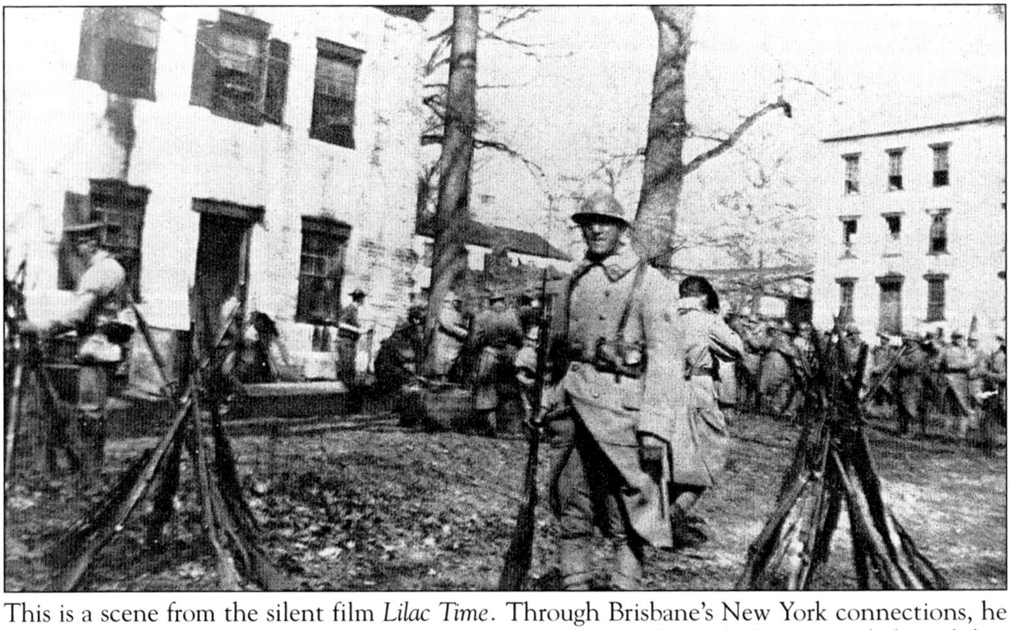

This is a scene from the silent film *Lilac Time*. Through Brisbane's New York connections, he allowed the village to be used as a backdrop for silent films in the early 1900s. It is believed that many of the village buildings endured another round of whitewashing for filming. Pictured are the bakery (left) and the rear of the general store (right) in a World War I scene.

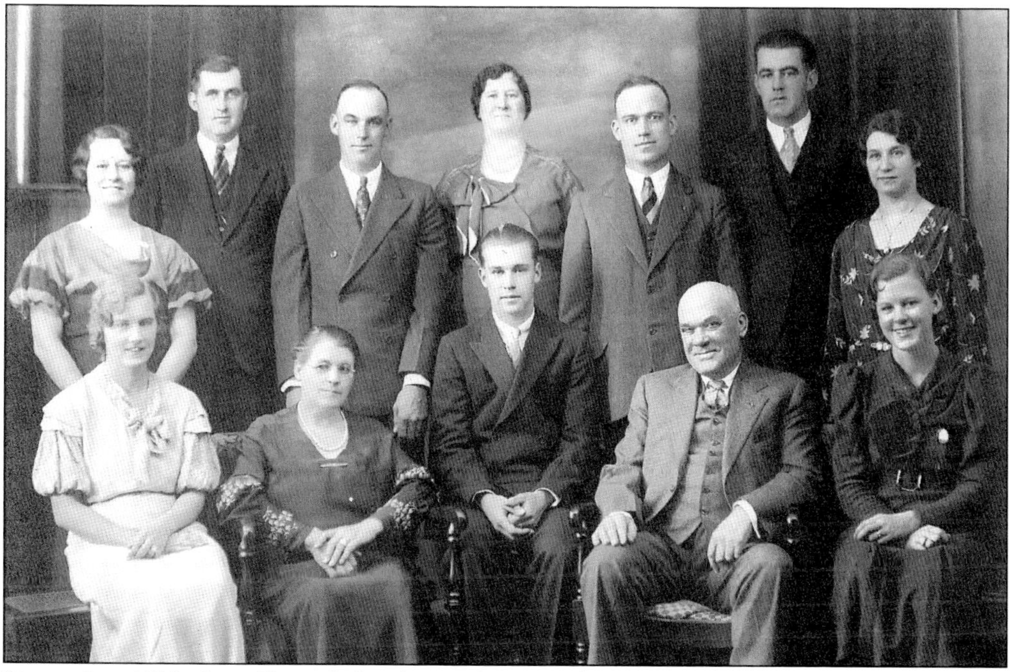

Pictured in 1938, these Frostick family members are, from left to right, as follows: (front row) Catherine, Janet (mother), Tom, William (father), and Helen; (back row) Mabel, William Jr., Ernest, Janet, Robert, George, and Ethel. Arthur Brisbane hired William Frostick in 1907 to serve as his superintendent. Frostick hired, fired, supervised, and paid the employees who maintained the grounds, worked in the orchards, and tended to the variety of horses and farm animals at Brisbane's Allaire estate. To the Frosticks, Allaire was their playground. The entire family chipped in to do work on the estate. Prior to his marriage in 1912, Brisbane would often dine with the Frosticks.

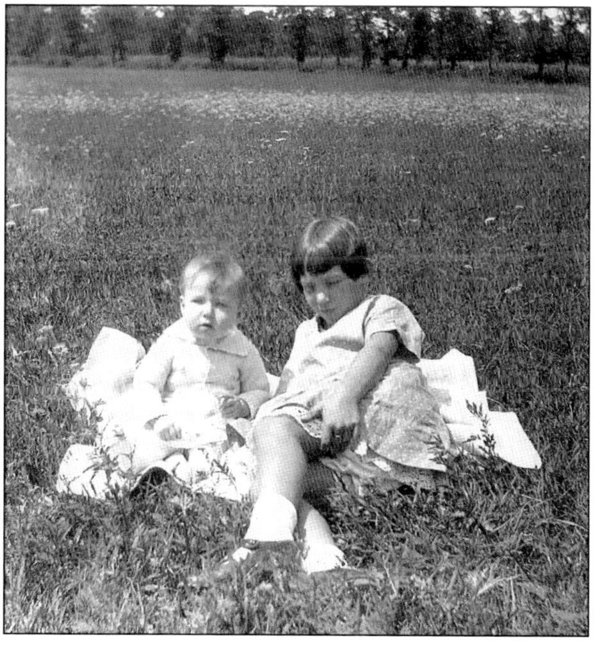

Enjoying a meadow near the Frostick homestead in 1926 are Evelyn Kessler Morton (left), granddaughter of William Frostick, and Helen Frostick Johnson, daughter of William Frostick. As superintendent, Frostick was instrumental in securing additional property for Brisbane's Allaire estate and served as Brisbane's agent in real estate purchases and sales. The grounds were neatly kept, and the tree lines serve as wind breaks for Brisbane's model farm. In the late 1960s, Morton served as president of the ladies auxiliary.

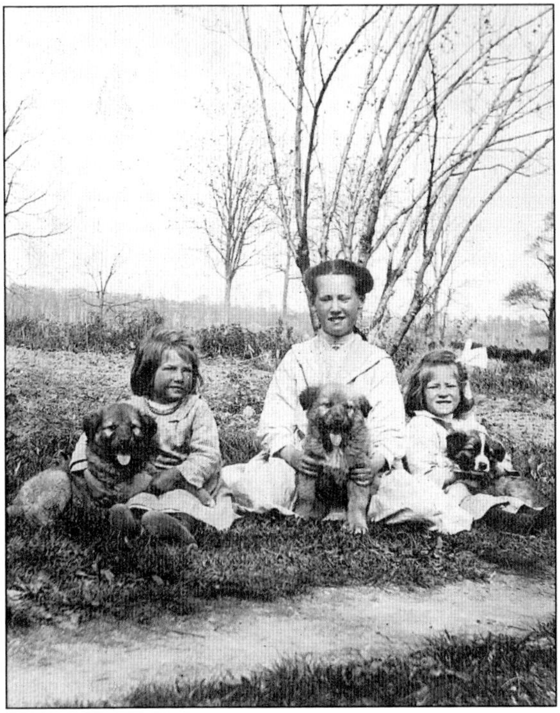

Posing *c.* 1912 with their puppies near the Allaire Big House are some of the Frostick children. They are, from left to right, Mabel Frostick Kessler, Janet (Jen) Frostick Pittenger, and Ethel Frostick Camp. The Frosticks immigrated to the United States in the late 1800s from England. George, Kathryn, Helen, and Tom Frostick were born at Allaire. The others were born in New York State or on their Long Island farm.

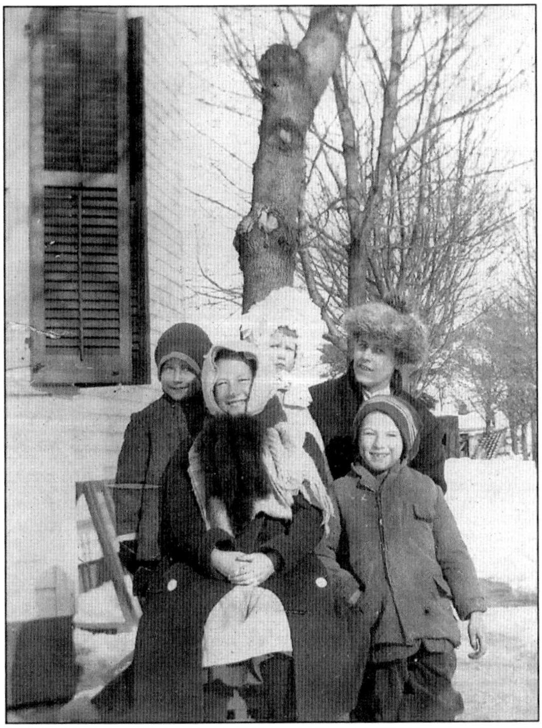

These Frostick family members are shown outside the Allaire Big House *c.* 1907. From left to right are Ernest, Janet, Mabel, Bill Jr. and mother Frostick. When they first came to Allaire, the Frosticks lived near Brisbane's orchards in Squakum. Later, they moved to the Allaire Big House, formerly the home of James P. Allaire. Frostick oversaw the building of Arthur Brisbane's mansion, completed in the 1920s. After it was complete, the Frosticks moved into the poured-concrete house Brisbane had formerly occupied. When the Brisbane family gifted Allaire to the state in 1940, the Frostick family received life rights to the concrete house. The home was torn down in 2000.

Tommy Frostick rides one of Brisbane's ponies c. 1923. Tommy Frostick's father, William, remained a loyal employee to the Brisbane family, lasting beyond Arthur Brisbane's death in 1936. In exchange, William Frostick was paid well (upwards of $150 a week), received many gifts from Brisbane, and paid no rent or maintenance fees for the use of the home they occupied. Frostick was called upon to go to California, Florida, and New York on business for Brisbane, who paid traveling expenses and allowed the family to travel with him.

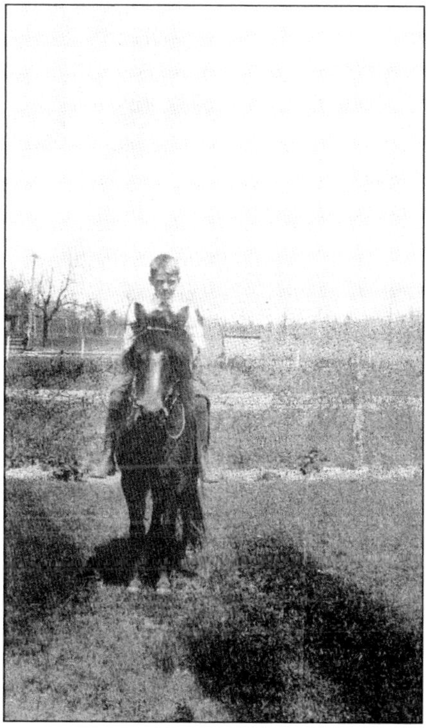

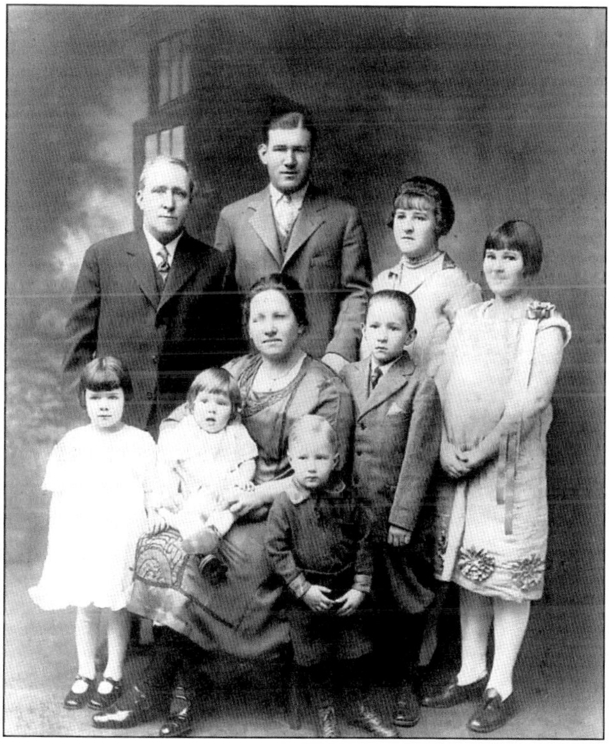

These Macauley family members are, from left to right, as follows: (front row) Genevieve, Frances, Maude (mother), Tom Jr., and Andrew; (back row) Tom (father), Dave, Ellen, and Alice. The family was employed by Brisbane to train and oversee Brisbane's farm animals and to maintain the buildings in which the animals were kept. Brisbane renovated the Enameling Building (the Lakeside House) and allowed the Macauleys to live there.

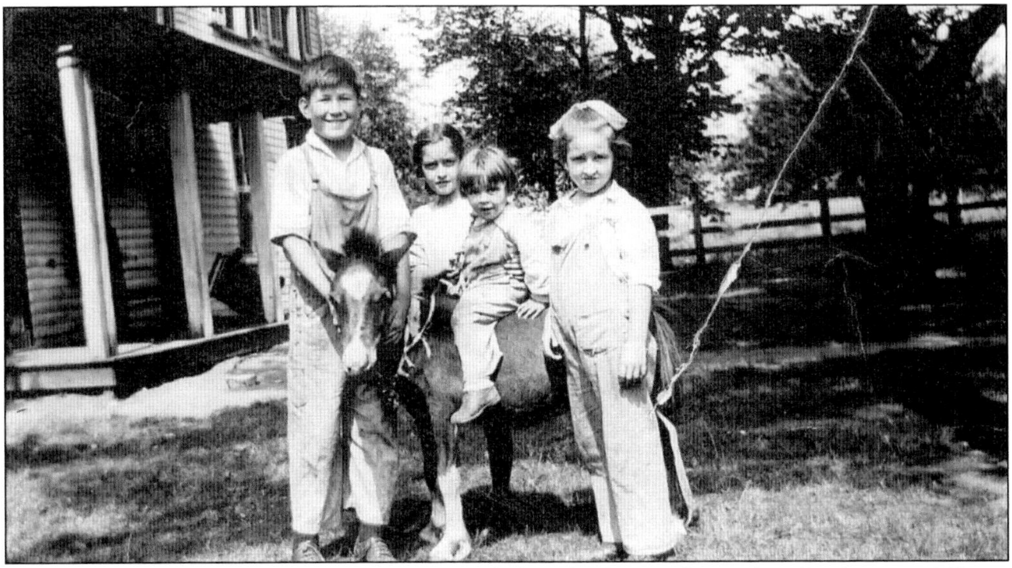

The Macauley family raised, trained, and tended to the horses for Arthur Brisbane at Allaire. Brisbane shipped horses by rail to Hearst's estate in California, accompanied by members of the Macauley and Frostick families. This view shows Dave Macauley (left), Ellen Macauley (right), and their friends with a pony by the Allaire Big House porch.

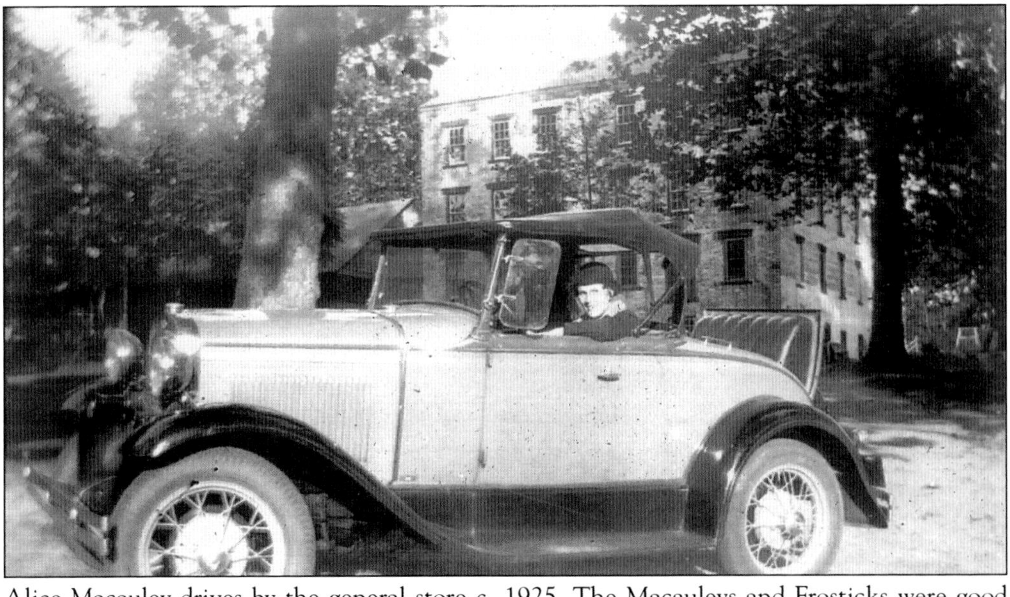

Alice Macauley drives by the general store *c.* 1925. The Macauleys and Frosticks were good friends and, like their employer, raised their own turkeys, guinea pigs, geese, rabbits, and chickens, making fine Christmas dinners.

Shown washing the horses c. 1934 are Tommy (Tim) and Frances Macauley with Porchie (one of Arthur Brisbane's ponies) near the Sears, Roebuck and Company barn at Allaire. Many local children remember the Macauley children allowing them to ride Brisbane's small ponies. The fee was 5¢ for one ride around the corral.

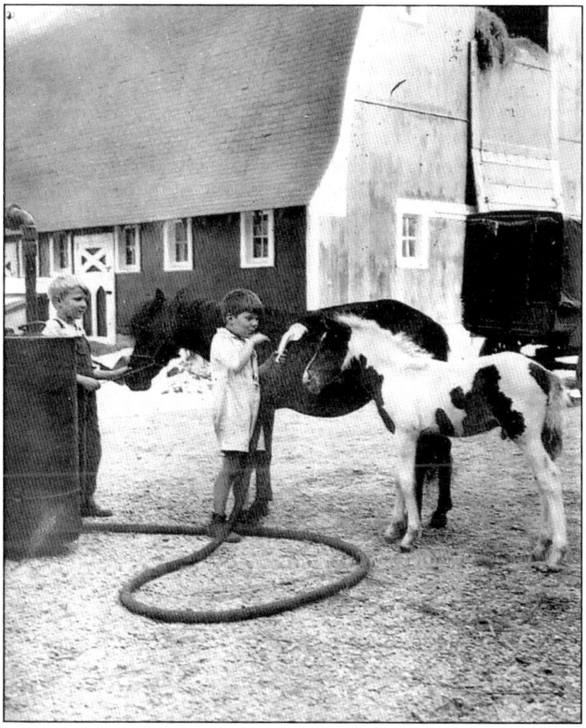

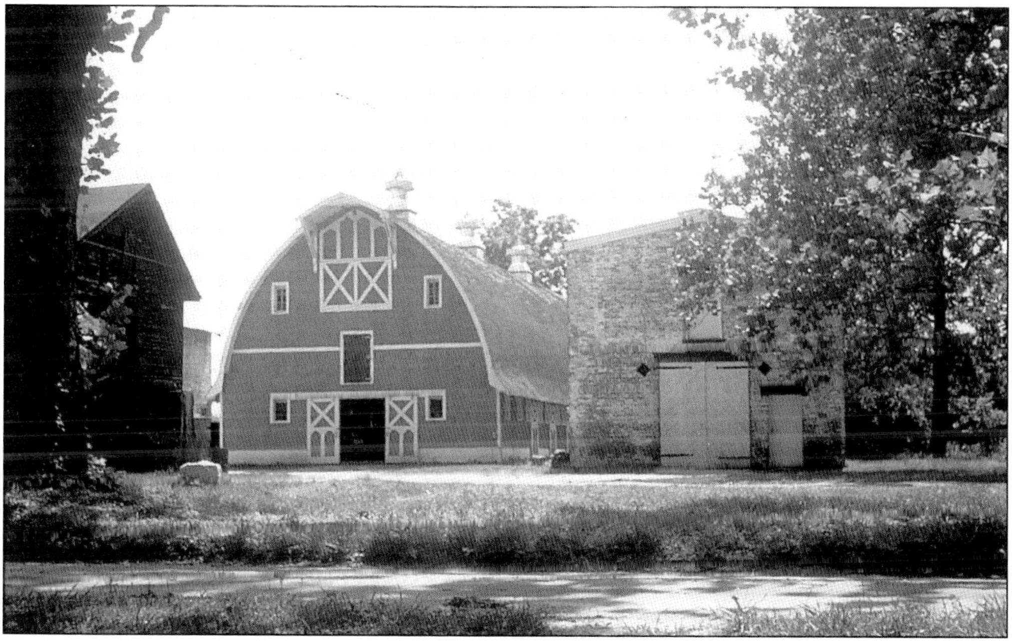

In addition to tending to Brisbane's farm animals, the Macauley family maintained the farm buildings at Allaire, including the huge Sears, Roebuck and Company barn (center). Ordered by Brisbane as a kit from the Sears catalog in the early 1930s, the barn housed Brisbane's increasing heard of riding horses, draft horses, and thoroughbred racehorses. Located next to the carriage house, the barn was dismantled in the early 1970s. Only the carriage house on the far right and barn on the left exist today.

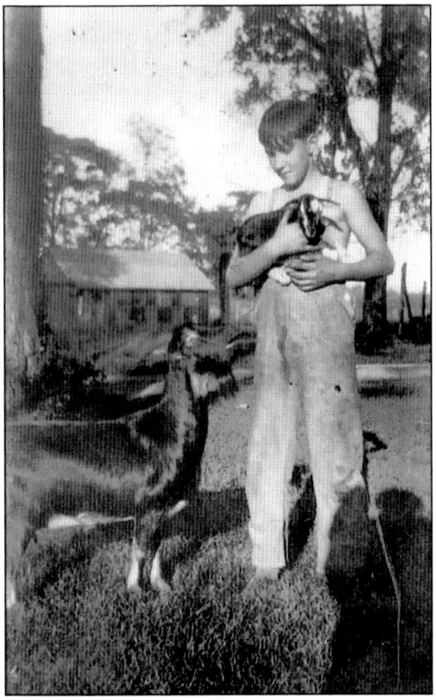

Andrew Macauley tends to goats in this 1927 view. In addition to goats, Brisbane kept sheep, chickens, cattle, guinea hens, horses, and other farm animals at Allaire. Among the more exotic animals kept was a flock of white deer.

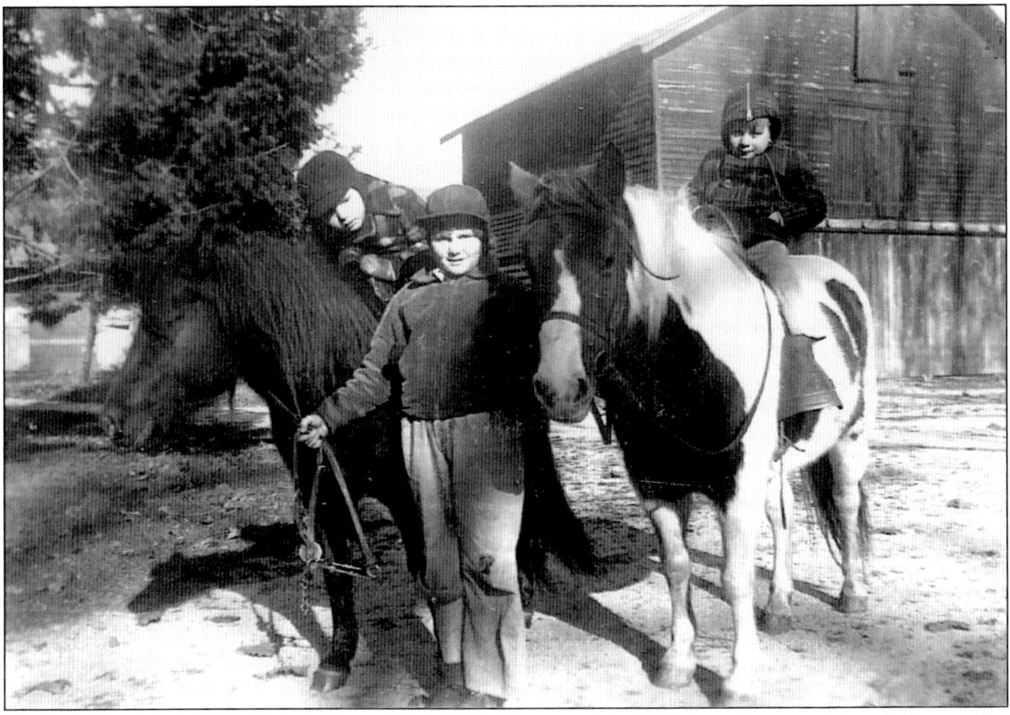

The Macauleys are shown *c.* 1940 just outside the barns and carriage house. From left to right are Tommy (Tim) Macauley, Kathleen Carmen, and Malcolm Carmen—grandchildren of Tom and Maude Macauley. These horses were kept at Arthur Brisbane's model farm. At the time this photograph was taken, the Carmens were living in the gardener's cottage (attached to the carriage house).

Four

THE RAILROAD AND THE ALLAIRE INN

From the 1890s to the early 1930s, the carpenter shop at Allaire Village was transformed into a restaurant and inn. It was called the Allaire Inn and was first under the proprietorship of the DeLisle family and, later, the Thorngreens. With the advent of the automobile in the early 1900s, the Allaire Inn evolved into a famous resort for sightseers and automobilists. The inn continued to operate after Arthur Brisbane bought the Allaire estate in 1907. The inn entered its heyday between 1905 and 1915. Most of what is known about the inn comes from postcards and brochures printed c. 1910. They give perhaps the best written description of the village and grounds during the early 20th century and shed light on the efforts Brisbane and possibly the inn's proprietors exerted to improve Allaire Village during this time. By 1935, the Allaire Inn had closed. One possible reason is a loss of business due to the Great Depression.

Passing through Allaire from the 1870s through the 1960s was the Freehold and Jamesburg Agricultural Railroad, Monmouth County's first railroad. Early railroads were chartered in New Jersey for two reasons—to transport raw materials and finished goods to industrial centers and to transport the state's bountiful agricultural products. The Freehold and Jamesburg was no exception. The discovery and use of greensand marl, a soil-enrichment agent, by Monmouth County farmers as early as 1768 (with an increase in agricultural products, population, and businesses of all kinds) created a demand in the central part of the county for an easier mode of transportation to the markets of New York, Philadelphia, and Trenton. Chartered in 1851 and opened in 1853, the Freehold and Jamesburg line was the solution. It was an extension of the Camden and Amboy Railroad and cost $220,000 to build. In 1866, a northwest extension from Jamesburg to Monmouth Junction was completed. At its southeast terminus in Freehold, an extension to Farmingdale was completed in 1868. In 1872, the Freehold and Jamesburg Agricultural Railroad reached the Jersey Shore town of Manasquan, passing through Allaire and Allenwood along the way. Hal and Calicia Allaire held a considerable amount of stock in the Freehold and Jamesburg. In 1876, the line boasted 27.5 miles of running track from Jamesburg to Manasquan with a connection to the New York and Long Branch Railroad in nearby Sea Girt. The Pennsylvania Railroad was attracted to the Freehold and Jamesburg due to its connection to the shore. It took over operations in 1879. The Pennsylvania Railroad made its first trial run on the Freehold and Jamesburg from West Philadelphia to Long Branch (84 miles) in 1 hour and 40 minutes. The line was in its prime from 1890 to 1920 while owned by the Pennsylvania Railroad.

The Freehold and Jamesburg's passenger and freight traffic paralleled the experience of other resort routes to the Jersey Shore. However, the decline of the railroad during the Great Depression was the most rapid of all the Pennsylvania Railroad's rail lines to the shore. In 1956, the Pennsylvania Railroad claimed that the Freehold and Jamesburg was losing $68,000 a year on passenger service. With the collapse of railroads in the Northeast looming, the Pennsylvania Railroad finally won its fight to discontinue passenger service on the Freehold and Jamesburg in 1962. It soon ripped up the tracks between Sea Girt and Farmingdale, and much of it is now part of the Manasquan bike path.

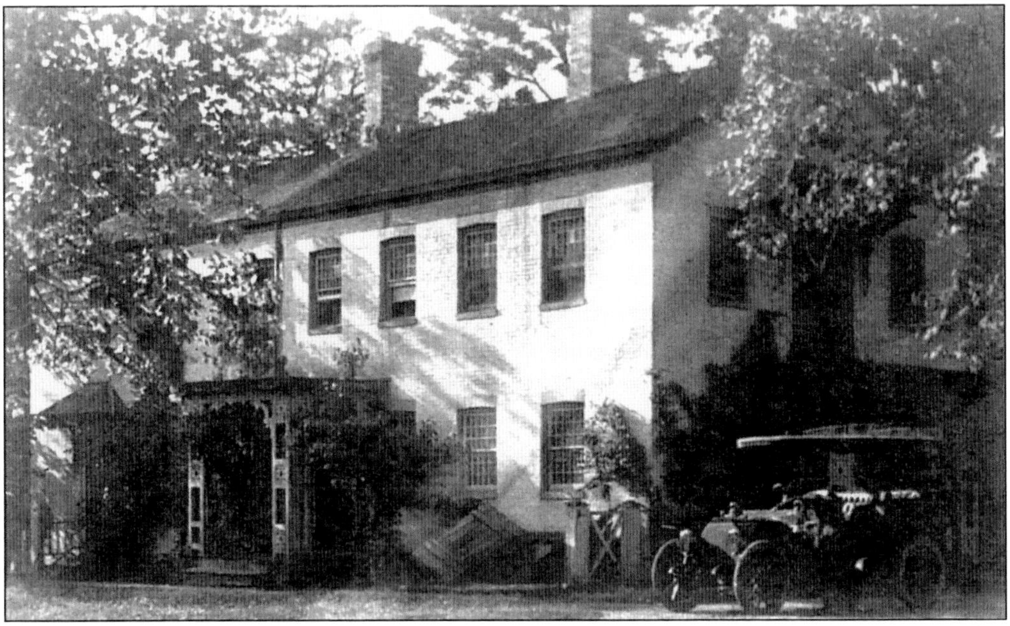

The Allaire Inn was operated by William DeLisle in the early 1900s. After iron making ceased at Allaire in 1846, much of the village lay idle. Hal Allaire allowed one major reuse in the village. William DeLisle transformed the old carpenter shop into a restaurant and inn *c.* 1890.

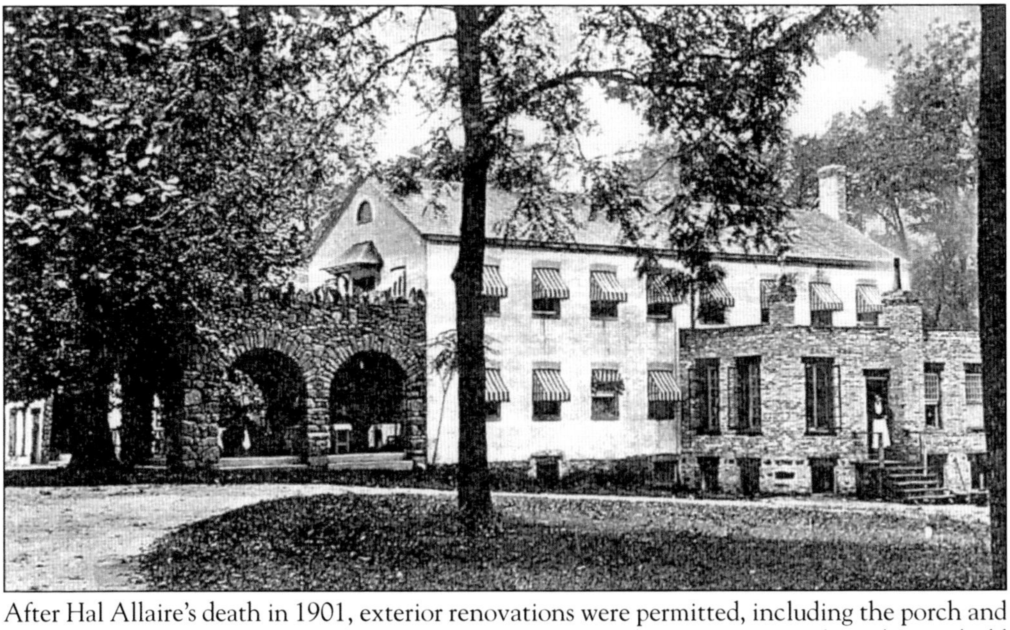

After Hal Allaire's death in 1901, exterior renovations were permitted, including the porch and a new kitchen, as seen in this *c.* 1910 postcard. In the early days, guests arrived via the Freehold and Jamesburg Agricultural Railroad or by horse and buggy.

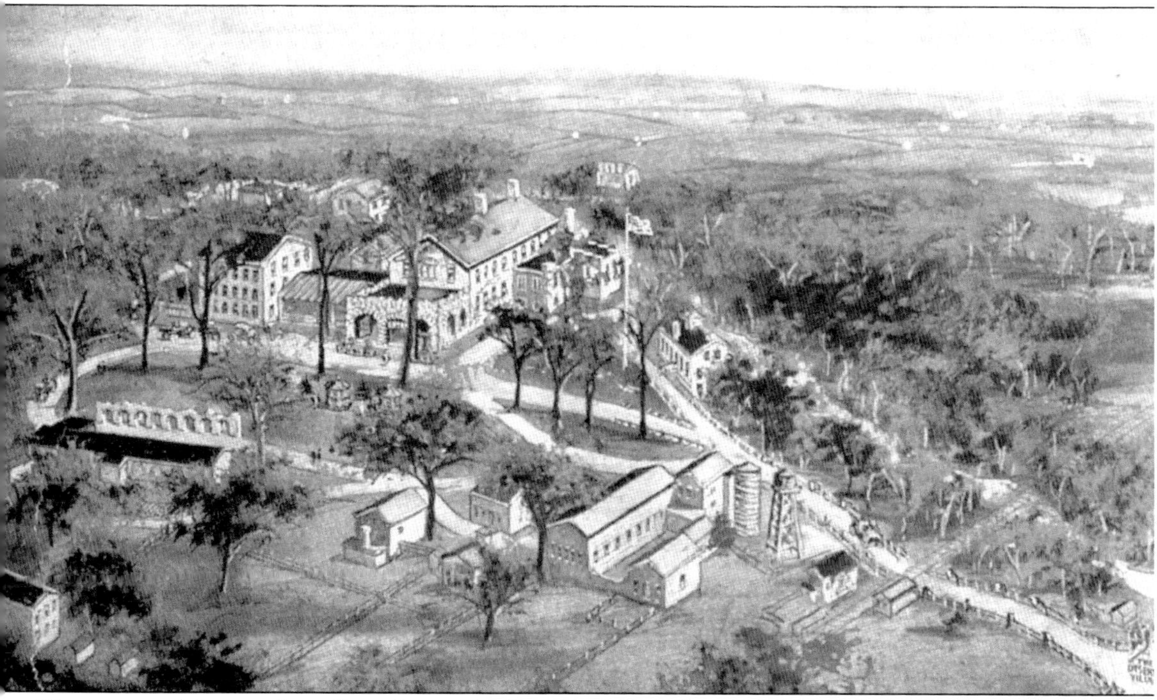

This postcard depicts the village during the height of the Allaire Inn, from 1905 to 1915. The Allaire Inn is seen in the center with the fieldstone porch. Between the inn and the general store was an open-air dancing pavilion. The charcoal depot, near the furnace on the far left, was a full-service garage for guests. At the time, Brisbane's employees occupied the homes in the village. The barns and farm buildings in the lower right (near the water tower) were the center of Brisbane's model farm. The grounds appear very neatly kept in this scene. During Arthur Brisbane's ownership of Allaire, the inn entered its heyday. Many visitors to Allaire do not realize the village's colorful history during the early 1900s. The village was never really deserted; this perception was a glamorization by newspaper journalists when the village was going through tough or changing times (the late 1800s and mid-1900s). This postcard, published c. 1910, shows the village full of life. The inn was located in the heart of Allaire Village and Brisbane's Allaire estate. As private automobile ownership grew in the early 1900s, an increasing number of guests traveled to Allaire. Sightseers flocked to the "deserted village," as it was often called, to see the ruins of this once flourishing bog-iron community. Brisbane allowed guests to use his expansive Allaire estate for their enjoyment.

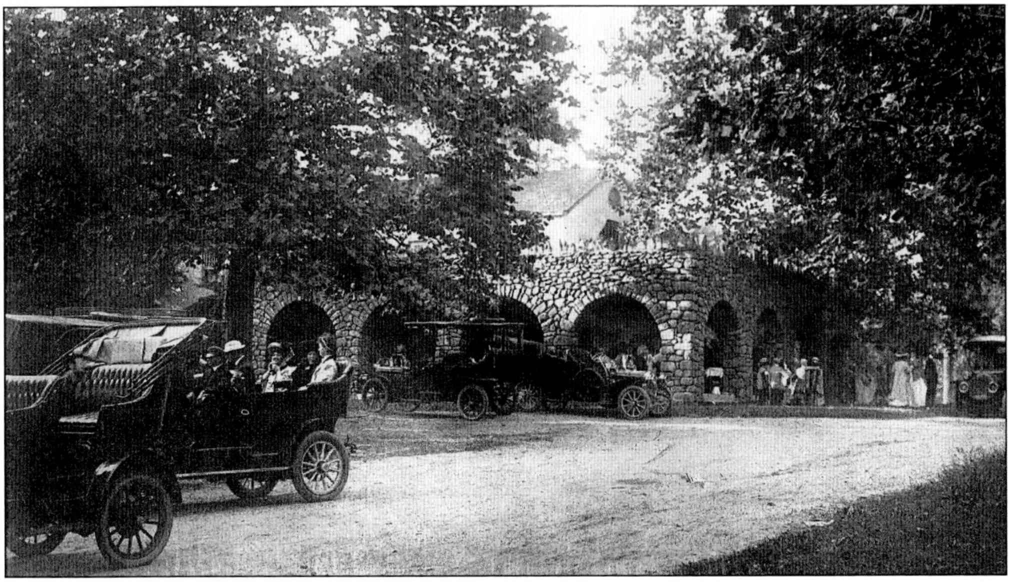

This picture, taken *c.* 1910 at the Allaire Inn, shows a crowd of diners spilling out onto the grass in front of the porch. The cars could be filled with patrons from fashionable estates in towns such as Lakewood, Spring Lake, Manasquan, Point Pleasant, or Sea Girt. The restaurant featured French cuisine. Brisbane's nearby model farm supplied the restaurant with the finest vegetables, milk, and fresh eggs. Refreshments were available at any time—including a bar service. Rumor has it that it was a famous speakeasy during Prohibition.

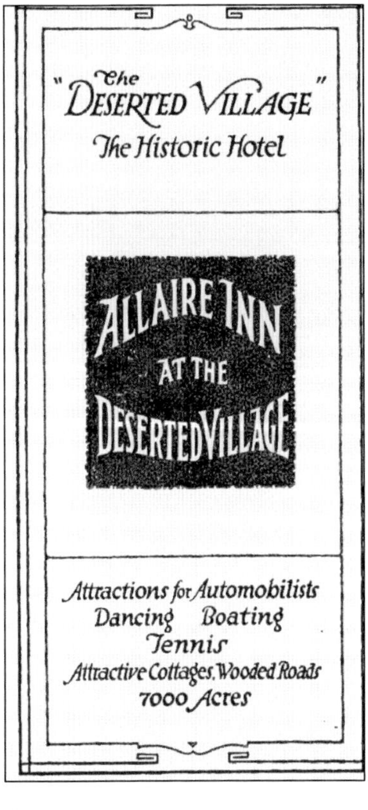

This 11-page brochure, printed *c.* 1910, gives the best description and pictures of what the atmosphere and grounds of Allaire Village were like during the early years of Arthur Brisbane's ownership. For the public, the focal point at this time was the Allaire Inn, with numerous recreational activities, including "attractions for automobilists, dancing in an open-air pavilion, boating, tennis, attractive cottages, wooded roads and 7,000 acres."

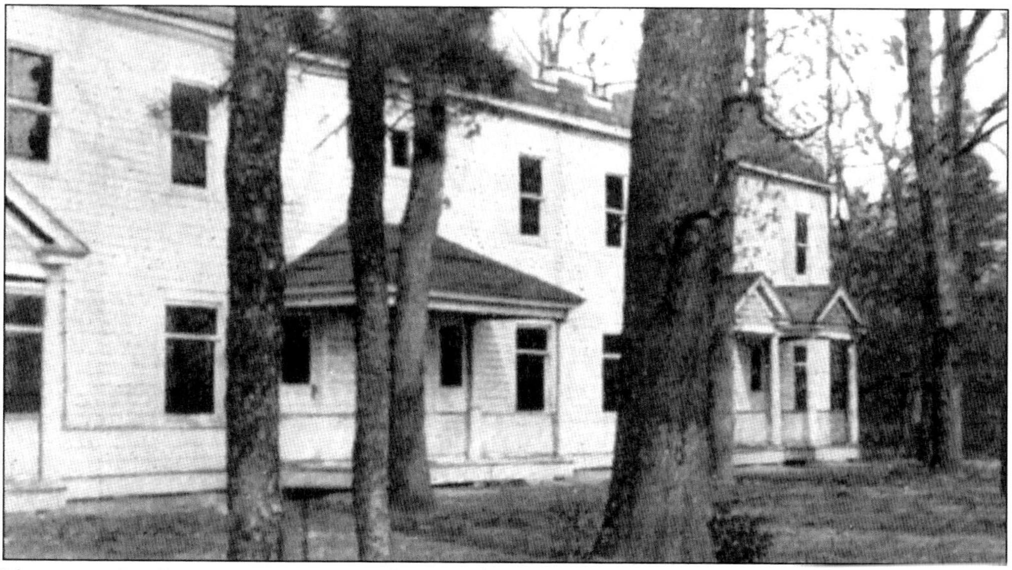

If staying for the season or overnight, as advertised, guests could stay in these comfortable cottages with charming surroundings. Guests, including Brisbane's wealthy friends, came from as far away as New York and Philadelphia to vacation at Allaire. These cottages, built in the early 1900s, no longer exist today. They were located outside the village on the north side of Atlantic Avenue (Route 524) between what is now the Arthur Brisbane Child Treatment Center and West 18th Avenue.

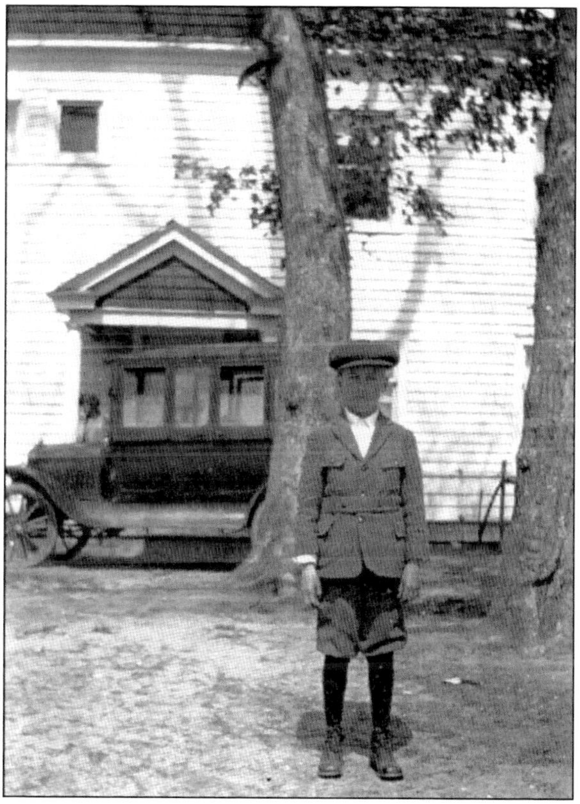

Tom Frostick poses at the Allaire Inn cottages c. 1925. There were about 13 cottages in this row. It is uncertain as to whether the second floor of the Allaire Inn had accommodations for overnight guests. Frequent buses would take guests to the beach and shore resorts. Eleanor Brisbane recalls her father allowing transient people during the Great Depression to live in the cottages.

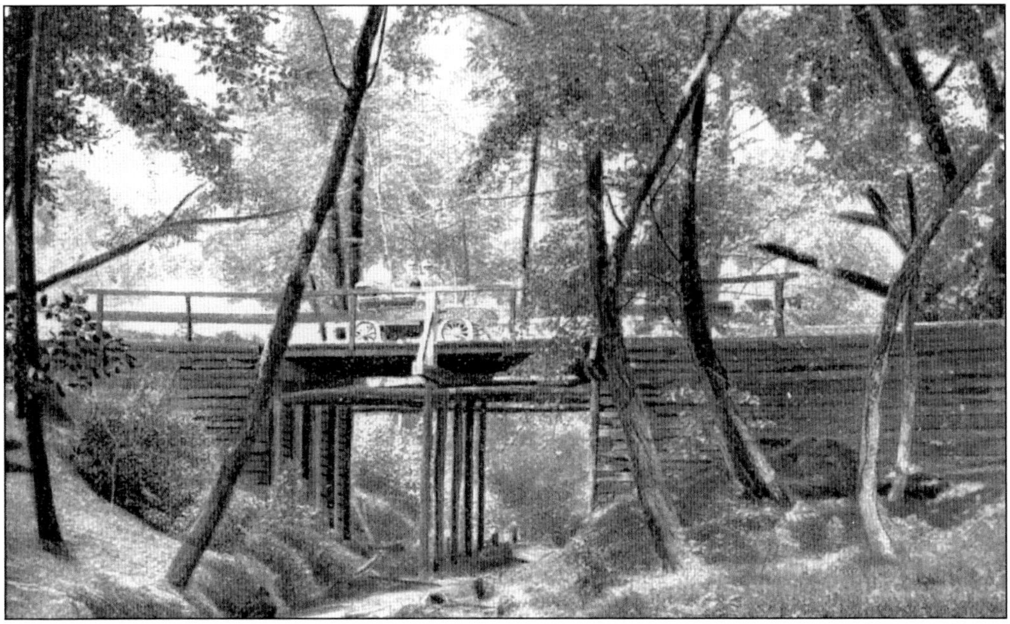

Picturesque landscapes such as this drew early-20th-century automobilists to Allaire Village. Visitors enjoyed outdoor sports, such as fishing, hunting, hiking, and boating. The brooks and streams at Allaire afforded an abundant catch of trout. Shaded roads and bountiful flowers were everywhere. Only wealthy Americans owned chauffeur or self-driven automobiles in 1910. The inn catered to these wealthy patrons.

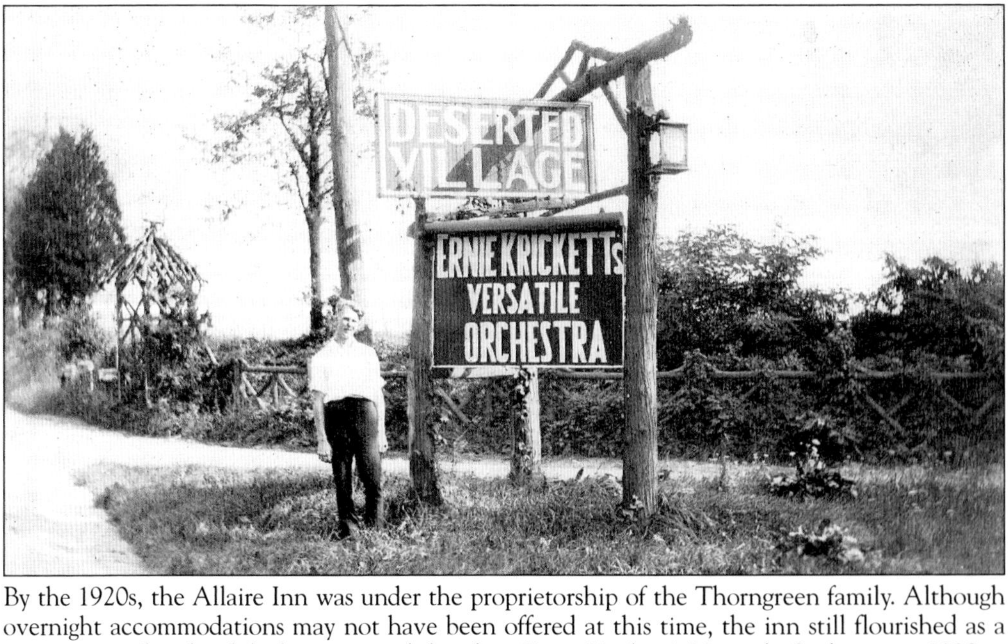

By the 1920s, the Allaire Inn was under the proprietorship of the Thorngreen family. Although overnight accommodations may not have been offered at this time, the inn still flourished as a restaurant and night club, featuring such bands as Ernie Krickett's Versatile Orchestra in 1923.

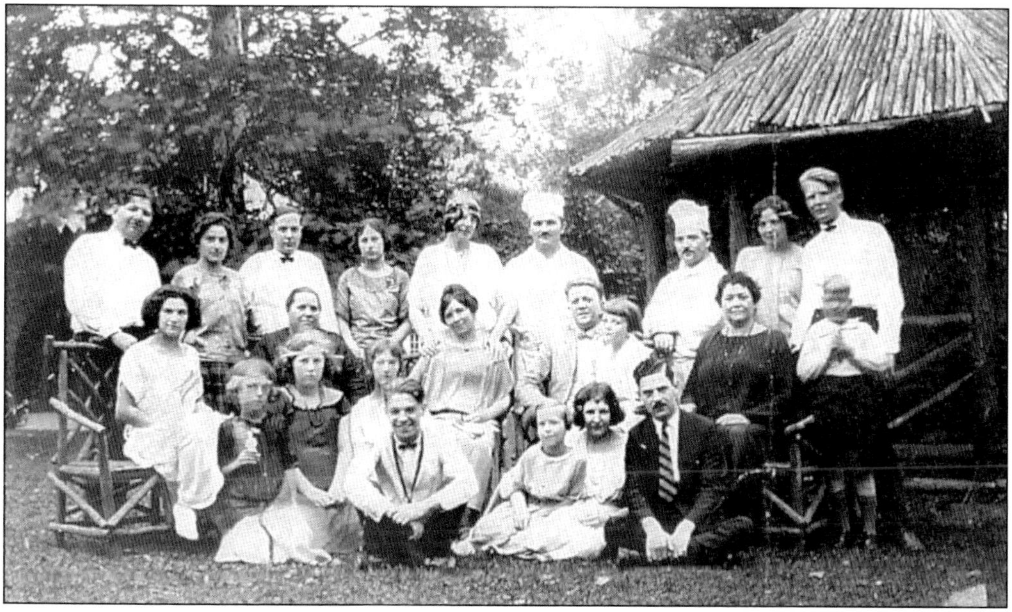

This photograph was taken at the gazebos by the charcoal depot c. 1920. Mabel, Ethel, and Helen Frostick, posing in the picture, served as cooks and waitresses at the restaurant and to Arthur Brisbane's Allaire mansion. The Thorngreens continued to operate a restaurant out of the old carpenter shop until it closed in the early 1930s. Thorngreen opened a restaurant in Farmingdale afterwards.

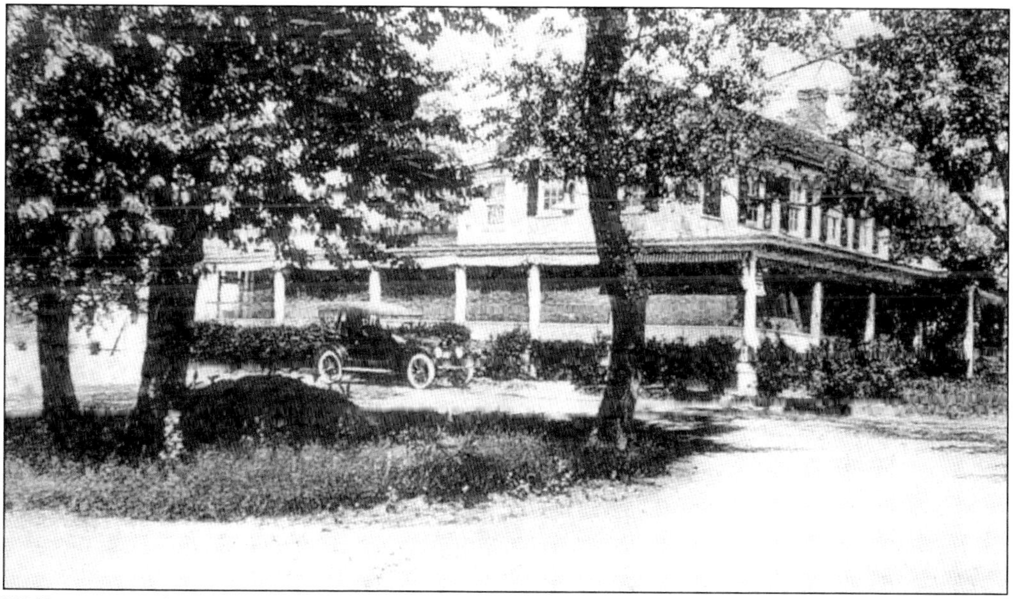

William DeLisle constructed and opened a new restaurant called DeLisle's Inn, seen here c. 1920. The Thorngreens took over operations at the Allaire Inn c. 1917.

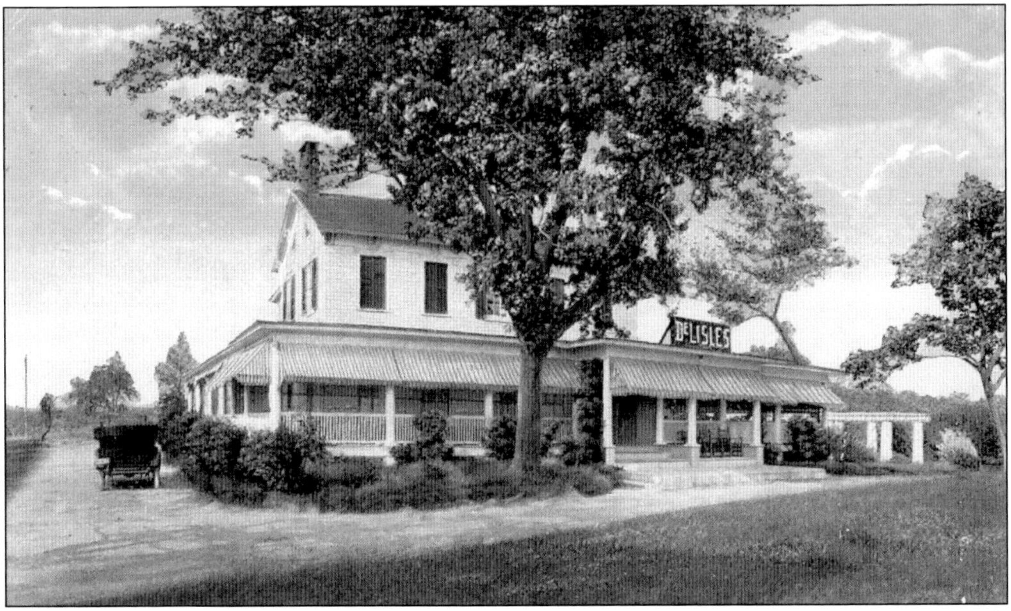

DeLisle's Inn was located on Atlantic Avenue (Route 524) near the corner of West 18th Avenue and Atlantic Avenue. This postcard depicts the inn c. 1930. At that time, Route 524 was the main road between the Jersey Shore, Trenton, and Philadelphia. The inn was destroyed by fire in the 1930s.

AMBOY DIVISION—Freehold and Jamesburg Agricultural Railroad.

TRAINS BETWEEN PHILADELPHIA AND NEW YORK AND LONG BRANCH, OCEAN GROVE, ASBURY PARK, SPRING LAKE, &c.

231	No. 299	387	No. 297	No. 383	291	381	Mls	*May* 21, 1893.	No. 360	No. 200	No. 292	296	No. 298	390	No. 224
P.M.		P.M.			A.M			(*Eastern time.*)				P.M.			
§5 55	†5 20 P.M.	†3 45	†12 15 NO'N	†7 40 A.M.	†7 10		0	lve. **Long Branch**..arr.	10 30 A.M.	11 50 A.M.	2 42 P.M.	5 55	7 25 P.M.		11 20 A.M.
5 57	5 22 "	3 47	12 17 "	7 42 "	7 12		1	.. West End (Hollywood) ..	10 28 "	11 48 "	2 40 "	5 53	7 23 "		11 18 "
6 01	5 26 "	3 51	12 21 "	7 46 "	7 16		2	........Elberon	10 24 "	11 44 "	2 36 "	5 49	7 19 "		11 14 "
6 04	5 29 "	3 54	12 24 "	7 49 "	7 19		3	..... Deal Beach.....	10 21 "	11 41 "	2 32 "	5 46	7 16 "		11 11 "
6 07	5 31 "	3 56	12 26 "	7 51 "	7 21		4	........Interlaken	10 18 "	11 38 "	2 29 "	5 43	7 13 "		11 08 "
....	5 33 "	3 57	12 28 "	7 52 "	7 22		5	...North Asbury Park...	10 17 "	11 37 "	2 27 "	5 42	7 11 "		....
....	5 35 "	3 59	12 33 "	7 55 "	7 25		6	... Asbury Park.... / ....Ocean Grove ...	10 15 "	11 35 "	2 25 "	5 40	7 09 "		....
6 14	5 39 "	4 04	12 38 "	8 00 "	7 30		7	....Avon (Key East)...	10 08 "	11 29 "	2 18 "	5 34	7 03 "		10 59 "
6 16	5 41 "	4 07	12 40 "	8 03 "	7 33		8	..Belmar (Ocean Beach)..	10 05 "	11 27 "	2 16 "	5 32	7 01 "		10 57 "
6 19	5 44 "	4 10	12 43 "	8 06 "	7 36		9	..........Como.........	10 02 "	11 24 "	2 13 "	5 29	6 58 "		10 54 "
6 21	5 46 "	4 14	12 47 "	8 09 "	7 40		10	.....**Spring Lake**.....	9 59 "	11 22 "	2 11 "	5 27	6 56 "		10 52 "
6 25	5 50 "	4 18	12 52 "	8 14 "	7 45		12	.........**Sea Girt**.....δ	9 55 "	11 18 "	2 07 "	5 23	6 52 "		10 48 "
6 27	5 53 "	4 22	12 55 NO'N	8 17 "	7 47		13	.......Manasquan.....δ	9 53 "	11 16 "	2 04 "	5 21	6 50 "		10 46 "
....	....	4 28	....	8 23 "	....		15	.......Allenwood.... ..	9 47 "	....	....	..	6 44 "		...
....	....	4 32	1 03 P.M.	8 27 "	....		17	.........Allaire.........	9 43 "	....	1 55 "	....	6 41 "		...
6 39	6 05 "	4 39	1 09 "	8 33 "	....		20	.....**Farmingdale**...δ	9 37 "	11 03 "	1 50 "	....	[illegible] "		10 33 "
....	....	4 43	....	8 37 "	....		22	.. ...Yellow Brook......	9 33 "	....	....	....	6 31 "		....
....	....	4 47	....	8 40 "	....		24	.... Fairfield........	9 30 "	..	....	..	6 28 "		....
....	....	4 51	1 16 "	8 43 "	....	A.M.	25	.........Howell.........	9 27 "	....	1 42 "	....	6 23 "	P.M.	....
6 51	6 18 "	5 02	1 23 "	8 50 "	8 08	†7 15	28	.... **Freehold**.....δ	9 21 "	10 51 "	1 37 "	6 02	6 20 "	7 10	10 21 "
....	....	5 10	....	8 56 "	....	7 21	31	....Tennent........	9 14 "	....	....	....	6 09 "	7 04	....
6 59	6 27 "	5 13	1 32 "	8 59 "	....	7 24	32	........Englishtown.....δ	9 11 "	10 41 "	1 24 "	....	6 06 "	7 01	10 11 "
....	....	5 18	....	9 07 "	....	7 28	34	.........Tracey.........	9 07 "	....	....	....	6 02 "	6 57	....
....	....	5 22	....	9 12 "	....	7 32	36	.... Hoffman........	9 03 "	....	....	....	5 58 "	6 53	....
7 09	....	5 28	1 41 "	9 17 "	....	7 37	38	....Lower Jamesburg....	8 58 "	....	1 15 "	....	5 53 "	6 48	10 02 "
....	6 41 "	5 31	1 44 "	9 19 "	....	7 40	39	arr...**Jamesburg**...lve.	8 55 "	10 30 "	1 12 "	....	5 50 "	6 45	....
....	6 41 "	5 45	1 44 "	9 25 "	....	7 46	39	lve...**Jamesburg**.δ arr.	8 51 "	10 30 "	1 12 "	....	5 45 "	6 27	....
7 19	6 49 "	5 52	1 51 "	9 31 "	....	7 53	43	.........Dayton.......δ	8 45 "	....	1 05 "	....	5 40 "	6 20	9 53 "
7 25	6 55 "	5 57	1 56 "	9 36 "	....	7 57	45	...**Monmouth Junc.** δ	8 40 "	....	1 00 P.M.	....	5 35 "	6 15	9 48 "
7 33	7 05 "	6 12	2 06 "	9 43 "	....	8 17		.**Princeton Junction**	7 58 "	10 09 "	12 51 NO'N	....	5 25 "	6 04	9 37 "
7 47	7 18 "	6 30	2 23 "	10 01 "	‡5 1	8 36		........**Trenton**........	7 45 "	9 55 "	12 35 NO'N	4 19	5 10 "	5 50	9 20 "
8 03	7 32 "	7 00	2 40 "	10 26 "	....	....		.. ..**Bristol**	7 29 "	9 32 "	....	..	4 45 "	5 34	0 04 "
8 31	8 00 "	7 37	3 13 "	d10 58 "	9 29	9 29		..**Germantown Junc.**.	7 01 "	9 12 "	11 52 A.M.	3 40	4 10 "	5 11	8 36 "
8 44	8 13 "	7 50	3 27 "	11 08 A.M.	9 40	9 40		..**Philad'a** (*Broad St.*)..	6 50 "	9 00 "	11 39 "	3 30	4 00 "	5 00	§6 25 A.M.
10 50	8 35 "	8 35	4 10 "	12 40 NO'N	10 50	9 30		.**Philad'a** (*Market St.*).	6 10 "	†7 20 A.M.	10 30 "	†2 30	4 00 "	4 30	....
9 05	9 05 P.M.	7 20	3 20 P.M.	11 30 A.M.	A.M.	9 20		..**New York** (Via Mon. Jn.)	†7 20 A.M.		†11 00 A.M.	P.M.	†4 00 P.M.	4 40	§8 30 A.M.
P.M.		7 43		11 13 A.M.		A.M.		.**New York** (Via S. Amboy).						†5 10	
		P.M.						ARRIVE] [LEAVE						P.M.	

* Daily; †daily, except Sunday; ‡ Sunday only; δ stops only to take on or let off passengers to or from points on the New York Division of the

The Freehold and Jamesburg Agricultural Railroad was operated by the Pennsylvania Railroad as part of its Amboy Division. In this June 1893 railroad schedule, it appears that three round-trip trains stopped at Allaire. You could board at Allaire and travel to New York, Trenton, Philadelphia, or Washington, D.C.

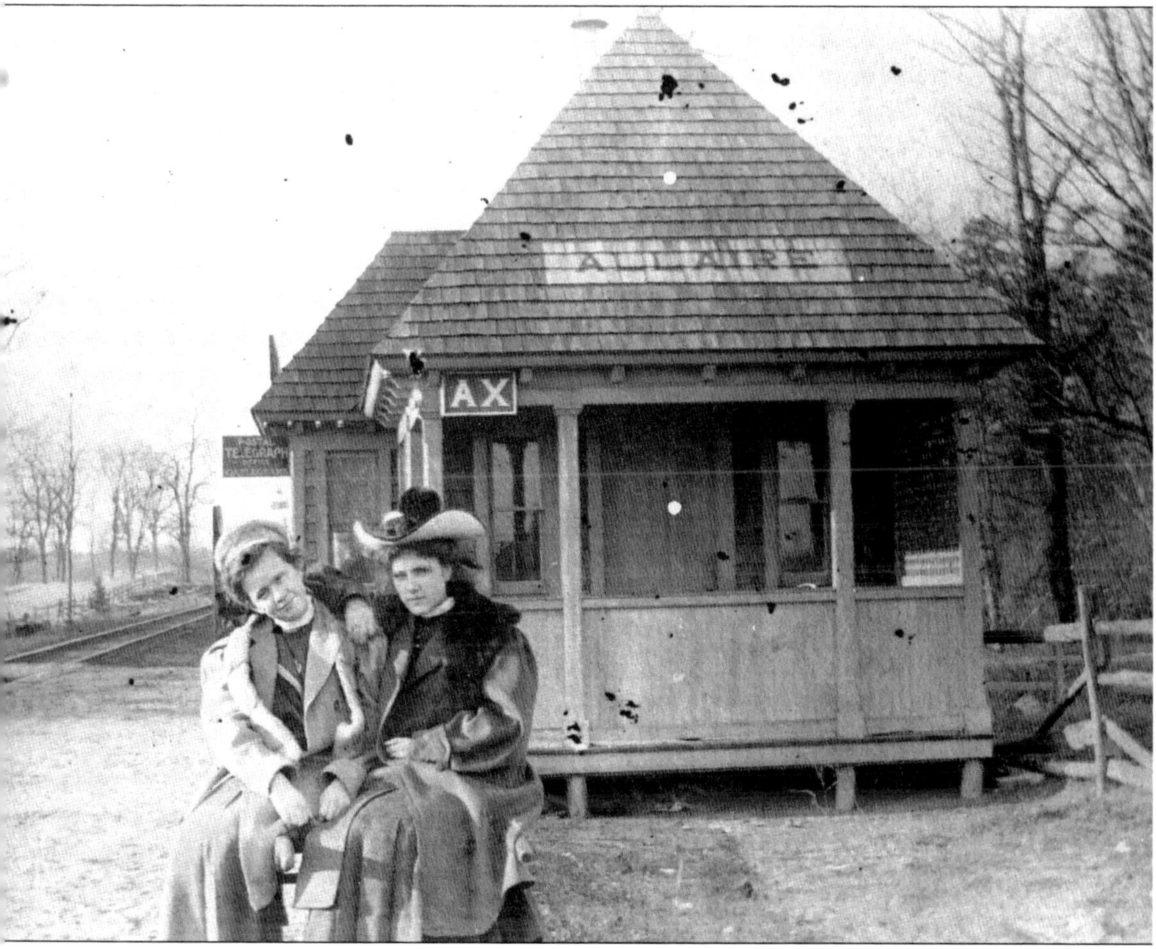

Hattie Height and Valetta Bennett are seen at the Allaire train station on the Freehold and Jamesburg Agricultural Railroad in 1907. The station, located just north of Allaire Village, featured telegraph service. The road behind the station leads to Allaire. Trains usually ran between Philadelphia and Long Branch. By the summer of 1908, nine trains to the Jersey Shore were reported to use the Freehold and Jamesburg. Some guests may have traveled by train to the Allaire Inn.

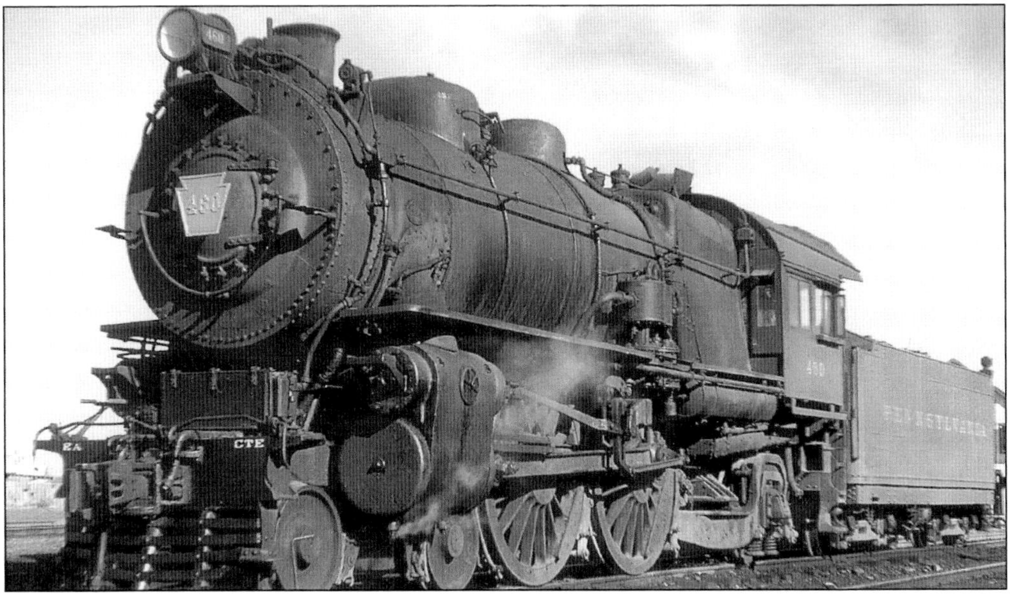

The Pennsylvania Railroad operated a variety of locomotive power over the Freehold and Jamesburg Agricultural Railroad, including Atlantic locomotive No. 460 (above), Pacific No. 3750 (below), and doodlebugs. No. 460 was the famous engine that raced an airplane from Washington, D.C., to New York and won. The Freehold and Jamesburg mainly carried passengers to the shore communities in the summer months but also had a local freight business. Customers on the route included several coal and lumber companies, as well as the Monmouth County Farmer's Exchange (Englishtown), Reed and Perrine (Tennent), A & M Karagheusian Inc. (Freehold), Stokes Brothers Manufacturing (Freehold), Monmouth Lumber Company (Farmingdale), United Canvas Products (Farmingdale), F.L.F. Farmers' Cooperative (Farmingdale), Monmouth Box Company (Allenwood), H.L Schafer (Manasquan), Stone Lumber Company (Manasquan), and Imperial Porcelain Works (Manasquan). Farmers in the Freehold and Adelphia area grew many potatoes that were transported to market via the Freehold and Jamesburg line.

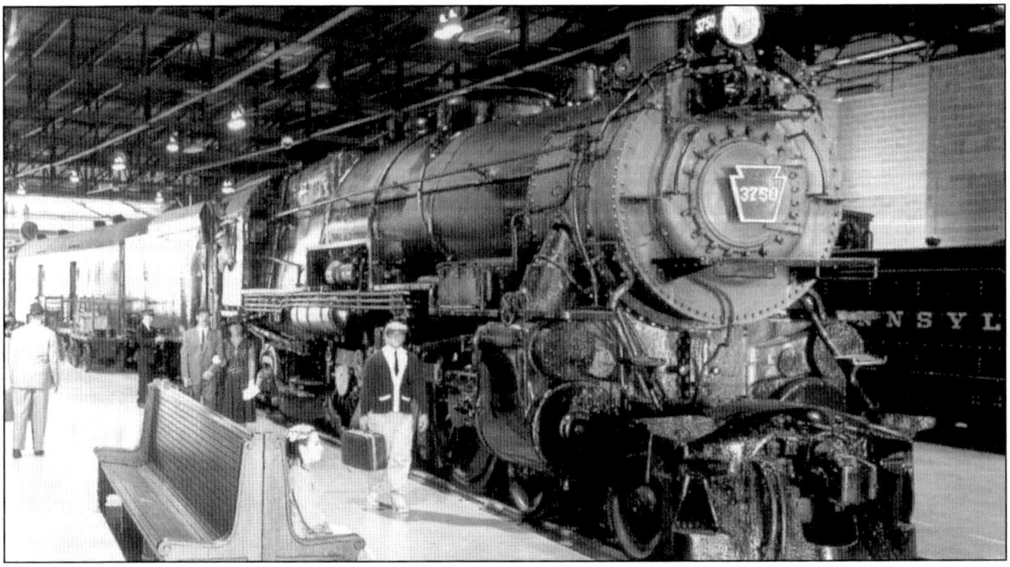

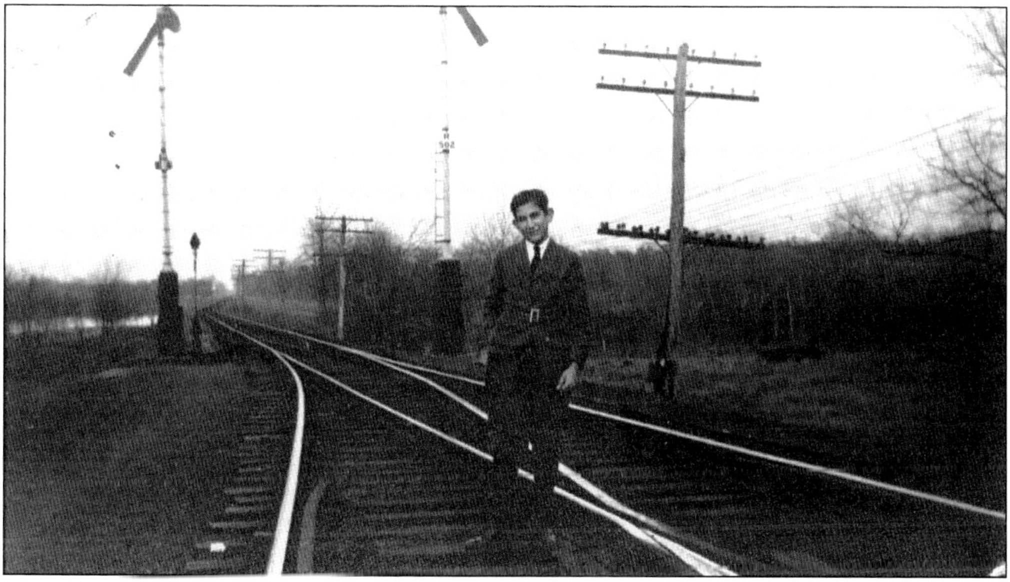

This photograph was taken along the Freehold and Jamesburg tracks *c.* 1920 near Allaire Village. At one time, passenger and freight traffic was so great on the line that the Pennsylvania Railroad came close to double tracking it. This never materialized, but the line did have several sidings, as seen here. (Note the old semaphores in the background.) Freehold and Jamesburg passengers were able to gaze out at central New Jersey fields, farms, and small towns.

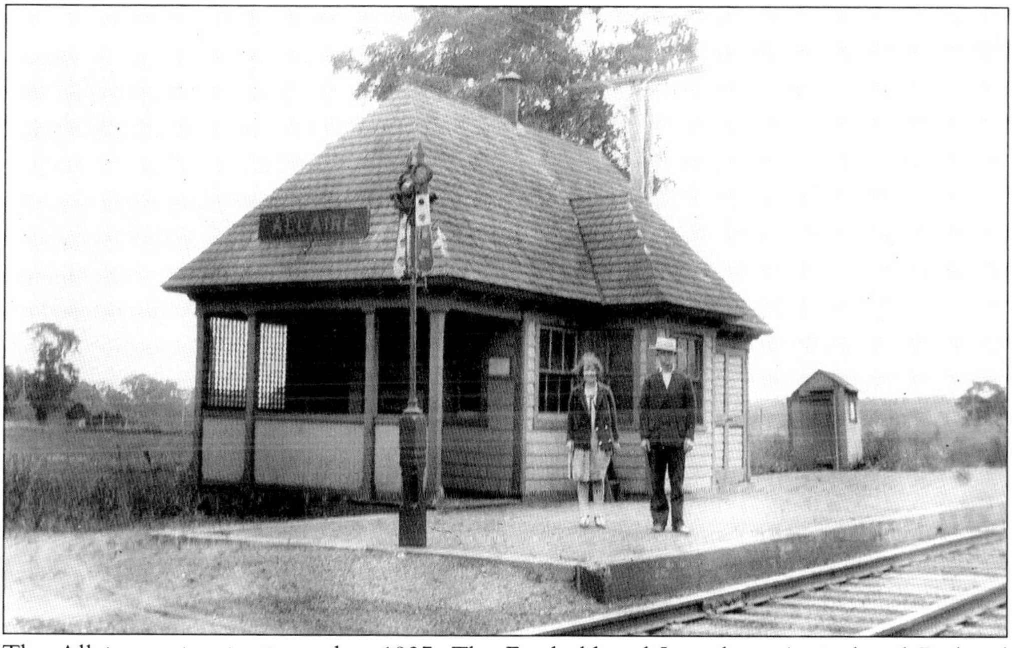

The Allaire station is pictured *c.* 1927. The Freehold and Jamesburg Agricultural Railroad carried some famous and wealthy people from Philadelphia to the Jersey Shore. A train bearing a mortally wounded Pres. James Garfield made its way to Elberon on the line in 1881. On June 10, 1939, a carefully guarded and specially prepared royal train bearing the king and queen of England followed the same route. Many circus trains passed through Allaire as well.

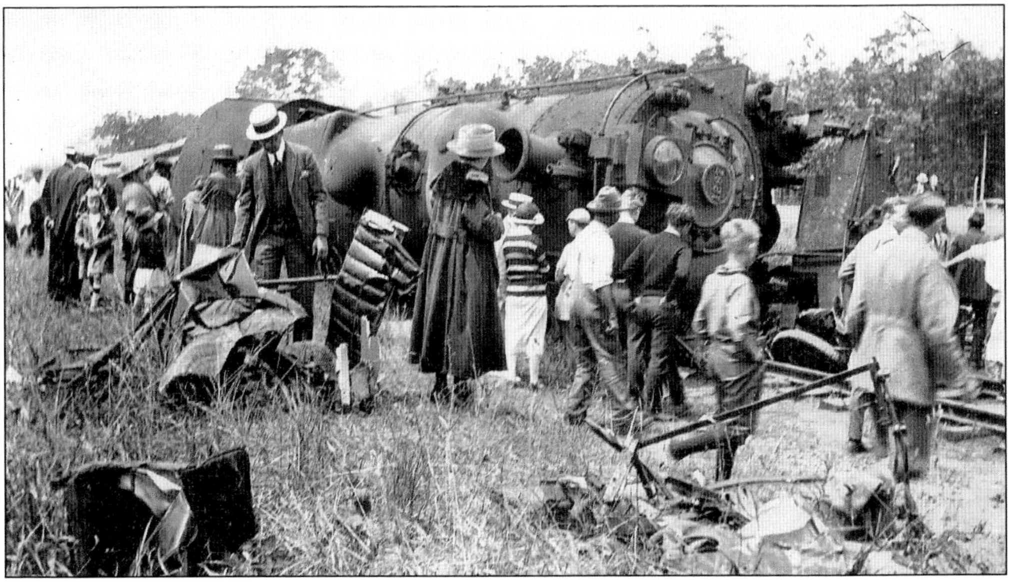

This train wreck occurred near a crossing Allaire in 1925. As the train was traveling eastbound, it struck a car. Wrecked was an RPO car, several coaches (probably carrying patrons to the Jersey Shore), and one of the Pennsylvania Railroad's Atlantic steam locomotives (No. 1287). Arthur Brisabane's property surrounded the Allaire train station.

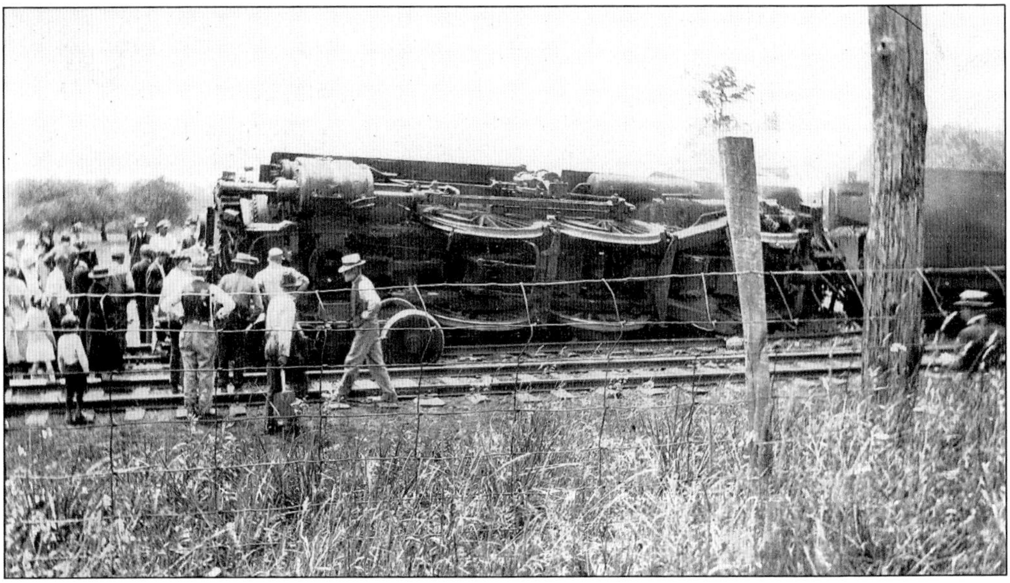

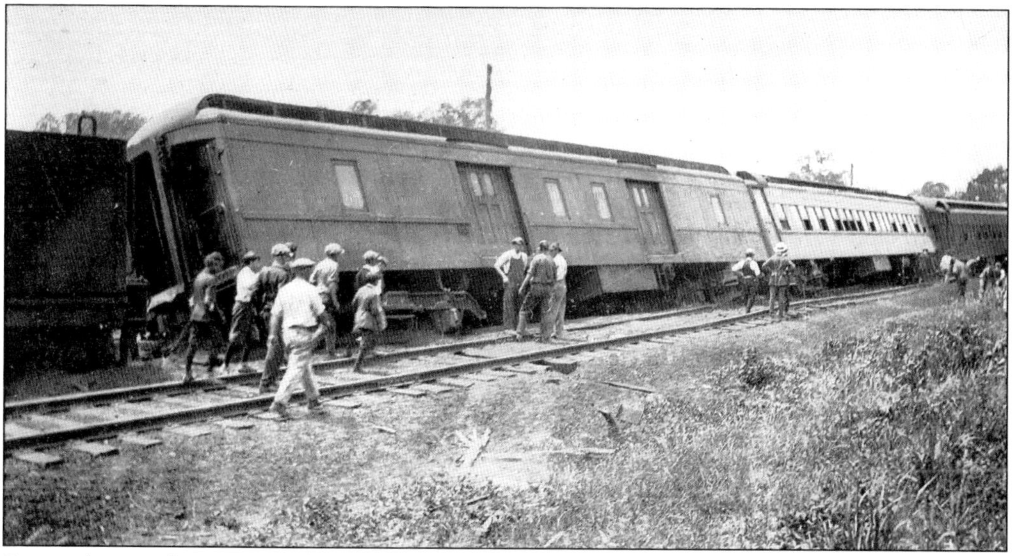

Pictured is another view of the 1925 wreck.

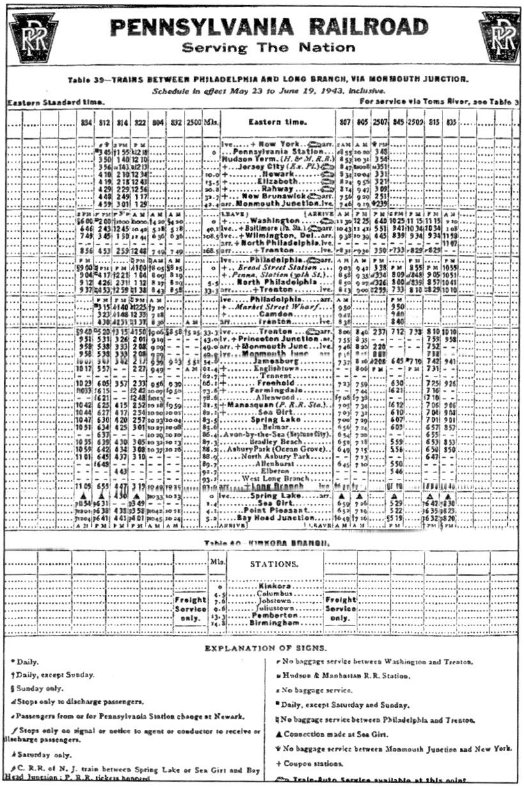

This Freehold and Jamesburg timetable dates from June 1943. In previous summers, the *Sea Breeze* had operated over the Freehold and Jamesburg Agricultural Railroad, leaving Broad Street in Philadelphia at 3:15 p.m. and arriving at Long Branch at 5:26 p.m. Allaire had been dropped as a station stop. Residents had to travel to nearby Allenwood. In the early 1960s, freight trains used the Freehold and Jamesburg regularly to carry jetty rocks (from a traprock quarry in Kingston) to the shore.

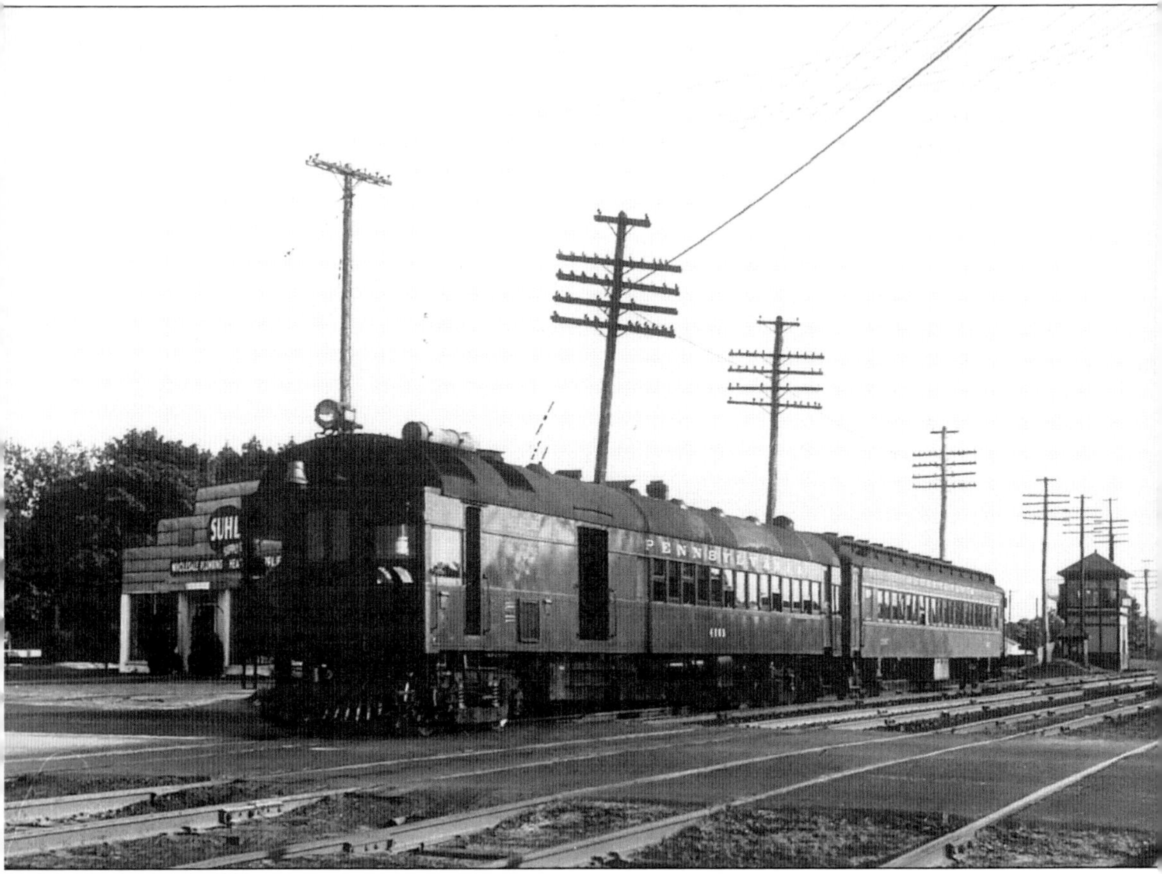

Pennsylvania Railroad train No. 812, operating Monday through Friday, is seen here on July 9, 1954, at 6:21 p.m. It is leaving the Freehold and Jamesburg line and taking the tracks of the New York and Long Branch at Sea Girt. Due to changing economic times, passenger service by 1953 had been reduced on the Freehold and Jamesburg to a single doodlebug. Representing the highest level of advancement, this doodlebug could accommodate 66 passengers and carry an empty passenger car or caboose. Its top speed was 60 miles per hour. Doodlebugs were self-propelled rail cars that combined the features of a locomotive, passenger car, and sometimes a baggage car into one vehicle. The Freehold and Jamesburg was seen as ideal for doodlebug service—a cheap, efficient way to serve agricultural areas, picking up mail, light freight, and passengers who relied on the railroad.

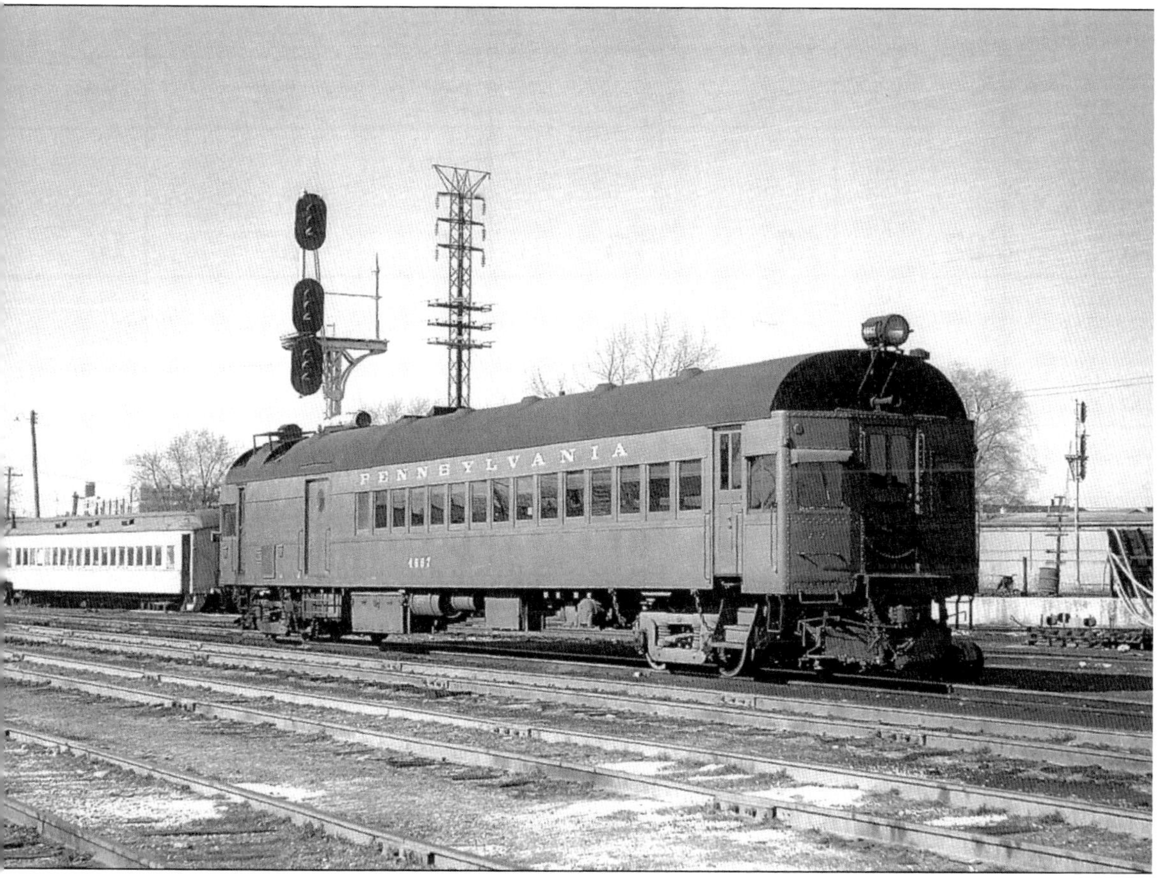

Doodlebug No. 4667 is shown at Red Bank in 1961, awaiting its run to Trenton via the Freehold and Jamesburg Agricultural Railroad. For 13 years (from 1949 to 1962), the doodlebug plodded from Red Bank to Trenton via the Freehold and Jamesburg. The last half of the doodlebug's life was spent in raging controversy as the railroad sought to end the service, politicians and riders battling to save it. The doodlebug had fans who came to greet it as it passed by. Passengers grew to know the conductors. Catholic high school girls heading for a parochial school in Trenton decorated it for Christmas. In the end, the girls were the reason it ran. The doodlebug departed Red Bank at 6:25 a.m. with a return journey from Trenton at 5:00 p.m., taking close to 2 hours and 15 minutes one-way. Its sister, doodlebug No. 4666, closed out passenger service on the Freehold and Jamesburg on May 29, 1962. On this final run, close to 100 people and a band showed up at the Allenwood train station, draped in black, to bid farewell. Many passengers boarded there and presented baskets of fruit and cheese to the three trainmen—engineer George T. Murphy, conductor C.S. Smith, and trainman Frank Riddle. People bowed their heads as the doodlebug crawled into oblivion. Today, the Freehold and Jamesburg west of Farmingdale to Jamesburg is still intact but is out of service between Farmingdale and Freehold.

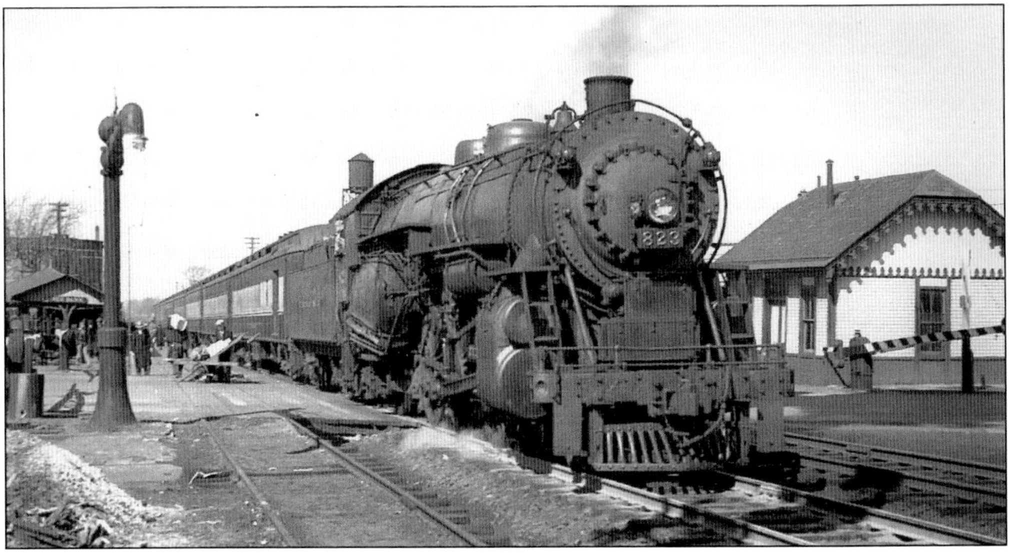

The *Blue Comet* is shown above at the Red Bank train station in 1938 before heading down the Central Railroad of New Jersey's Southern Division for Atlantic City. Below is the *Blue Comet* wreck near Chatsworth. The *Blue Comet*, a luxury coach express train, ran from New York to Atlantic City in three hours from 1929 to 1941. It was operated by the Central Railroad of New Jersey. For Allaire residents, it was entertainment for the day when it passed through nearby Collingswood and Farmingdale. The *Blue Comet*'s color scheme of Jersey cream, Packard blue, and royal blue represented the sand, sky, and sea of New Jersey's seashore. A cream-colored band ran the length of the train so that when it sped by, it resembled a comet streaking through space.

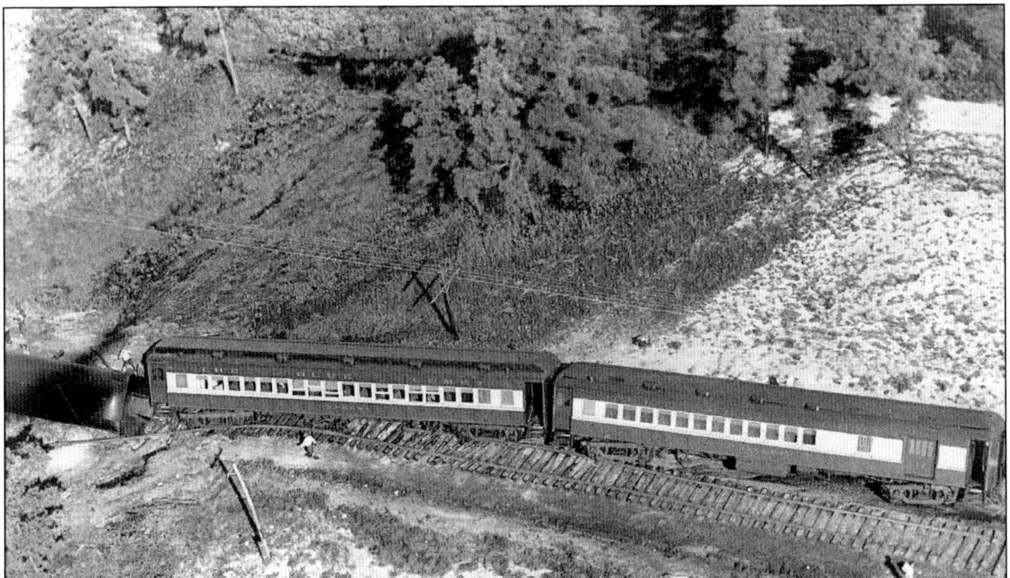

Five

Arthur Brisbane, the Benefactor

In the 1920s and 1930s, Arthur Brisbane, wife Phoebe, and their five children made Allaire their permanent residence. This chapter contains photographs of Allaire Village during the later years of Brisbane's ownership as well as Brisbane's generosity. This generosity included allowing various clubs and private organizations, such as the Boy Scouts, to use Allaire Village from 1928 to 1939. His model farm entered its prime in the 1930s. Brisbane was also influential in allowing Allaire Village to be used by Depression programs, such as the Civilian Conservation Corps (CCC). If it had not been for Brisbane's generosity of allowing various clubs and organizations to use the former village buildings during his ownership, complete devastation or severe damage would have ensued before the state received the property. Through these endeavors, the same 16 buildings that stood when Arthur Brisbane bought Allaire in 1907 were still standing upon his death.

Brisbane's personal real estate holdings during his lifetime were considerable. Believing in the future development of the Jersey Shore as a vacation and beach resort, he owned and developed Arnold and Richmond Avenues, the business center of Point Pleasant. He also owned large estates in Arizona, California, New York, and Florida, as well as Kingscote Mansion in Lakewood, later given to Georgian Court College. Believing Manhattan real estate to be the safest investment in the world, he bought heavily in the upper 50s. He owned property with Hearst, including the Warwick Hotel and parcels around Columbus Circle. He helped finance the building of the Ritz Tower, New York City's first high-rise apartment building.

Brisbane knew the future real estate value of his Allaire property, let alone its historical value. He sought to protect its development, beginning in the late 1920s. In 1927, Brisbane expressed an interest in making much of his Allaire estate a forest reserve with a historical center. He wrote to Allaire descendants to learn the history of the property.

In the midst of the Great Depression, Brisbane was hit hard with real estate taxes. His real estate holdings in the United States were extensive. Brisbane, although a wealthy person, found Depression tax rates a burden. His Allaire estate, once as large as 10,000 acres during the early 1920s, would be reduced to 3,000 acres by 1940. One of the first parcels he sold was the outlying sandpits and farmland including his orchard. Later, the property that now comprises Monmouth Executive Airport was sold to Edward Brown. Brisbane, however, held on to strategic parcels of land. The village was retained as well as much of the property that contained picturesque landscapes, watersheds, and forests.

On December 25, 1936, Arthur Brisbane died quietly in New York City with his family at his bedside. Newspapers across the country announced the editor's death. Headlines read, "Nation Mourns Brisbane's Death." The *New York Evening Journal* ran a seven-page spread on Brisbane's life and included numerous condolence letters sent by the leading politicians, celebrities, and journalists of the time. He was buried with other family members on the highest knoll at his Allaire estate, not far from his mansion. He was moved in the 1960s to Batavia, New York.

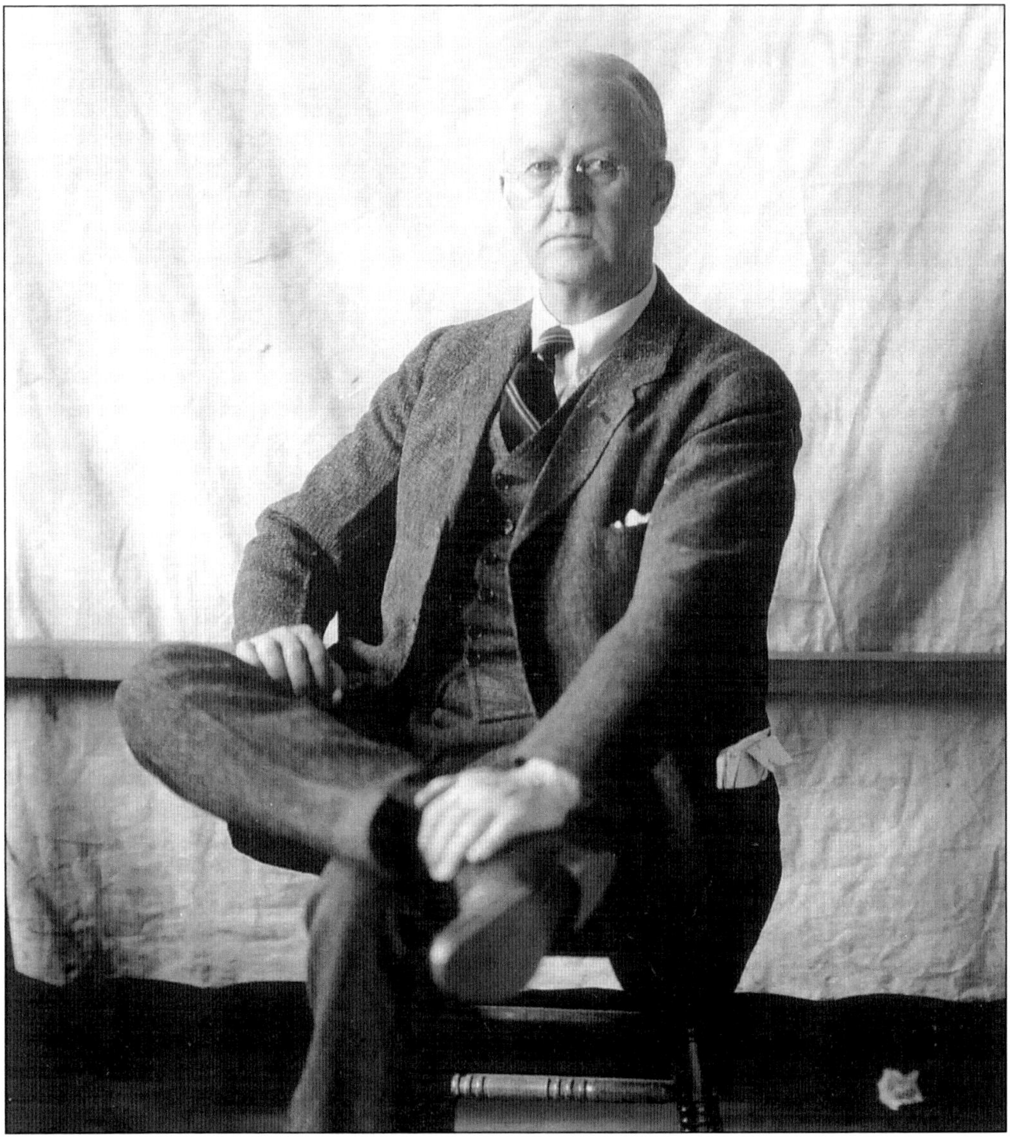

Arthur Brisbane is pictured *c.* 1930. Prior to his death in 1936, negotiations were under way to give much of his Allaire estate to the state. It was not until 1940 that his widow, Phoebe Brisbane, completed her husband's plan of gifting the village proper to the state. More land gifts followed. By 1944, the Brisbane family had gifted more than 1,200 acres—the heart of Allaire State Park today. They even gifted the Brisbane family home (called the Castle), which was to be used as a child-treatment center. Restoration of the village did not begin until a decade after World War II. By then, more than 20 years had passed since the death of Brisbane. Mother Nature had certainly taken a toll on the village, buildings, and grounds. Nonetheless, Brisbane's vision of a recreational park and restored village was being realized by 1957 and continues today. Commonly forgotten in the history of Allaire Village, Brisbane is clearly an important person responsible for its existence today. Brisbane and his family spared Allaire from any future commercial and residential development, for the land deeds contained strict stipulations on how the property was to be used. Since the 1940s, additional property has been added to the park through the Green Acres Program.

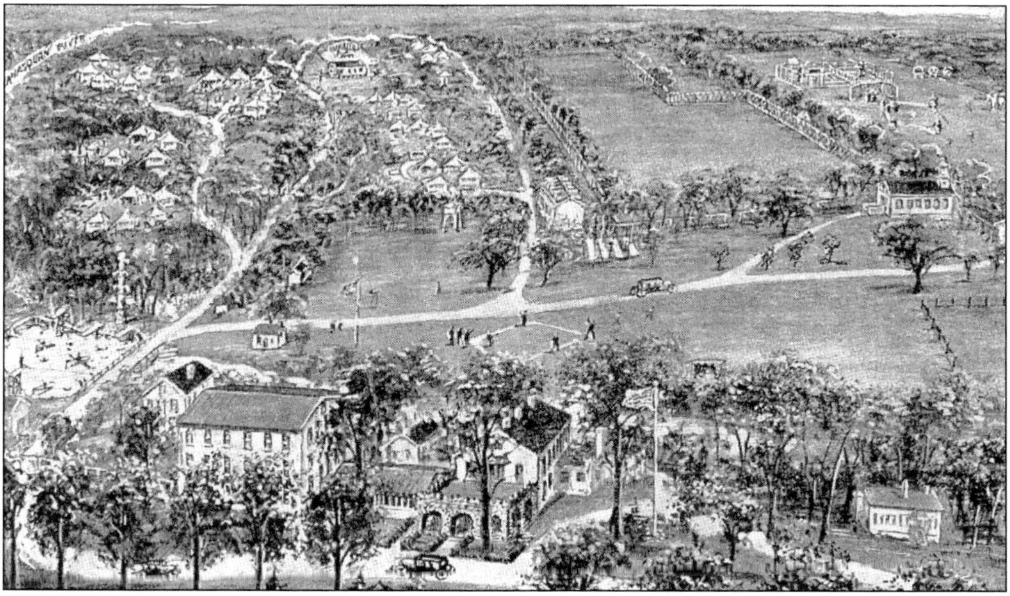

The Boy Scouts' Camp Burton is shown c. 1930. In 1928, a few spirited men, following a suggestion made by Arthur Brisbane, considered developing Allaire Village into a Boy Scout camp. The result is depicted in this early-1930s postcard. To the left is the swimming pool, built by damming up the old millpond. Brisbane made available 200 acres, occupied with playgrounds, two baseball diamonds, tennis courts, campsites, an archery range, volleyball courts, and horseshoe pits. The rent was $1 a year.

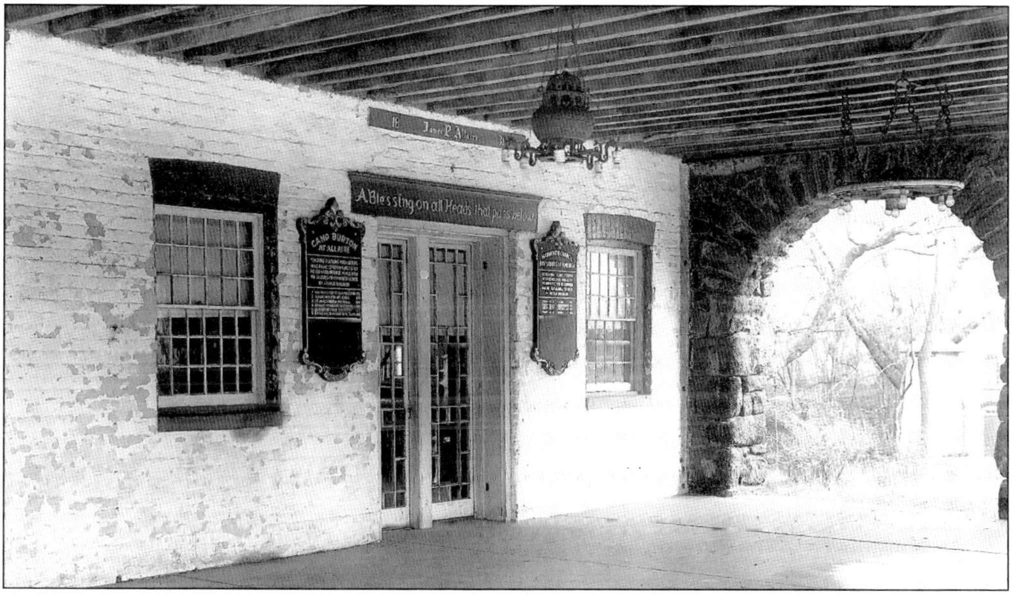

Arthur Brisbane did not like to accept publicity for the camp he allowed to occupy his property. However, evidence hints that he influenced the camp's philosophy, operations, and development. Other private organizations also helped restore Allaire Village for the Boy Scouts (as seen with these plaques, which once adorned the carpenter shop), including the Housman family, the Asbury Park Kiwanis, St. James Church in Red Bank, the Belmar Kiwanis, Leonard Newman, and the Asbury Park Elks Club. The Boy Scouts assisted in restoration projects, too.

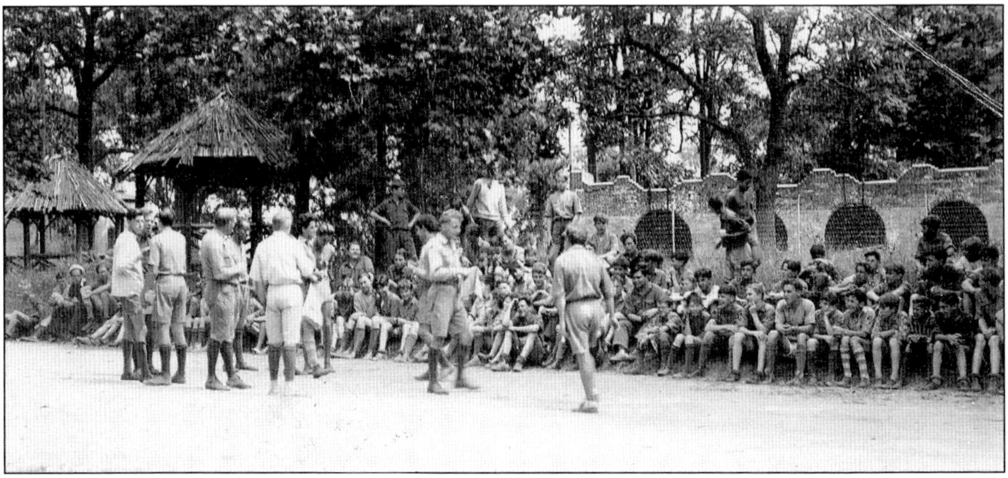

Boy Scouts assemble near the gazebos and charcoal depot ruins c. 1934. Upon arriving at Camp Burton, the Boy Scouts came face to face with the department heads, including the hobby and training director, camp physician, and scoutmaster. Scouts registered their hobby and training interests on the first day.

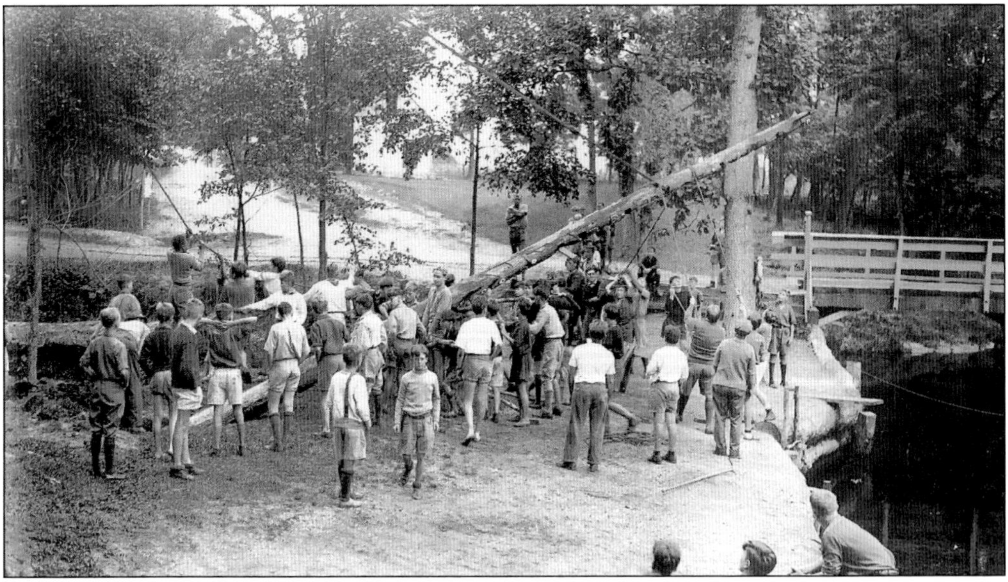

Scouts are shown raising a totem pole into place near the millpond c. 1934, a common sight at the camp. Numerous educational programs were offered at the camp, including Native American lore. The bridge across the millpond can be seen to the right. In addition to swimming in the millpond, the Boy Scouts canoed on the Manasquan River and went on excursions as far as Barnegat Bay.

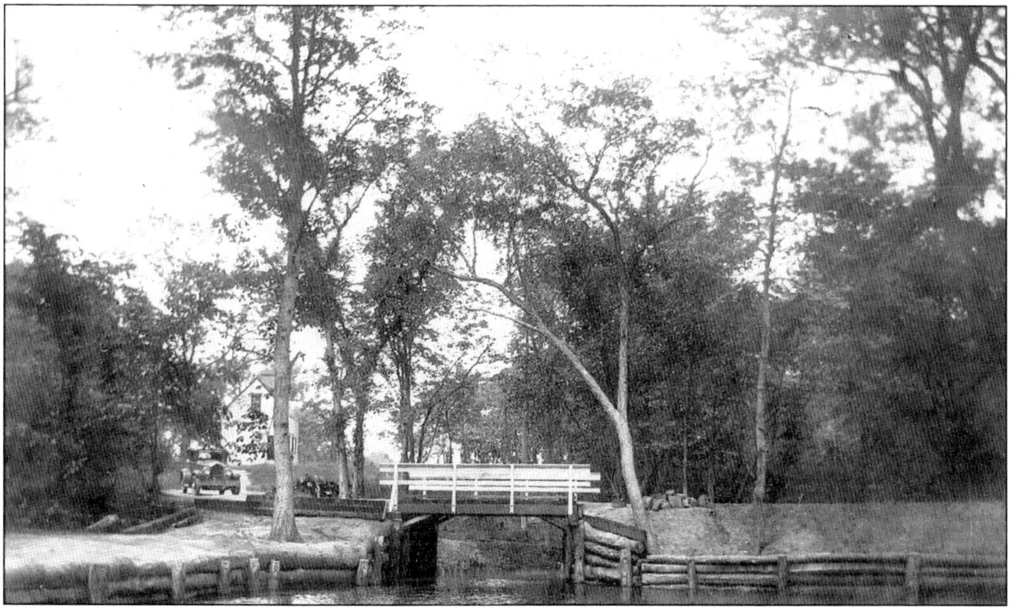

This is a view of the millpond *c.* 1935 at Allaire Village, south of the dam that crosses near the blacksmith shop. A car is about to cross the bridge. The Boy Scouts had dammed up this section to create a large swimming hole. Part of the dam can still be seen today. They practiced good safety with the buddy plan, a check system, and a well-organized corps of American Red Cross lifeguards. Today, this section of the millpond is a small brook.

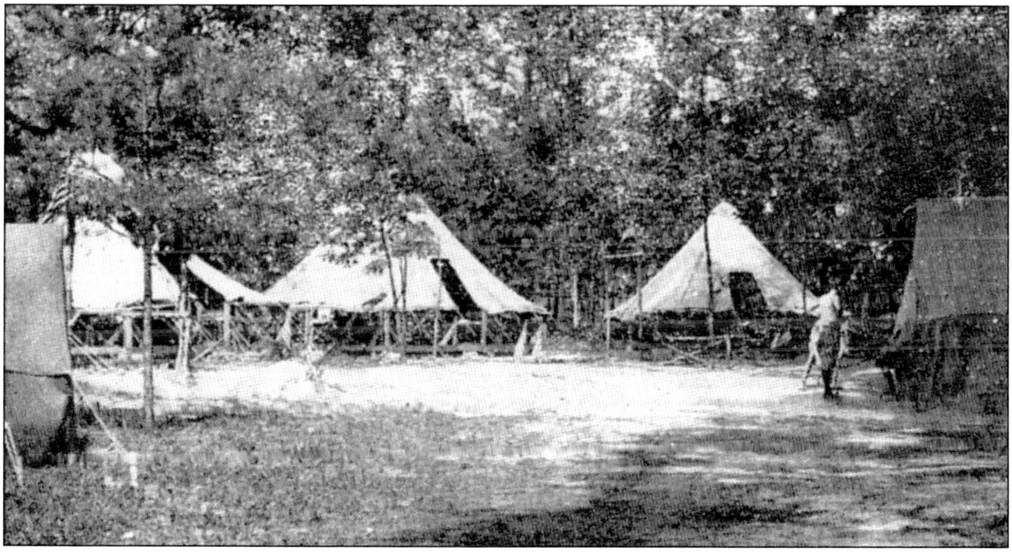

Campsites were established for the Boy Scouts with funding from the Housman family. Scouts were taught family units of living and democracy. Unit campfire programs were conducted regularly. In 1931, the *Asbury Park Press* reported, "The roads and paths have been improved, brush cut to make way for campsites and woods immediately surrounding these sites thinned to bring more light and air to campers."

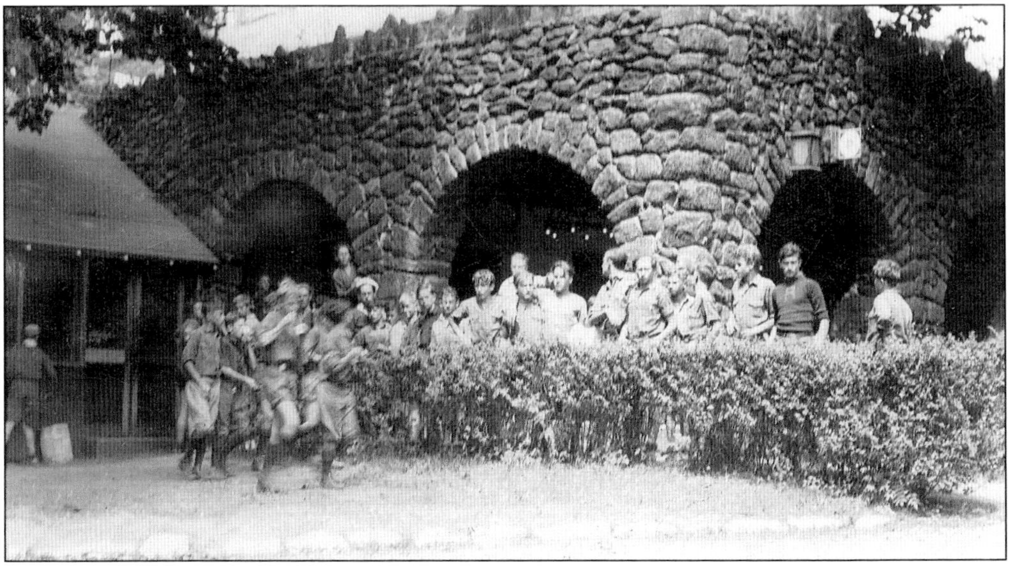

Boy Scouts are seen assembled outside the carpenter shop *c.* 1935. After the Allaire Inn closed, the Boy Scouts used the former Howell Works carpenter shop as their kitchen and dining hall. Some 300 Boy Scouts could dine at one time, assembled in groups of 8 and served family style. Scoutmasters and counselors were distributed among the tables. The carpenter shop also served as the camp headquarters building, housing the camp director and department heads.

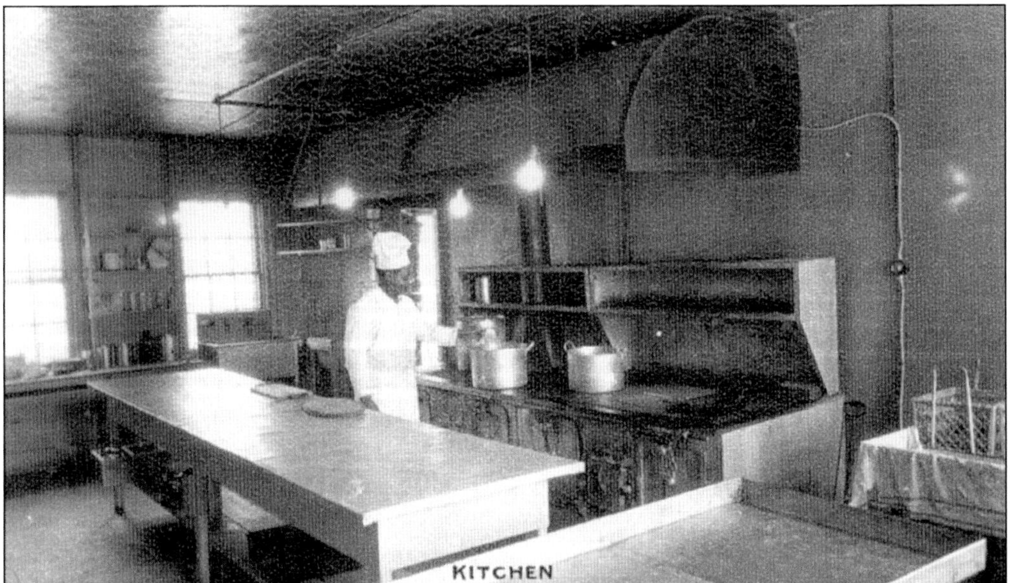

Everything in the kitchen was planned for the convenience and comfort of the chef and assistants. Equipped with the most up-to-date equipment, the kitchen included two huge ranges and an electrical dishwashing machine.

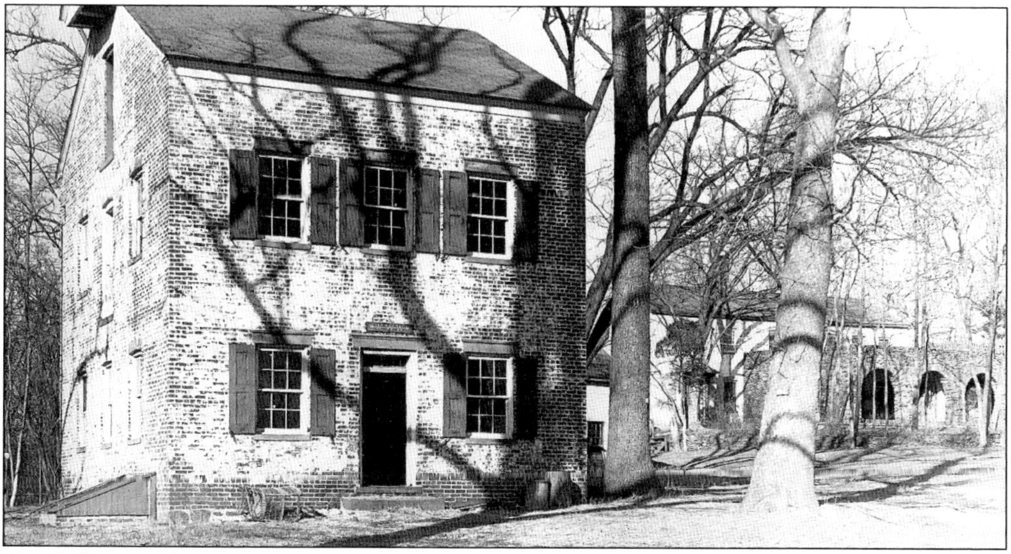

The bakery is shown c. 1931. During the Howell Works era, the school was located in the church. By the 1870s, however, local children attended school on the second floor of the bakery until 1900. A few pupils who attended school at the bakery were present for the dedication of Allaire State Park in 1957. In the 1930s, the Boy Scouts nicknamed the bakery Bamford Lodge, and it served as their winter sleeping quarters and general training facility.

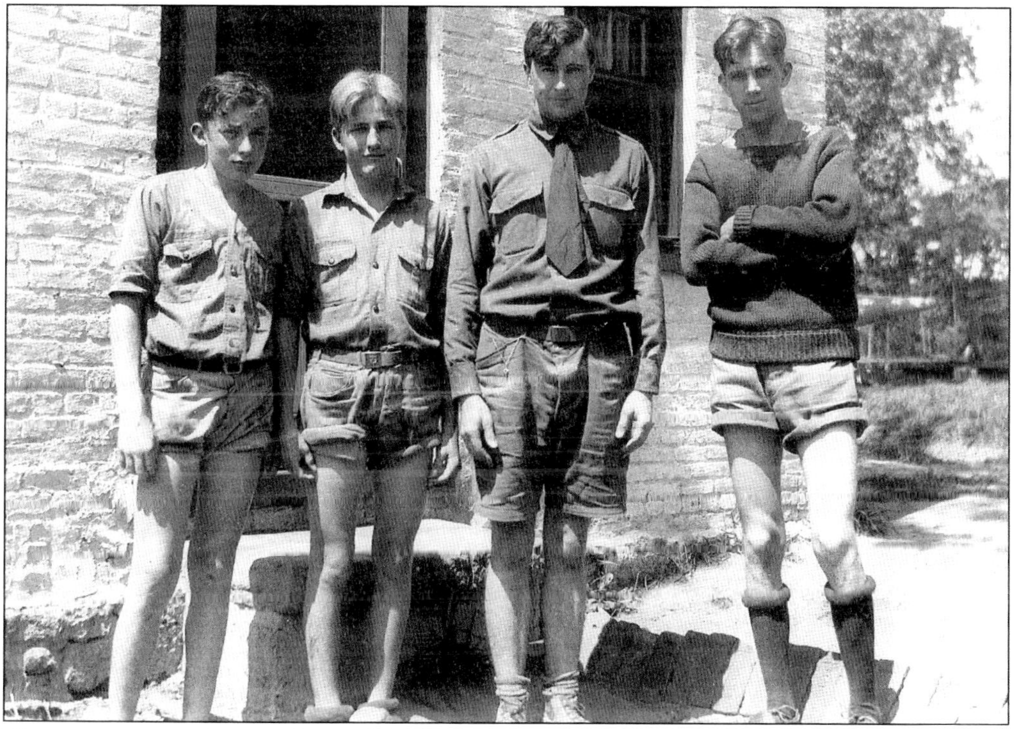

This picture was taken in front of the bakery c. 1933. The Boy Scouts helped a local mason construct a Colonial oven in the bakery. During the late 1920s and 1930s, hundreds of Boy Scouts at Allaire enjoyed handicrafts and activities, such as trail making, camping, pioneering, photography, and modeling. At the bakery, records were kept on each member's advancement.

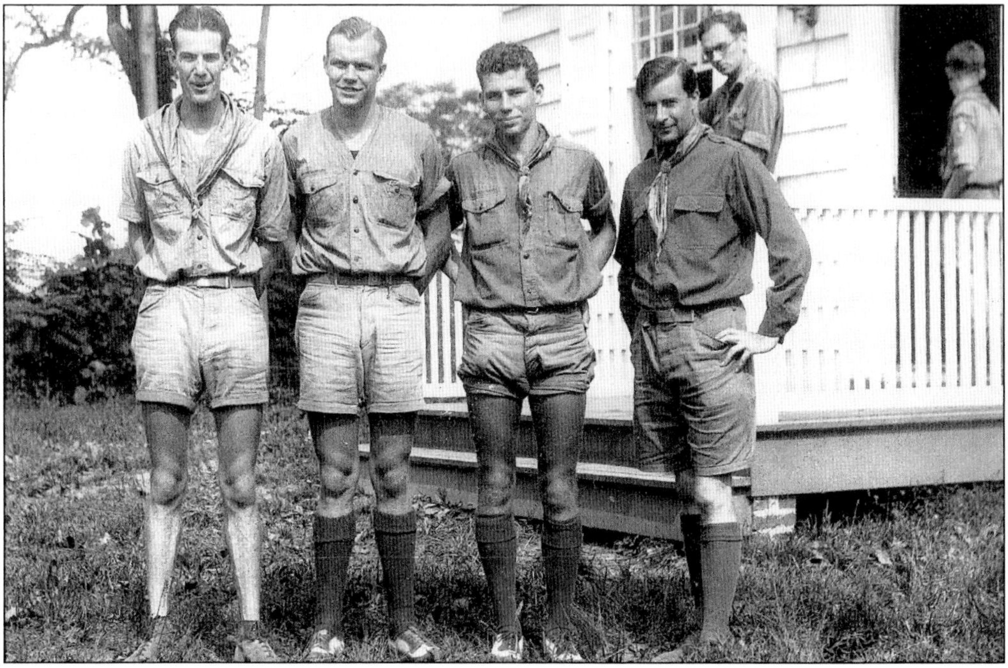

The photograph above shows Boy Scouts near the church in the early 1930s. The view below shows the church as it appeared *c.* 1935, after being restored for the Boy Scouts by the Asbury Park Elks Lodge. The church looks very much like it does today, except for the shutters. It fell into disrepair after Arthur Brisbane's death in 1936. Local farmers and residents of the village continued to attend the church well after iron making had ceased. During the Boy Scouts' occupation of Allaire, devotional services were held for every denomination in camp under their own church leadership. The church was also used for meetings and featured writing and reading areas, including a library of 500 books. A Boy Scout was always reverent and could use the church at any time for meditation and prayer.

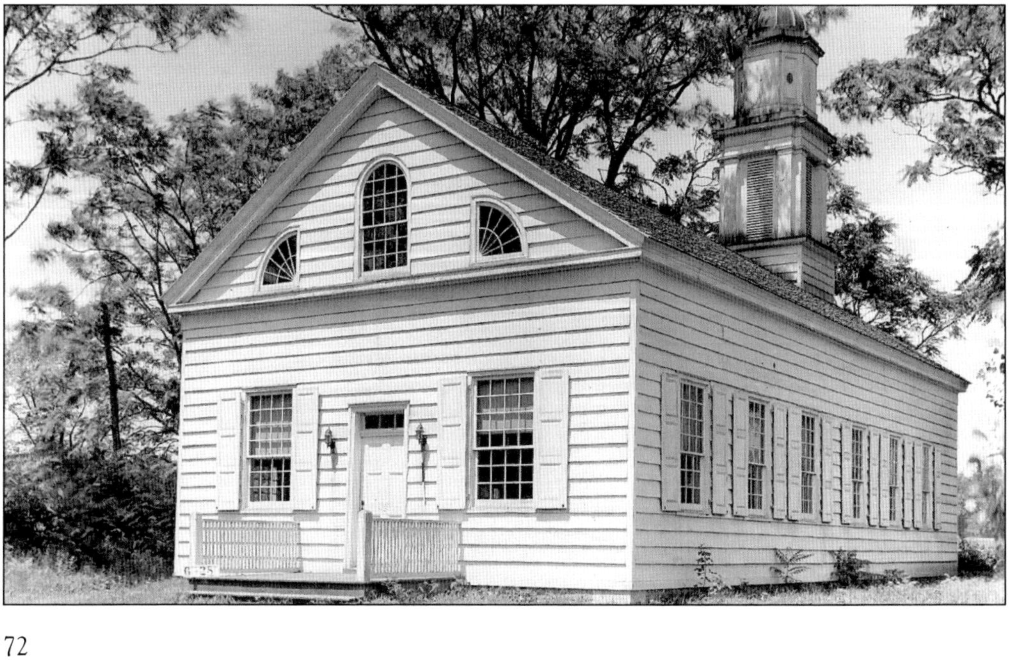

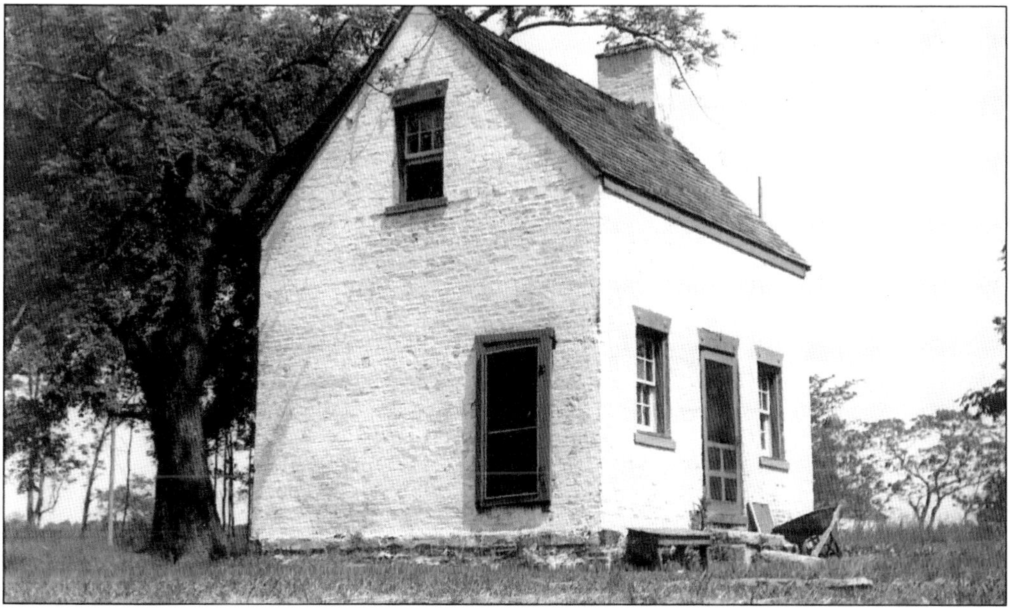

The foreman's cottage is pictured *c.* 1932 after it was restored by the St. James Church in Red Bank. It served as a first-aid station to the Boy Scouts. The wooden addition that was built in the late 1800s had been removed.

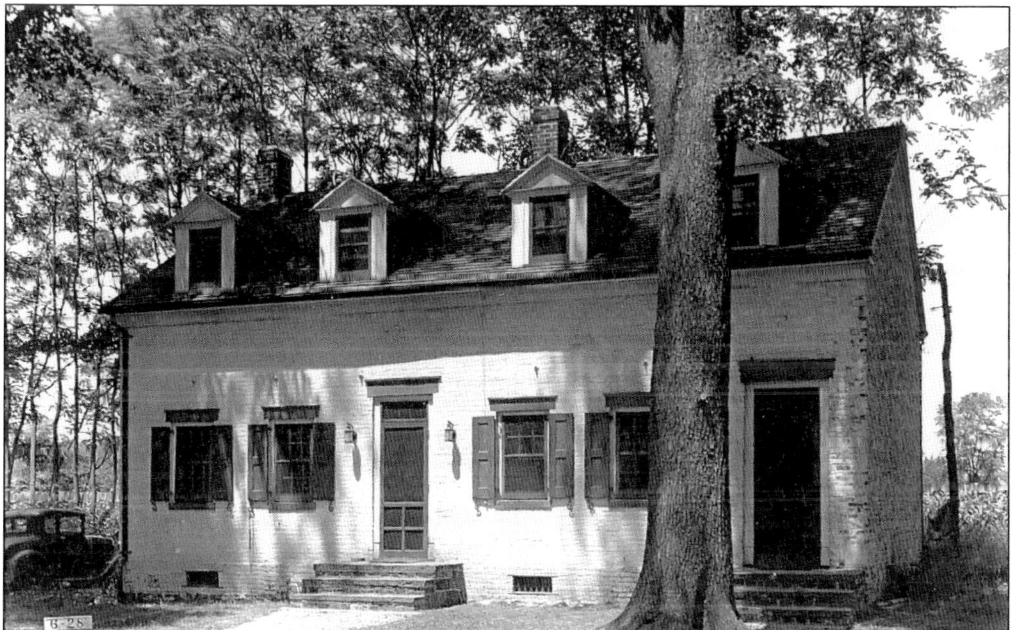

From the late 1920s through the mid-1930s, these row houses were used as a headquarters for the Boy Scouts. This photograph of the remaining two row houses at Allaire was taken in 1936. It is now part of the visitor center.

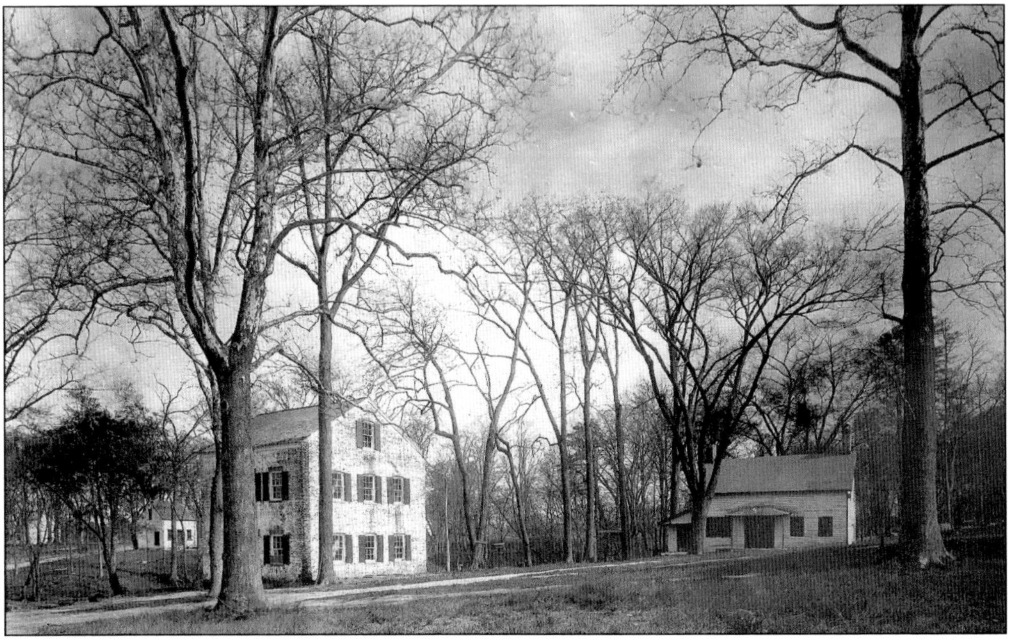

This village view was taken *c.* 1929 just after Arthur Brisbane allowed the Boy Scouts to begin using the village grounds. The Boy Scouts helped maintain the village during their use of Allaire from 1928 to 1939. They were also instrumental in recruiting private organizations to fund various restoration projects at the village. Notice the shutters on the bakery (left). The manager's house served as residence for the caretaker (employed by Brisbane). The village is shown here in relatively good shape.

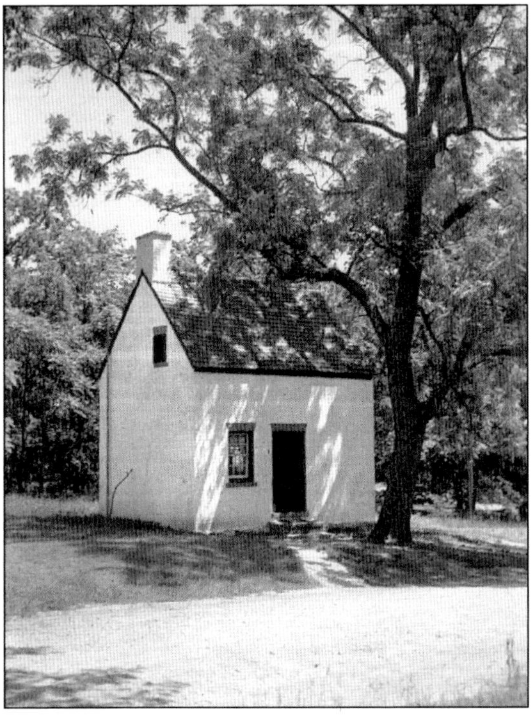

The foreman's cottage, serving as a first-aid station for the Boy Scouts, is seen in this 1935 photograph. The main road now passes by the rear of the cottage, as it does today.

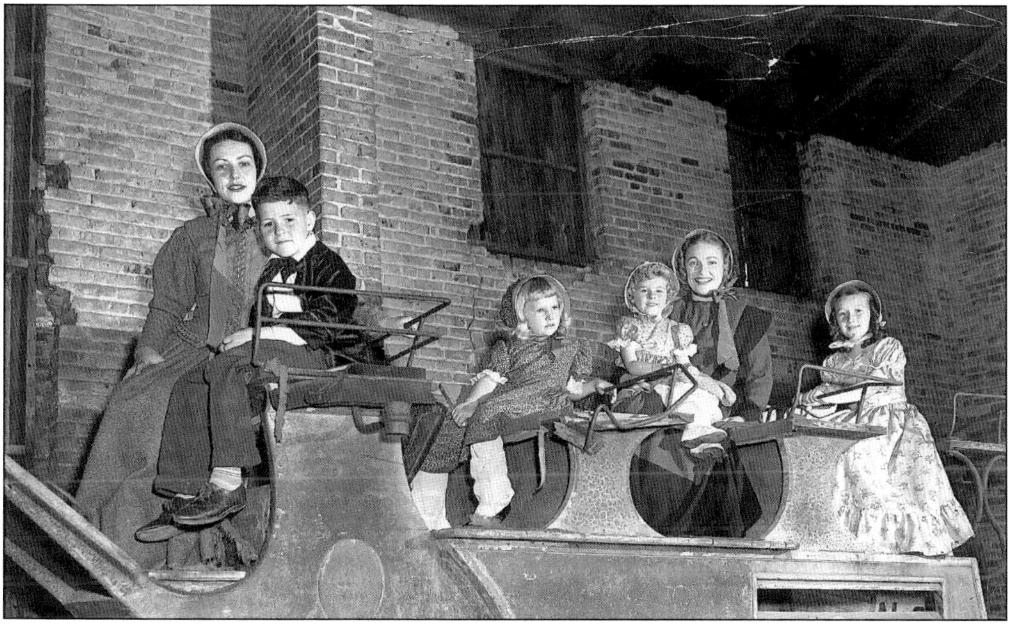

Stored in the blacksmith shop, this carriage may have been used to transport guests to Allaire during the Howell Works era. This group of local residents came to give life to the village in July 1949. They are, from left to right, Audrey Bonello, Dewey Moser, Nancy Peterson, Eleanor Riddle, Alice Waud, and Marina Mulvey. They gave a touch of authenticity to the scene by their 19th-century costumes. The Brewster Wagon was restored in 1975 and is on exhibit at the carriage house.

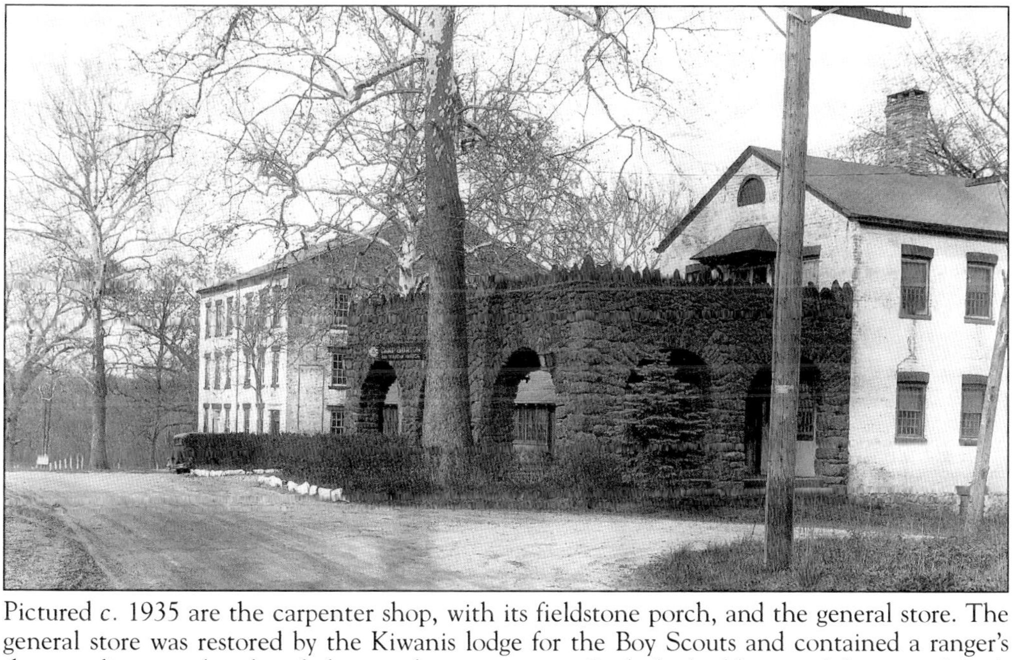

Pictured *c.* 1935 are the carpenter shop, with its fieldstone porch, and the general store. The general store was restored by the Kiwanis lodge for the Boy Scouts and contained a ranger's shop, trading post, handicraft shop, and camp museum. Both the buildings and the grounds look pretty good in this picture. Notice the evidence of whitewashing on the buildings. Cars used the roads through the village, and telephone poles lined the streets.

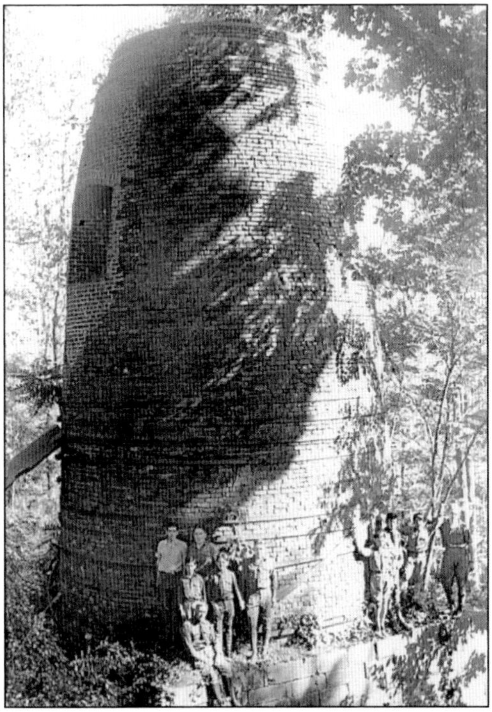

Boy Scouts pose near the blast furnace in the mid-1930s. The huge building that once surrounded the blast furnace no longer stands. The only existing requirement at the camp was good human relations. Any deviation was settled democratically in council under guidance of an experienced adult leader. A regard for others was fostered.

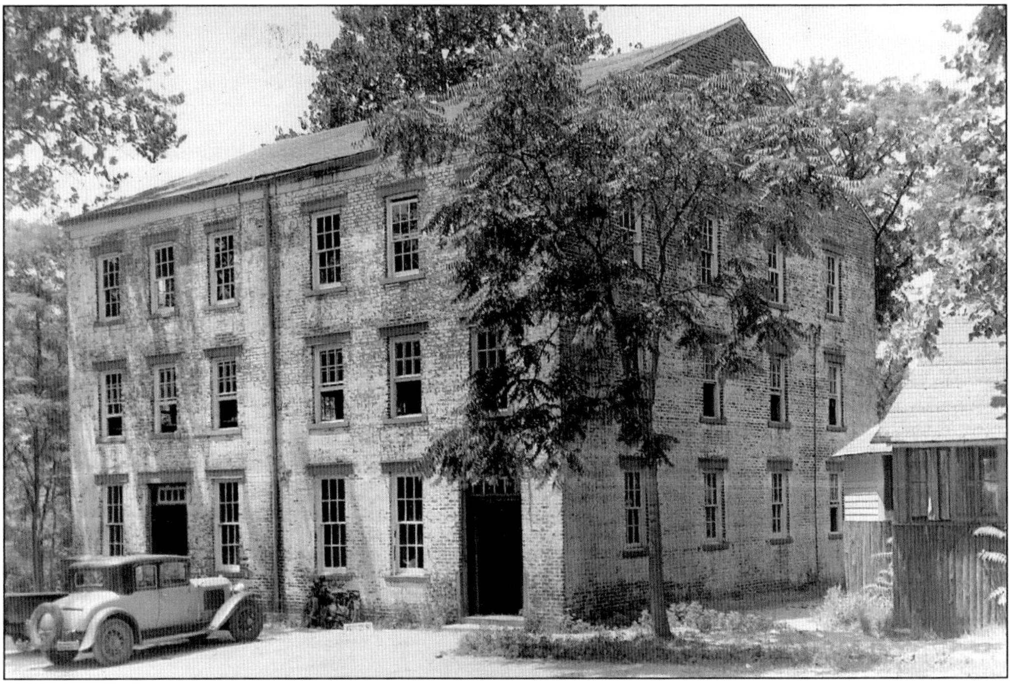

The general store, shown *c.* 1935, was used for various manufacturing concerns during the Brisbane ownership, most notably a toy factory in the early 1900s. The author's great-grandfather worked at the toy factory in 1920. The store was built in 1835 and, at that time, was the third-largest building at Allaire Village. Of the three largest buildings, only the store survived into the 20th century. The store here looks today much like it did in the 1930s.

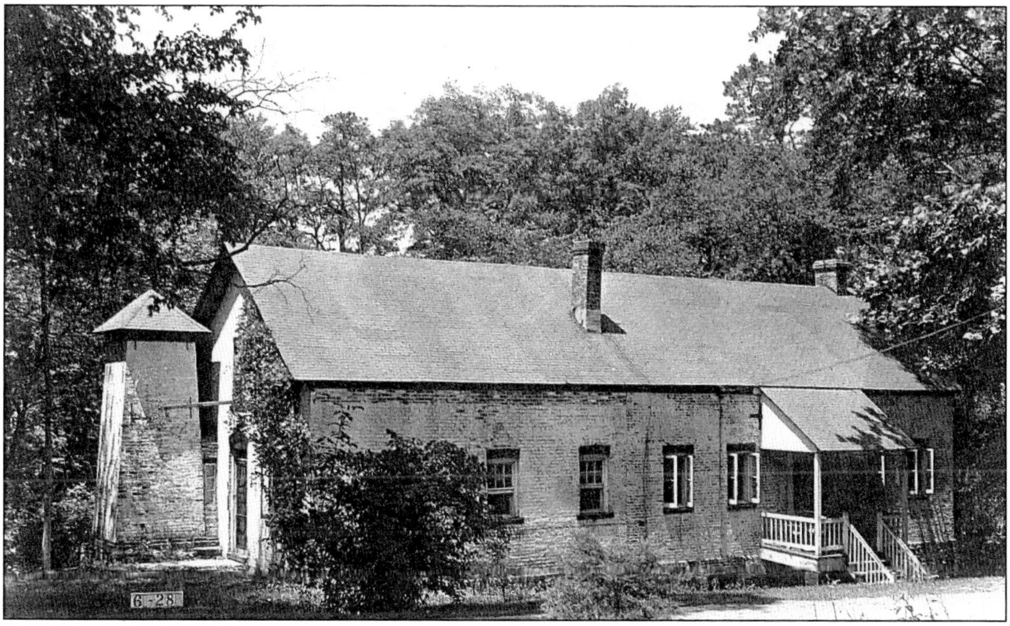

At the time of this 1936 photograph, the Enameling Building was serving as a private residence for the Macauley family, employees of Arthur Brisbane.

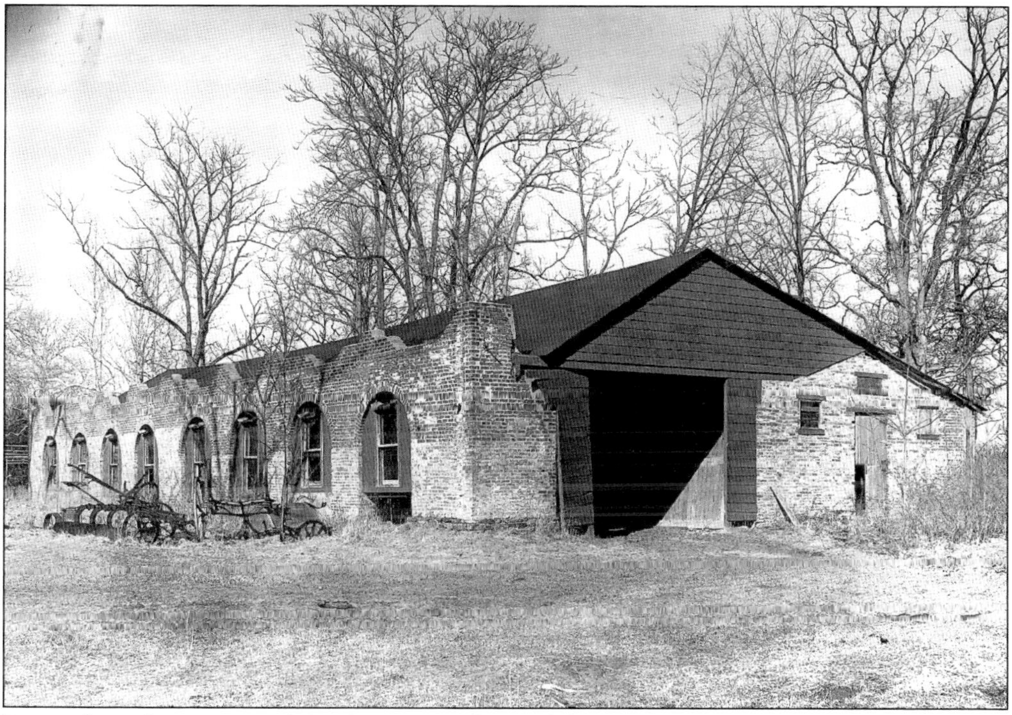
Pictured are the remains of the three-story charcoal depot in 1934, reduced to a single level by 1900. During Arthur Brisbane's ownership of Allaire, the charcoal depot served as a garage and service center for guests of the Allaire Inn. In the 1930s, after the Allaire Inn had closed, the charcoal depot was used by the Boy Scouts and Brisbane to store maintenance equipment. By 1960, only a small corner of the charcoal depot remained.

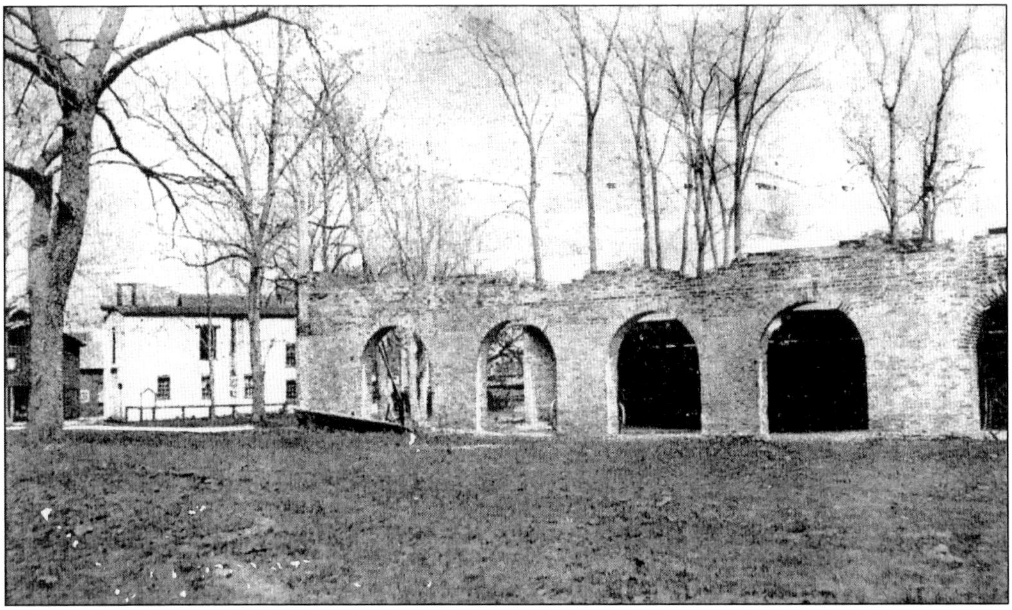

This view shows the charcoal depot archways (once three stories high), the carriage house, and barns. The grounds appear to be neatly kept. The carriage house and barns, where he kept a variety of horses and farm animals, served as the focal point of Arthur Brisbane's model farm.

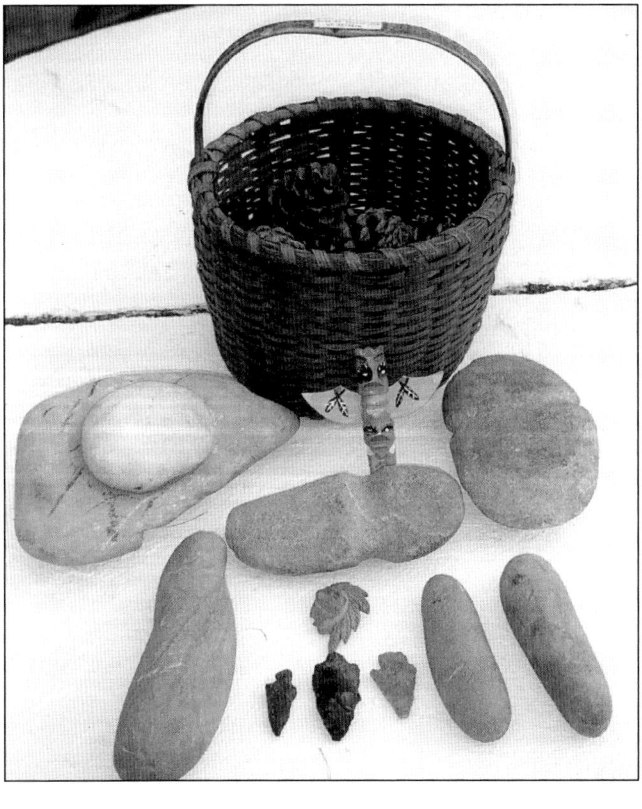

These stones were found in the Allaire area. Indian Joe, who lived in a lean-to in the Allaire woods during the early 1900s, made the basket. He was raised in Nova Scotia and was a member of the Micomac or Penobscot tribe. He made some money by carving war clubs and fashioning canoes, baskets, and wooden handles. He sold his wares in nearby Farmingdale, Allenwood, and Manasquan, hopping on the train as it slowed through Allaire. He died in the 1930s.

Six

From Hard Times to Restoration

Although the Brisbane family had gifted much of their Allaire property, including the village, to the state in the early 1940s for development into a recreational park and historical center, restoration funds were unavailable until 1957. From 1941 to 1957, most of the village buildings were unused and remained idle, leaving the grounds and buildings to be overrun with dense vegetation. Between 1890 and 1905, postcards and journalists first labeled the former Howell Works as the "deserted village of Allaire." Writers compared the Howell Works to a prominent iron-producing community with a population of more than 300 during its height in 1836 to one of crumbling ruins and home to a few lonely souls by 1900. Its former glory as an iron-producing community was a memory. Journalists and visitors often think the village was deserted for the entire time period from 1846 (the closing of the Howell Works) to 1957 (the first signs of restoration for public use). Few realized the village's colorful history in the early 1900s. This same image of crumbling ruins and desertion was captured in newspapers and postcards from 1941 to 1957—long after Arthur Brisbane had died and his family had given the state the property. The village was simply awaiting restoration funds, and World War II delayed the attention of any major maintenance or upkeep.

In 1954 and 1956, the grounds of Allaire Village were cleared, and the New Jersey State Division of Parks and Forestry began landscaping projects. In 1957, the Monmouth Council Advisory Board, under the guidance of E. Donald Sterner, helped to form the Deserted Village of Allaire Inc., today known as Allaire Village Inc. This organization was formed to help the State of New Jersey Department of Conservation and Economic Development with initial restoration efforts. The New Jersey Federation of Women's Clubs, Monmouth County Historical Society, and the Monmouth County Planning Board sponsored Allaire in the early years and conducted fund-raisers to help the restoration process. A ladies auxiliary was formed in 1961 to assist and to staff the buildings.

Today, Historic Allaire Village, a community listed on the New Jersey and National Registers of Historic Places, celebrates the life and times of James P. Allaire's Howell Iron Works Company, a major industrial center in the 1830s. It stands in a beautifully preserved section of southern Monmouth County as a reminder of the bog-iron industry that existed here in the early 19th century. Allaire Village Inc., a nonprofit educational organization, is licensed by the state to interpret the history and culture associated with the village, located within the confines of Allaire State Park. The unique partnership between Allaire Village Inc. and the Division of Parks and Forestry (the agency responsible for the administration and operation of Allaire State Park) still exists.

The Green Acres Program has enabled Allaire State Park to grow beyond its original 1,200 acres. Today, the park encompasses close to 3,500 acres and offers numerous outdoor sports and recreational activities, such as canoeing, picnicking, hiking, fishing, hunting, camping, and horseback riding. This chapter contains photographs of the village buildings before restoration in 1957 and how the buildings look and are interpreted today.

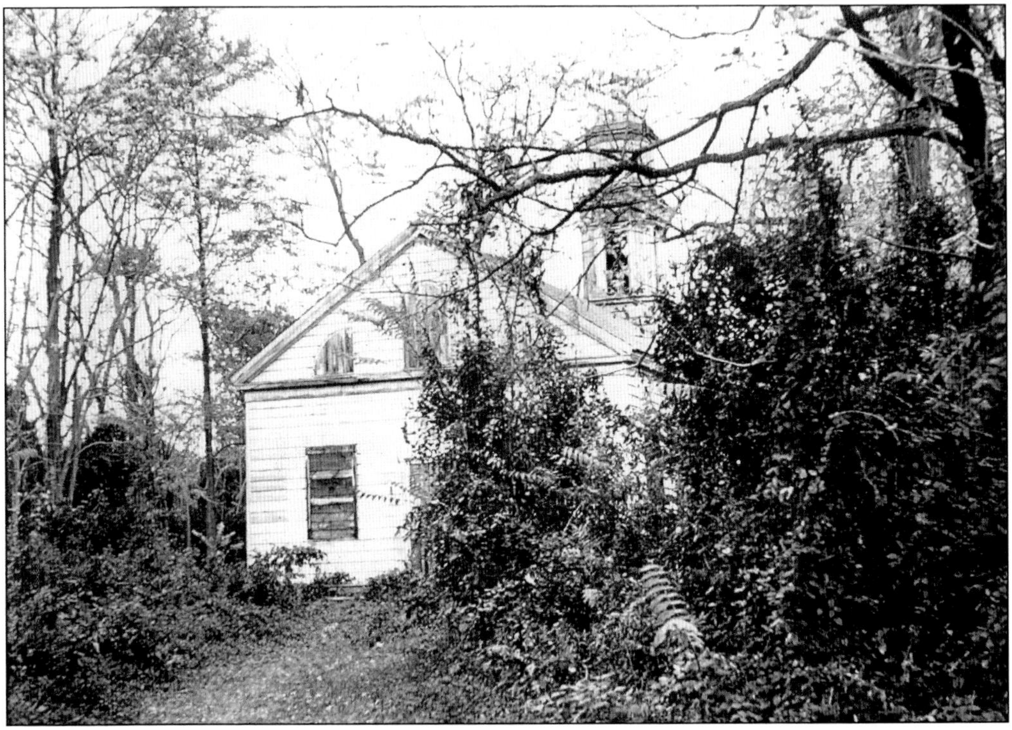

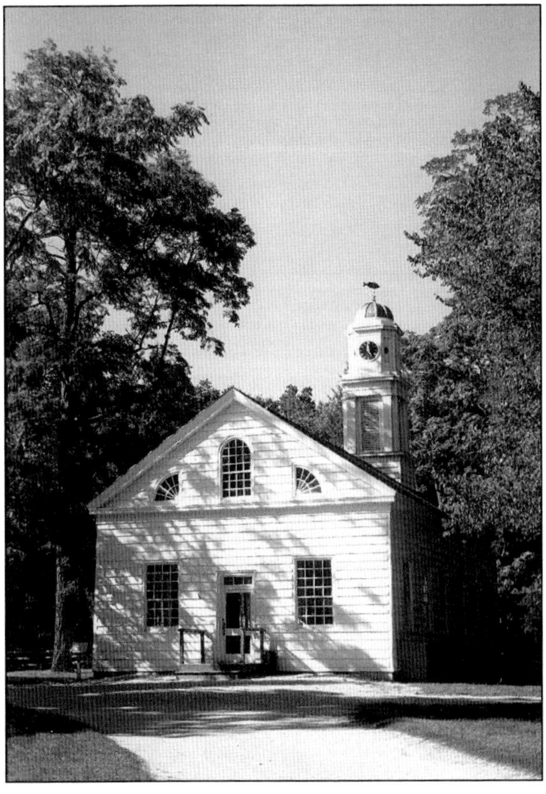

The church is pictured above in 1954, before restoration, and to the left in a present-day view. Visitors today learn how the church served as a place of worship (Episcopal), a meeting place, and a school during the Howell Works era. The church was constructed in two sections, the older section built in 1832 and the newer section built in 1834. The newer section was built to sustain the weight of the steeple, normally not located on the rear of a church. All the children living at Howell Works were required to attend school up until age 12, even the girls. James P. Allaire believed strongly in education and personally financed the school. They were taught using the Lancasterian method, a technique of memorization whereby the older children taught the younger children, making the schoolmaster only an overseer. The church can be rented out for weddings, christenings, and other functions.

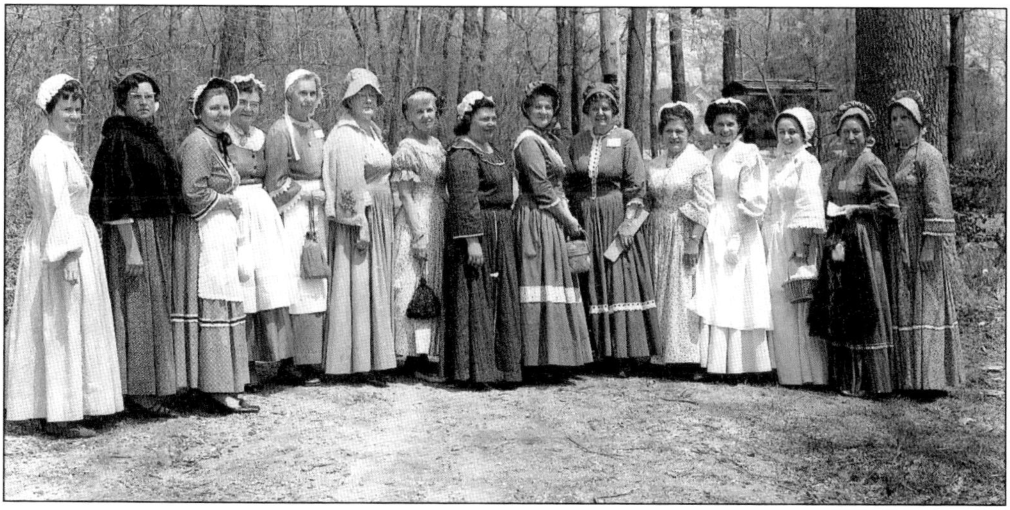

The ladies auxiliary was formed in 1961 under the leadership of Joan Creveling. Some of the original founders can be seen in this photograph, taken *c.* 1969 during the sawmill site dedication. Pictured are Evelyn Kessler Morton (2nd from left), Doris Holloway (3rd from left), Janet Frostick Pittenger (6th from left), Dot Young (7th from left), Jean Schneider (8th from left), Fran Beck (9th from left), Mae Shellham (10th from left), and Joan Creveling (12th from left).

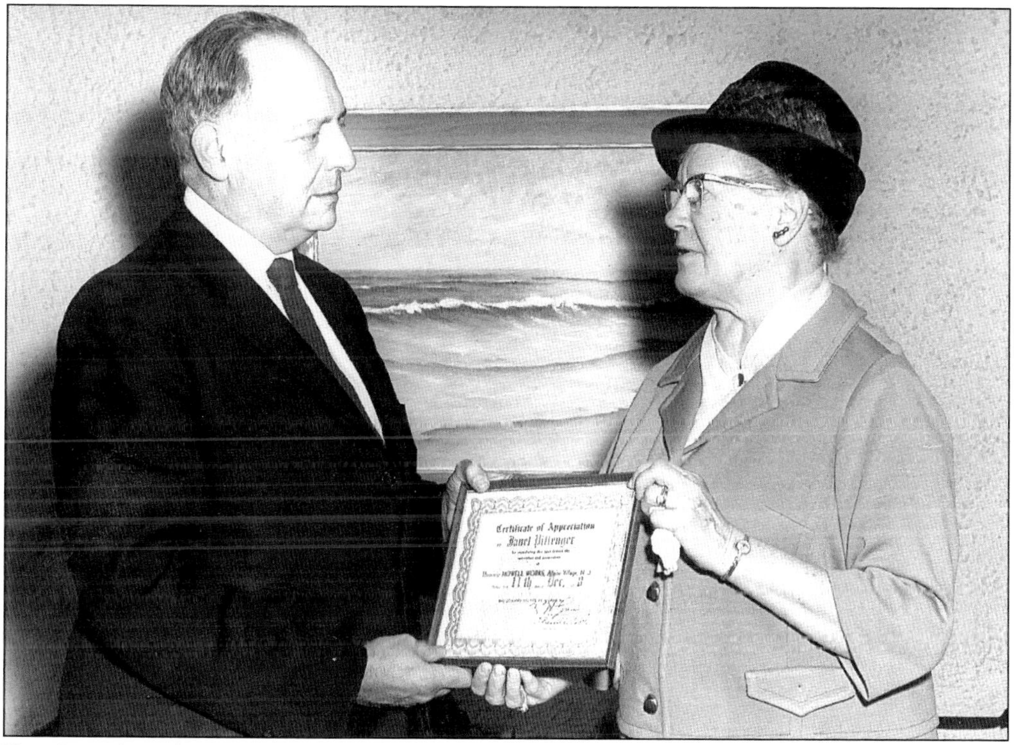

Ken Creveling, first executive director of Allaire Village Inc., and Janet Frostick Pittenger, one of the original founders of the ladies auxiliary, are receiving a certificate of appreciation at an awards banquet. As Allaire Village became a more popular historic site, a professional museum staff, including an executive director, was hired by Allaire Village Inc. The auxiliary continues to sponsor fund-raisers and sell hand-made crafts to support museum operations.

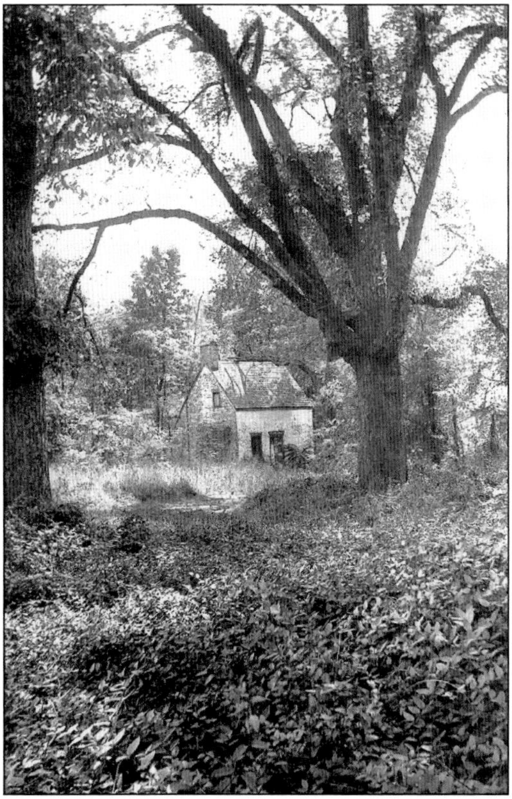

The foreman's cottage is pictured in 1954. Twenty-one years would pass between the death of Arthur Brisbane in 1936 and the opening of Allaire State Park in 1957. The village was deeded to the state in 1940 but stood idle and largely unused until 1957. Shrubs and vegetation overtook the village and choked the streets during that period. World War II delayed restoration, and funds were unavailable.

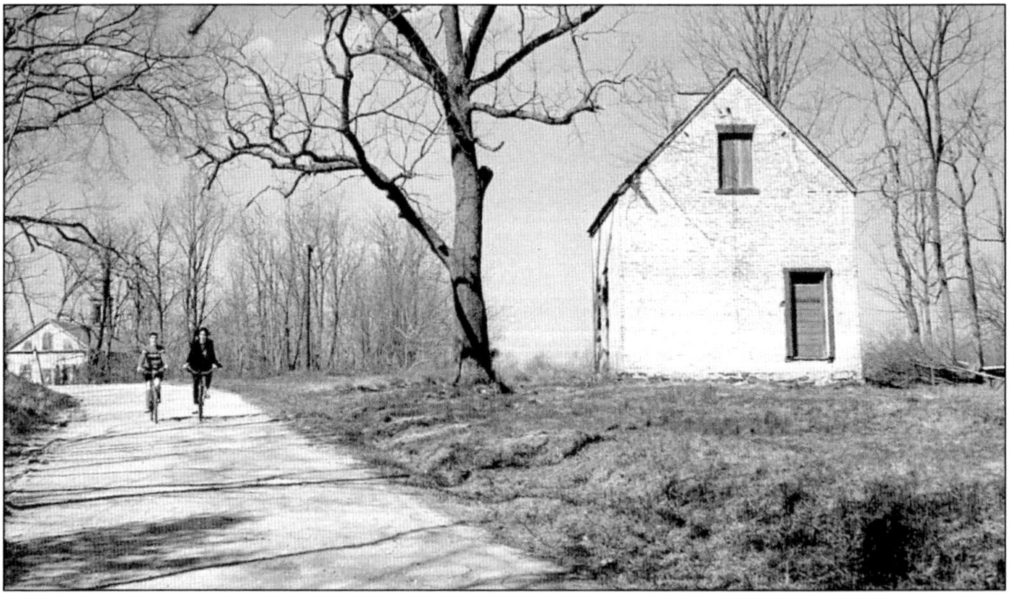

The foreman's cottage is still boarded up just after the park opened in 1957. On August 5, 1967, the post office was reestablished here. The post office now operates in the general store at Christmastime. Allaire replaced the wooden buildings predating his ownership and built in their place, strong brick buildings. The foreman's cottage is the oldest brick building in the village, dating back to 1827.

Today, the roadbed passes by the rear of the foreman's cottage, and visitors enter the building using the back door. Currently, the foreman's cottage is interpreted as if the Johnson family lives there during the Howell Works era. Joseph Johnson was the foreman who oversaw furnace workers at the Howell Works. The downstairs served as a kitchen, living room, and parents' bedroom. The upstairs featured a sleeping loft for the children and guests.

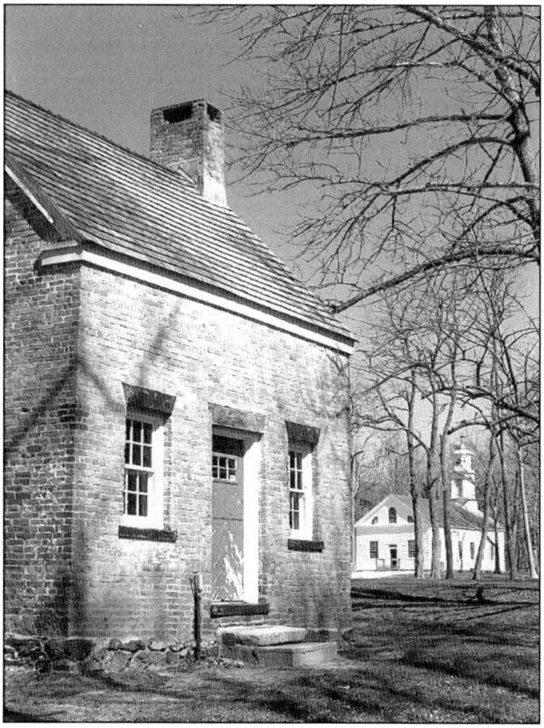

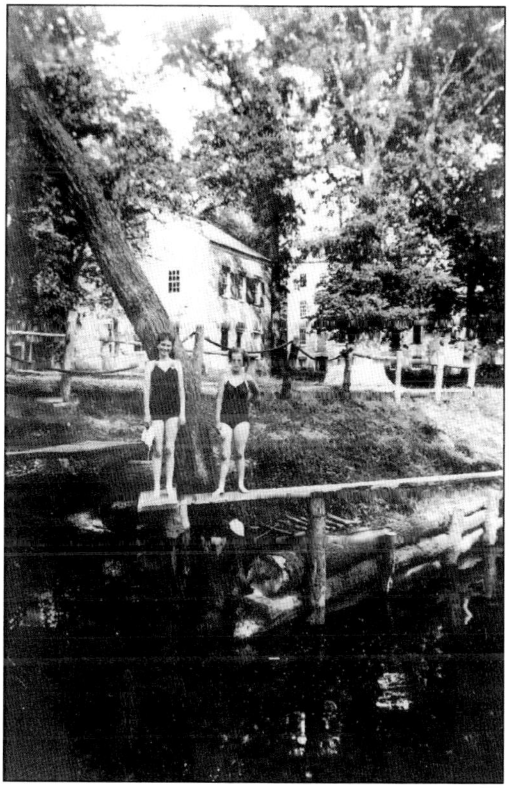

Theresa Frawley (left) and Mabel Kessler are about to take a swim in the millpond in July 1940. The bakery and general store are in the background and appear in pretty good shape. By 1950, the millpond was all dried up.

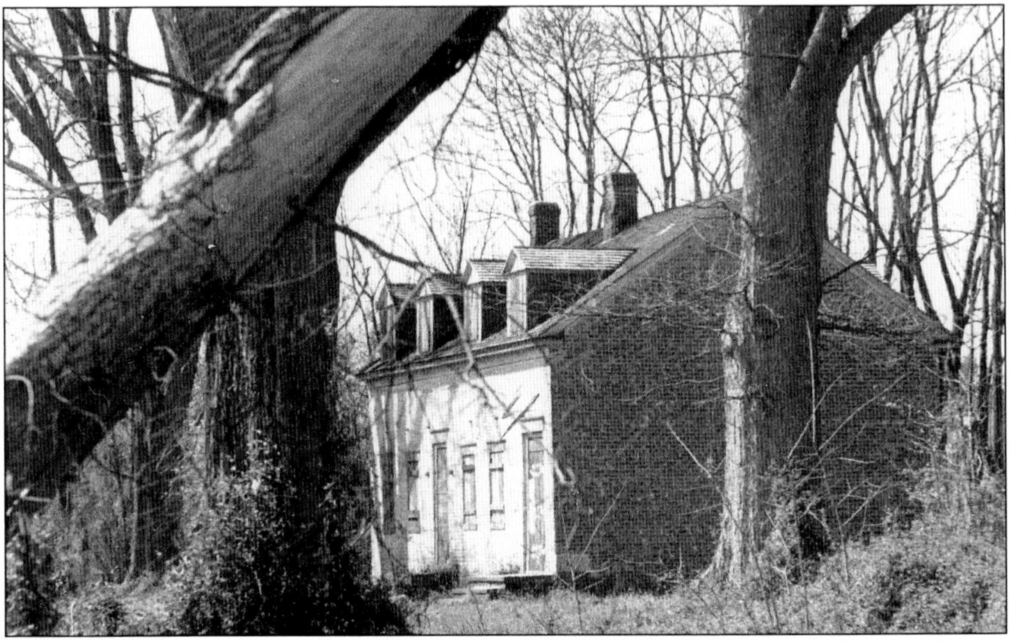

The row houses are pictured above as they appeared before restoration in 1951. In 1956, the row houses were restored and became the home of park superintendents. Of the original 11 houses in this row, only 2 remained after 1900. In 1985, the other 9 were reconstructed to house a modern visitor center and museum (below), which features information on the life of James P. Allaire, the iron-making process at the Howell Works, and the village's development. This museum, run by state staff, is open year-round and offers special programs, activities, and walking tours. The interior of one row house, principal dwelling places for James P. Allaire's workers, resembles the 1830s. This row of houses, the only one of four units remaining today, was the largest of the workers' houses with the luxury of private kitchens. Thus, it is believed that skilled workers and privileged employees lived there.

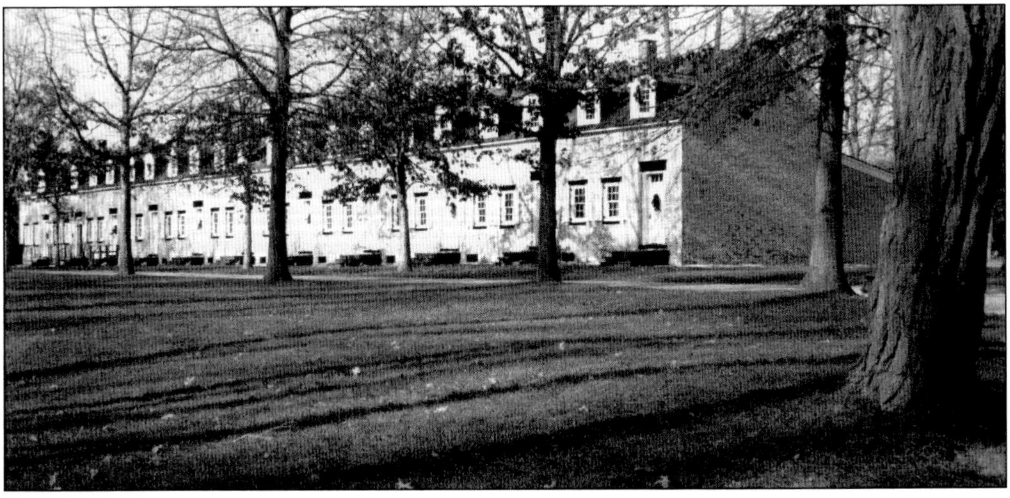

A relation to James P. Allaire, Betty Allaire Taylor donated many Allaire family pieces to the museum before her death. She was a very active member of the ladies auxiliary and was influential in starting the Allaire Village Library.

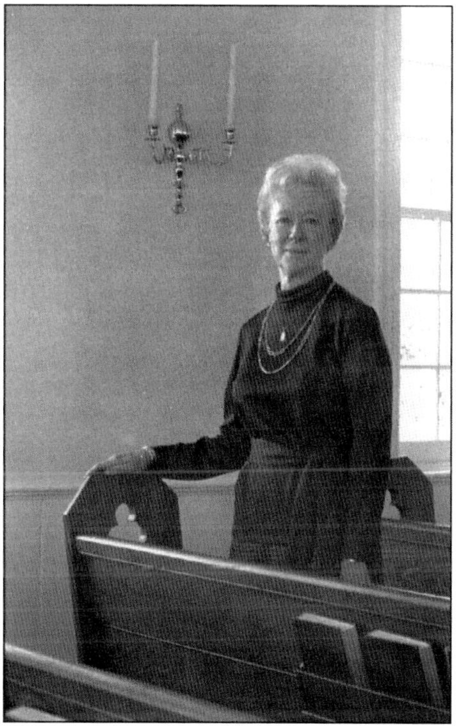

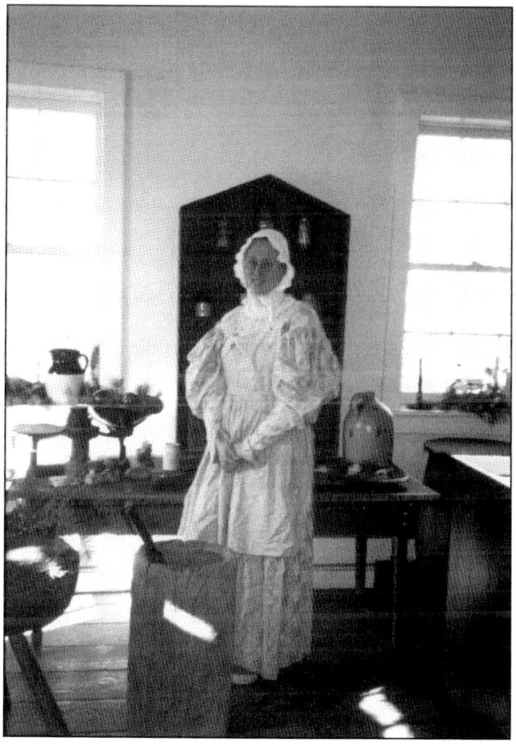

Janice Juralewicz, related to Valetta Bennett (pictured on page 57), served as the bakery interpreter in the 1990s. Her family developed and owned Spring Meadow Golf Course. The first floor of the bakery was used for mixing the dough and preparing the baked goods during the Howell Works era. A beehive oven existed off the rear back and was the most modern of its time. The upper floors were used for storing grain and flour, processed across at the gristmill.

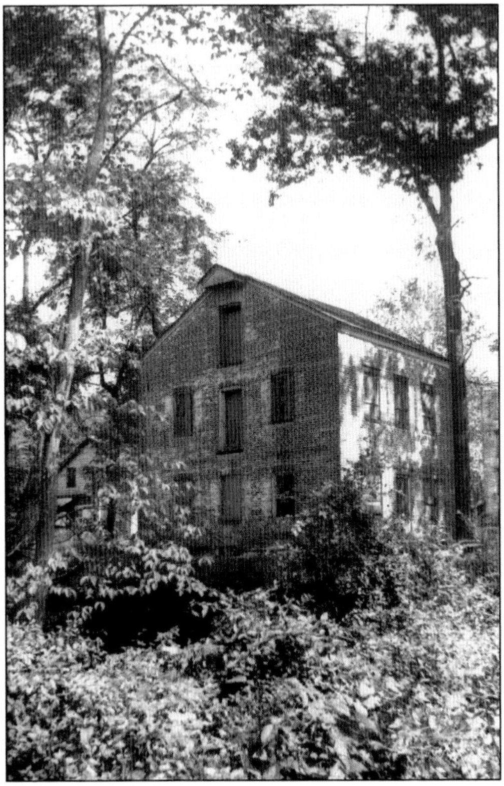

To the left, the bakery and millpond are surrounded by vegetation in 1954 before restoration. The image below shows the bakery today. During World War II, the army out of Fort Monmouth used the village grounds for training. They used the bakery as a base. The bakery opened in 1957 and was the first village building to open for public visitation. Built in 1835, the bakery was restored with funds from the New Jersey Federation of Women's Clubs and served as a museum. Starting in the 1980s, Allaire Village Inc. began selling baked goods out of the bakery and presenting its history during the Howell Works era. It is uncertain if this was a communal bakery for residents of the village or if a full-time baker was employed.

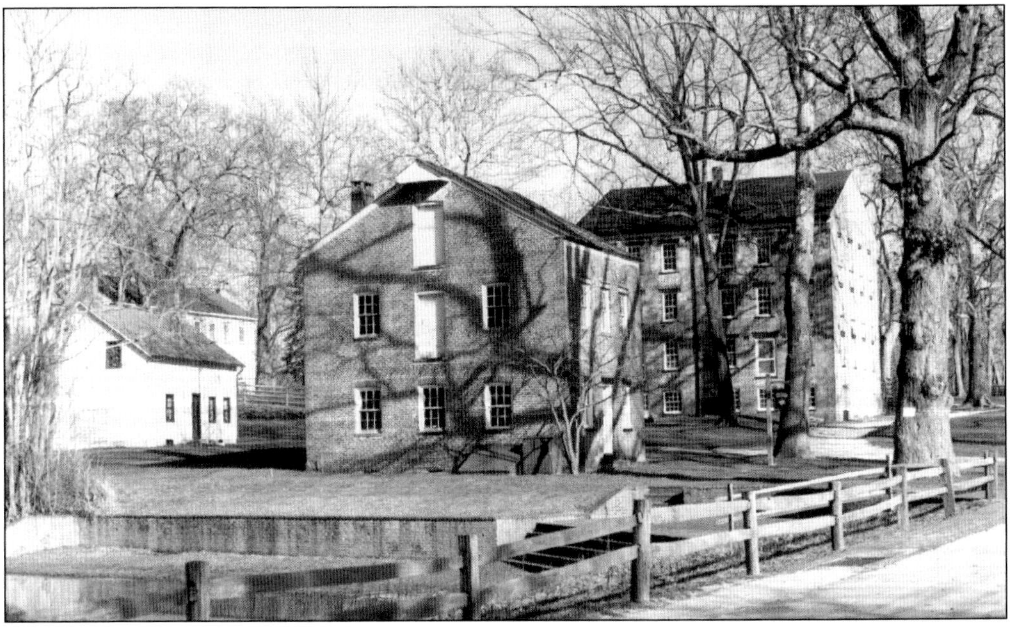

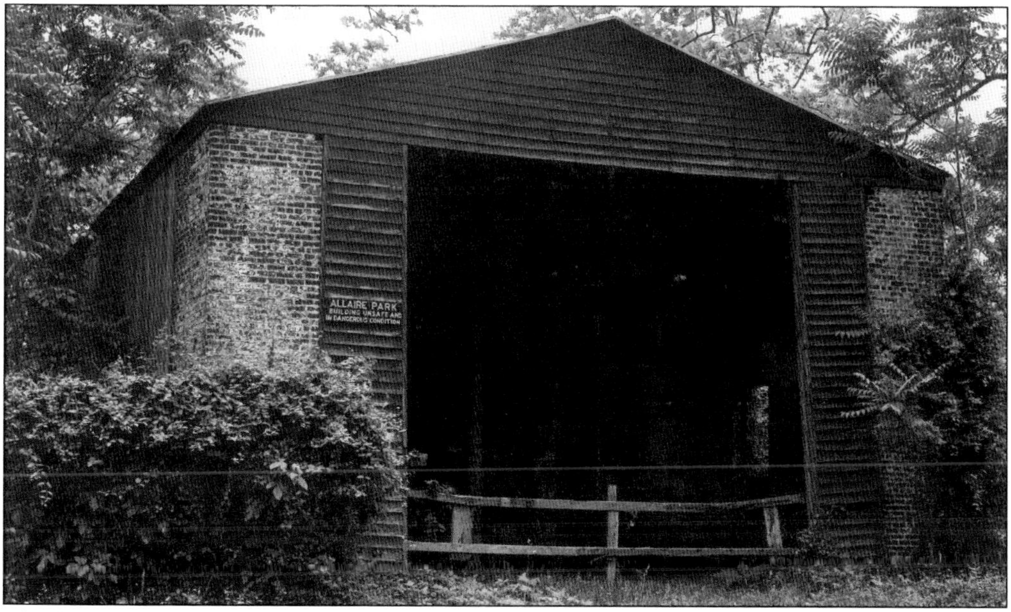

The blacksmith shop (above) was in such disrepair that it was entirely reconstructed in the early 1960s. The original roof of the blacksmith shop collapsed sometime before 1900, and only the three brick walls remained. During Brisbane's ownership of Allaire, he transformed what was left of the blacksmith shop into a general storage facility—adding a new wooden roof (as seen in the above photograph). Today, (below) the Blacksmith Guild and various historic interpreters demonstrate the age-old craft of blacksmithing, using four forges. The most important task blacksmiths performed at the Howell Works was shoeing the draft animals and repairing carriages, tools, and other iron items. Wagons, carriages, and carts transporting pig and cast iron operated regularly to and from the village and James P. Allaire's steamship docks in Red Bank. (Above courtesy Division of Parks and Forestry, New Jersey State Park Service.)

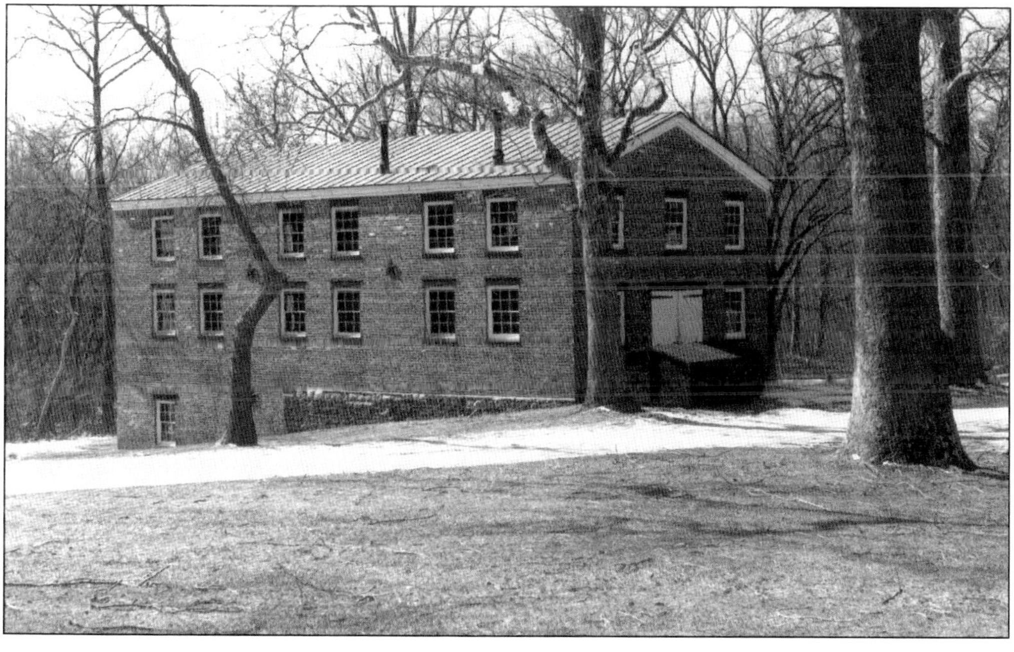

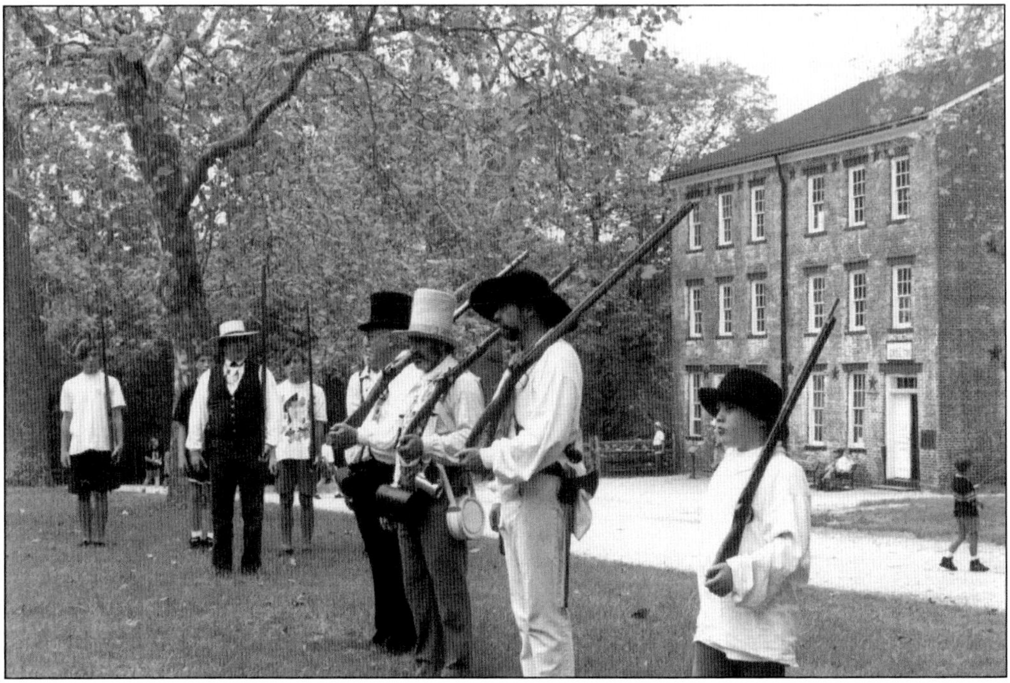

More than 30 special events are sponsored by Allaire Village Inc. throughout the year, including an 1830 militia muster, as seen here. Historic Allaire Village promotes itself as being a living-history museum. Historic interpreters, in period costumes, re-create what it was like to live and work at James P. Allaire's Howell Works during its height in 1836.

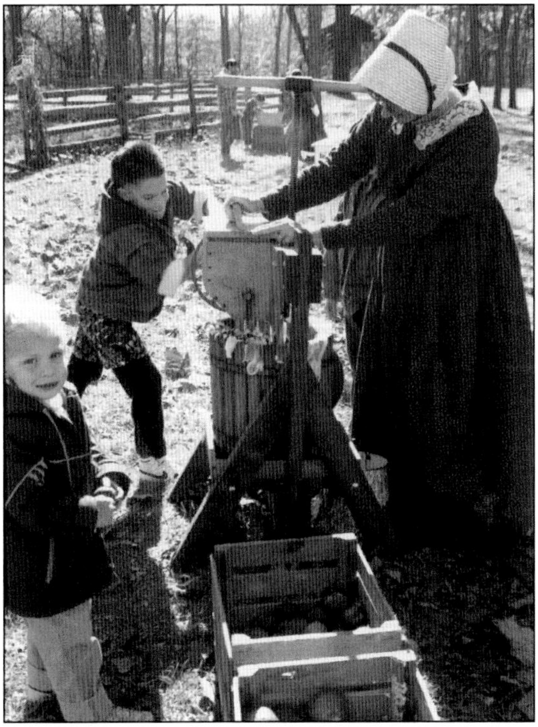

Children help press apples into cider. In the fall, visitors at Allaire come to enjoy Allhallows Eve, cider pressing, evening lantern tours, and the fall foliage.

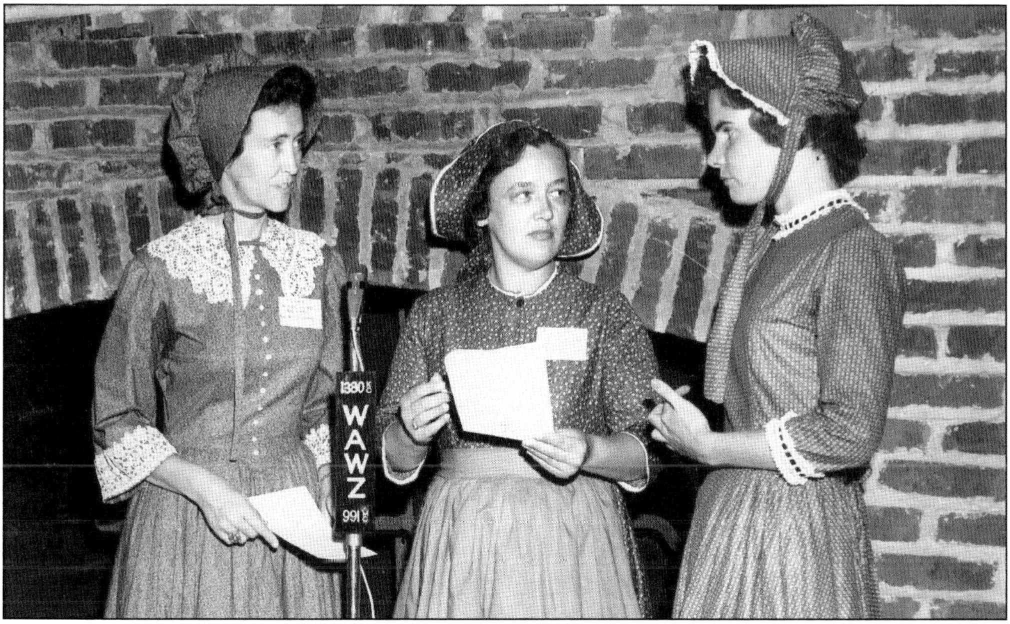

As part of a fund-raiser, Betty Turner (left), Jeanne Bennett Riker (center), and Jeanne Gilroy reenact a historical sketch in the early 1960s on WAWZ radio. Carl B. Ogilvie of Howell produced the program. In the background is the bakery's Colonial oven, built as part of the Boy Scout restoration in the 1930s. Jean Riker later served on the Allaire Village Board of Trustees.

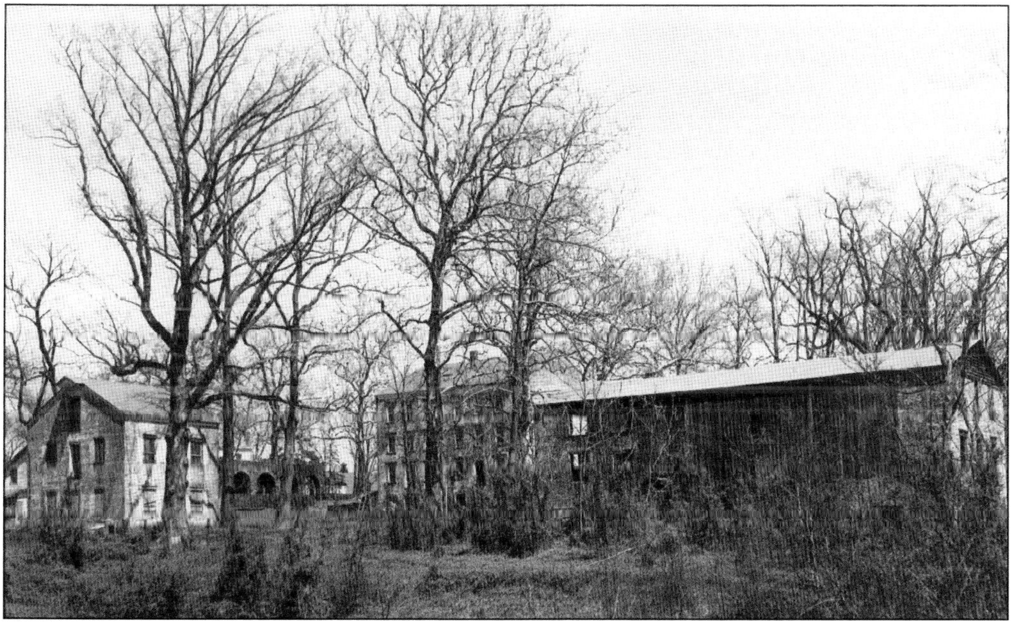

Depicted in this village scene in 1954 are, from left to right, the bakery, the fieldstone porch of the carpenter shop, the general store, and the blacksmith shop. The millpond next to the blacksmith shop is dried up. The state has concentrated on restoring existing structures. Partial restorations were done in the late 1950s and 1960s and, as more state funds became available later, a complete and historically accurate restoration was undertaken.

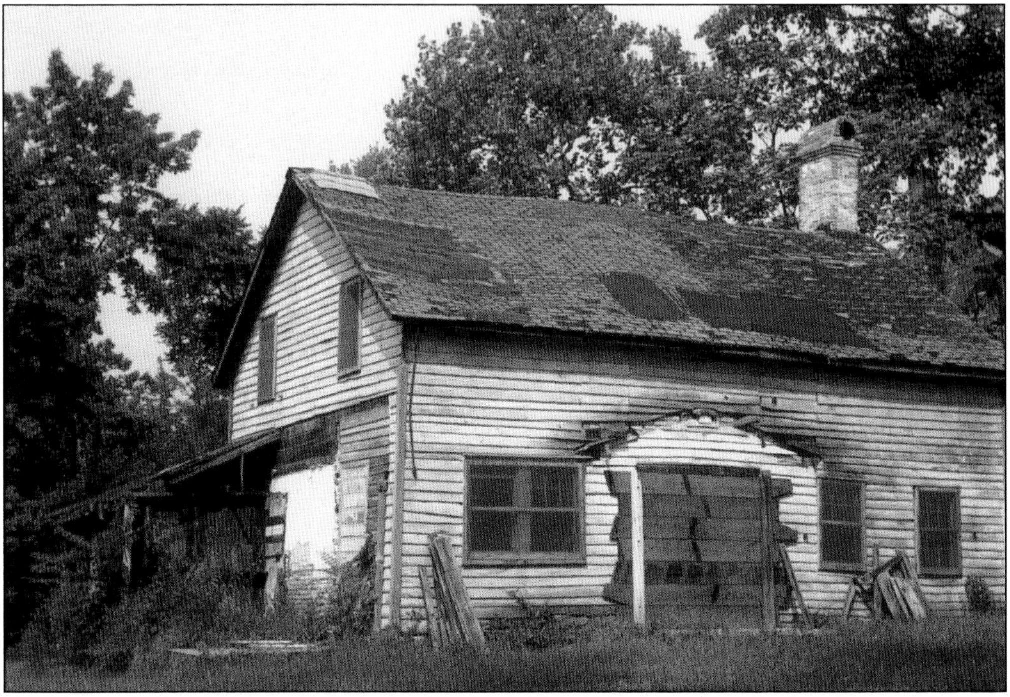

The manager's house is pictured above in 1951 prior to restoration and below after restoration. The house is the oldest building at the village and dates back to 1750. Isaac Palmer, who operated a sawmill back then, probably built the home. Today, the manager's house is interpreted as if the Smith family lives there. Since James P. Allaire resided primarily in New York City near his Allaire Works, a manager was needed to oversee operations at the Howell Works. The Smith family was an upper-middle-class family and had a more spacious home that included two parlors and a kitchen downstairs and four bedrooms upstairs.

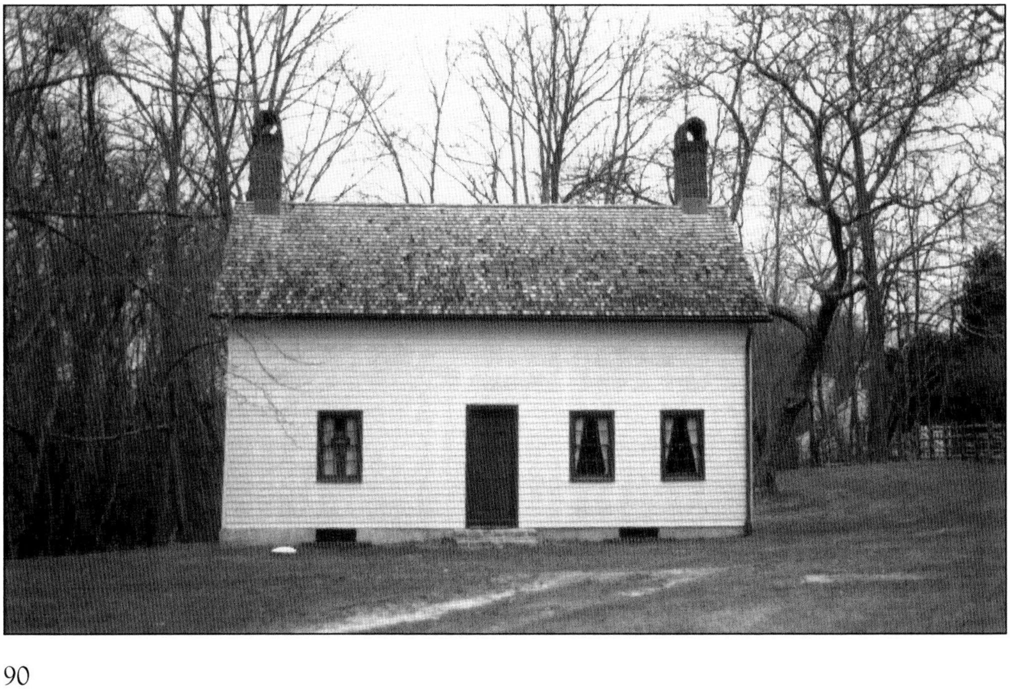

Joanna Mulkiewicz (standing) leads a twill-making demonstration. Children and adults volunteer their time at Allaire Village to preserve age-old crafts. Allaire Village Inc. is licensed to operate the state-owned Allaire Village and has more than 200 volunteers as well as a small paid staff.

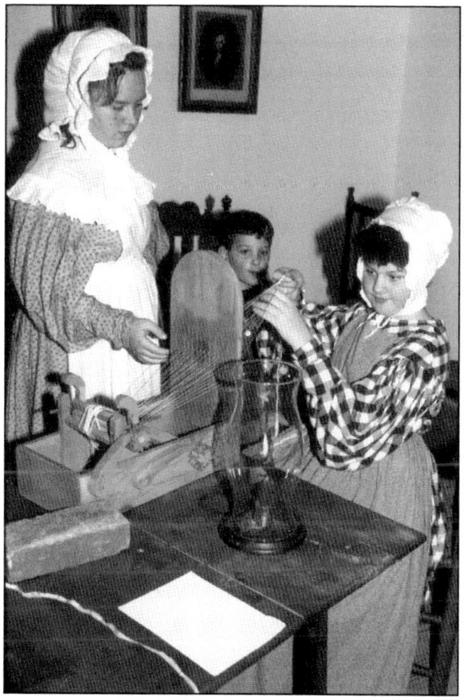

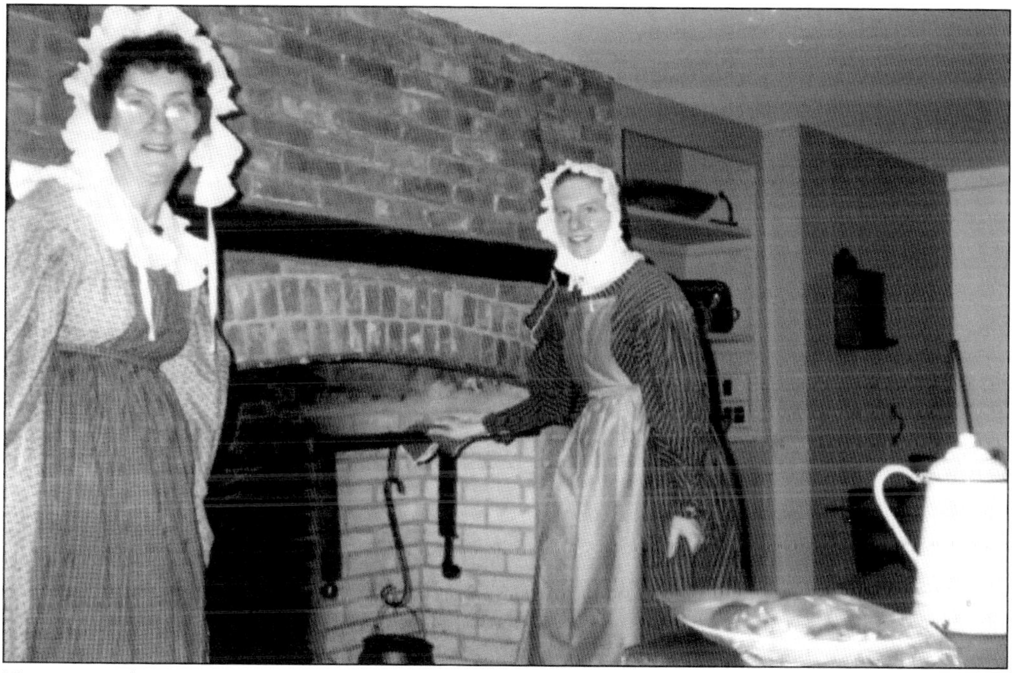

Victoria and Connie Dzenis are engaged in one of many open hearth cooking demonstrations at the manager's house. During the village's Thanksgiving and Christmas events, meals are prepared on the hearth today just like they were in the 1830s. Connie, a volunteer and member of the ladies auxiliary for many years, served as interim executive director and chairman of the board of trustees. Her daughter Victoria started volunteering at Allaire when she was just a child and later served as the coordinator of museum education and interpretation.

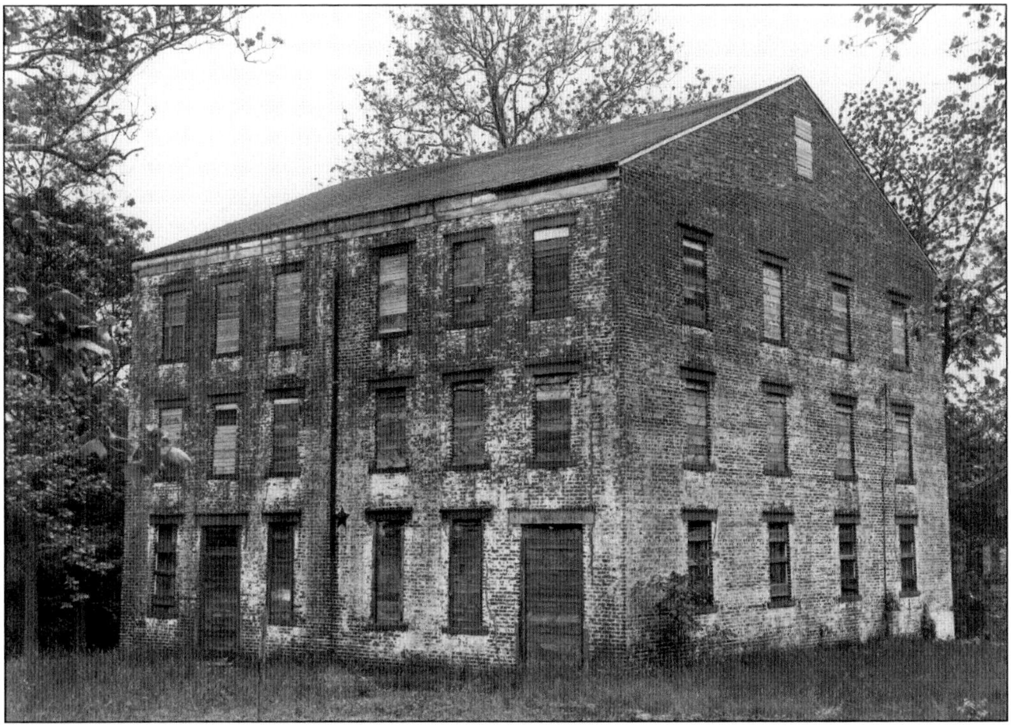

In the picture above, the general store is seen boarded up in 1955. After the Howell Works closed in 1846, the general store was used sporadically for all kinds of manufacturing concerns and was used regularly by the Boy Scouts in the 1930s before being boarded up in the late 1940s. The store, once the third-largest building in the village, is the largest still standing today. The store today, as seen below, houses a gift shop and museum.

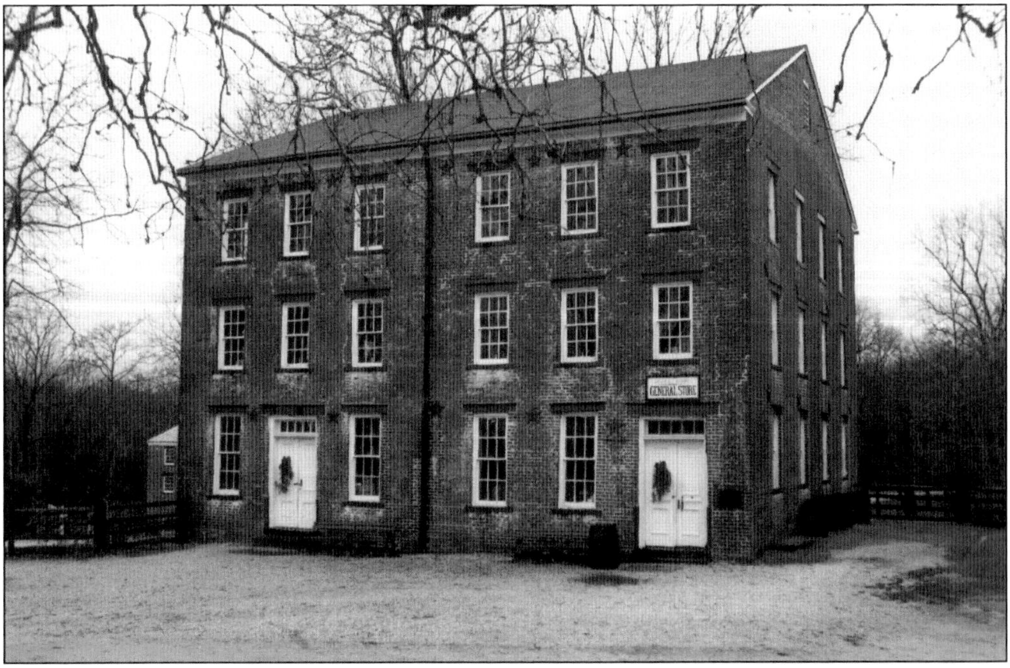

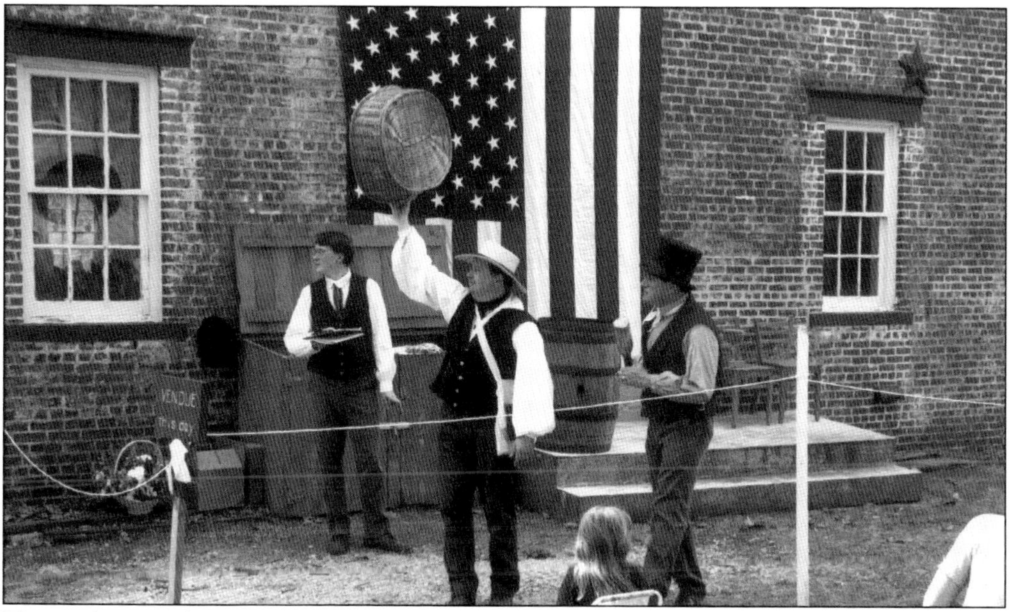

These photographs feature volunteers and staff re-creating a spring market day at Allaire Village. In early-19th-century villages, residents would get together and host a spring market day to sell their crafts and wares made during the winter months. Above, the author (left), retail sales manager and auction coordinator; Sibley Smith Jr. (center), executive director; and Charles Casagrande (right), Allaire Village trustee, re-create an auction in 1995. Market Day in 1997 featured a variety of peddlers, including Linda Ann Morton Sitkus, retail sales manager, selling spring plants and herbs. In the late 1990s, visiting the store was an educational experience. Most of the items for sale were antique reproductions from the 18th and 19th centuries. Customers were greeted by historical interpreters dressed in period costumes and provided with historical interpretation of items for sale.

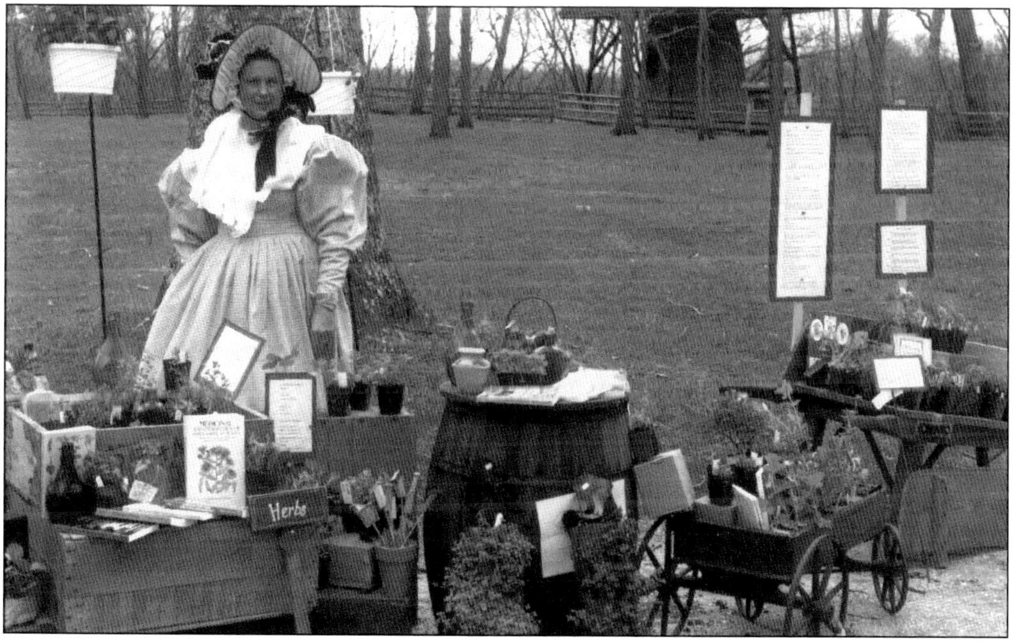

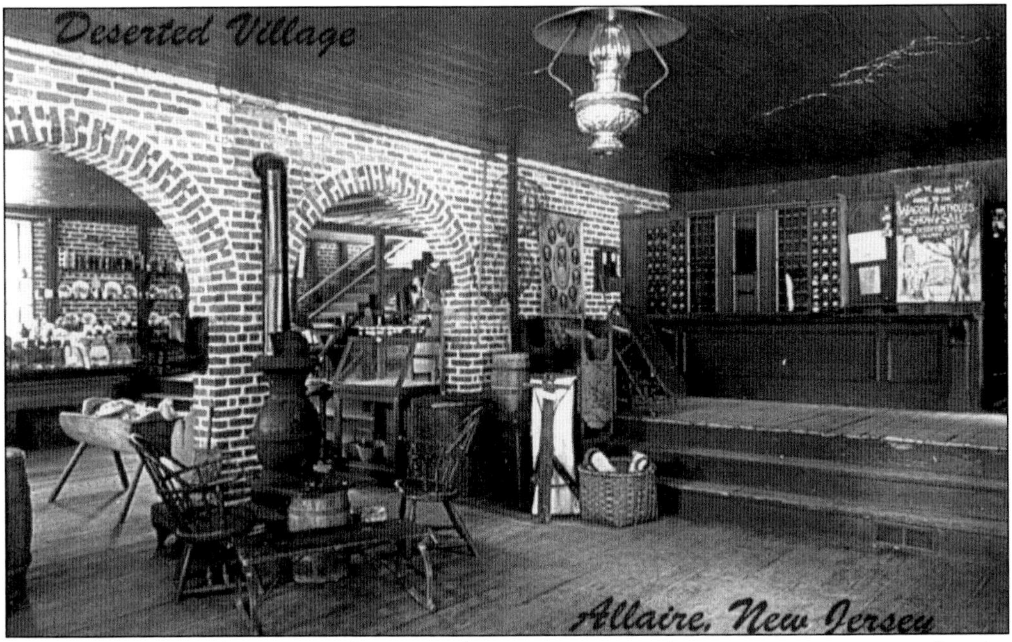

After being restored c. 1960, the general store was opened as a country store under the proprietorship of Charles Vanderveer, as seen here. Vanderveer later donated many of the antiques that are now displayed in the store. The store still awaits a complete restoration, estimated to take several years and a significant amount of money. In the late 1970s, Allaire Village Inc. took over direct operation of the store's retail business. The store is equipped with a manually operated freight elevator, one of the oldest in the state.

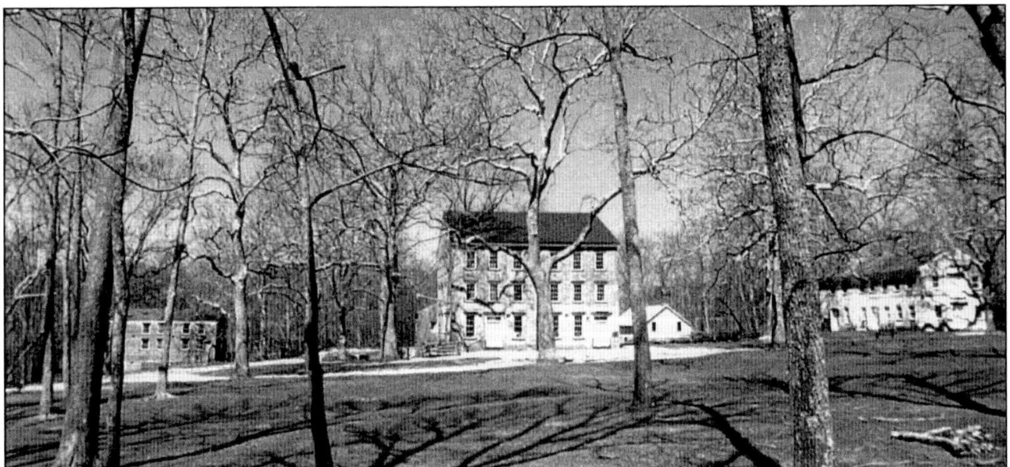

Pictured from the village green are the blacksmith shop (left), general store (center), and carpenter shop (right). During the Howell Works era, the store carried everything the residents of Howell Works and surrounding communities needed, including a drugstore and post office. Meat, molasses, fish, coarse groceries, and merchandise requiring a cool temperature were kept in the basement. The first floor contained the sale of dry goods, hardware, groceries, liquor, flour, meal, and ironware. The upper floors contained unpacked merchandise, grain, furniture, and flour. The store was a social center for Howell Works residents and a stop on the Toms River and Red Bank stagecoach line.

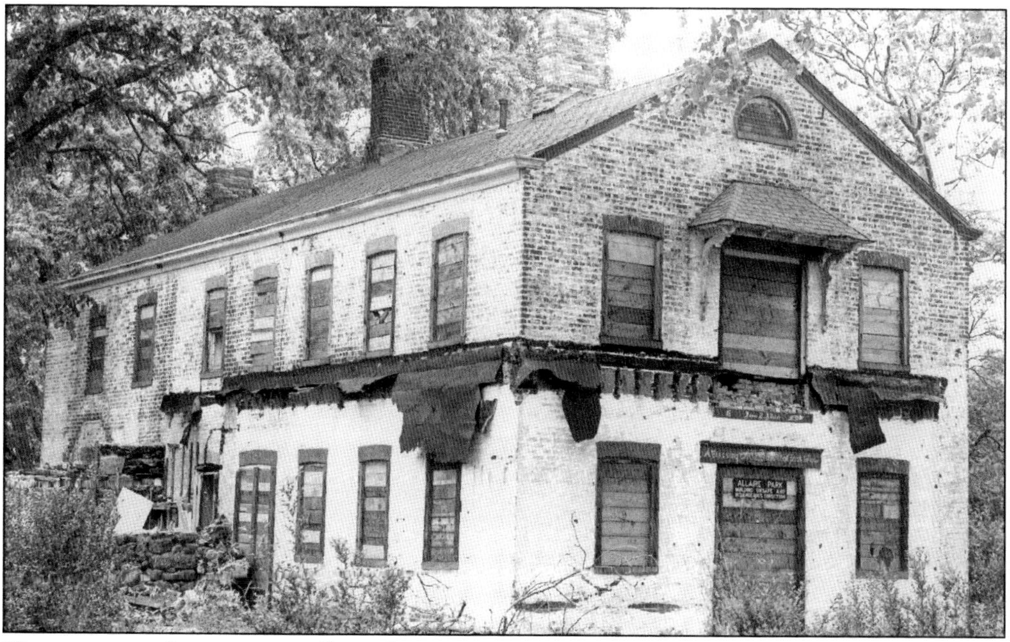

The carpenter shop is sitting idle and awaiting restoration funds in the 1955 photograph above. Restored to its original 1830s appearance, the large fieldstone porch (added much later) has just been removed. The carpenter shop, built in 1835, opened as an antique shop under the proprietorship of Marjorie and Urban Lohnes after being restored *c.* 1960. The large sycamore trees near the carpenter shop were planted in 1853 and stand today. The photograph below shows the carpenter shop restored. The shop was where patterns were made for casting iron products during the Howell Works era. At least three carpenters were employed during the Howell Works era, one serving as a wheelwright. They were the highest-paid workers at the works. The carpenters today demonstrate their age-old craft and also make toys for sale at the general store. (Above courtesy Division of Parks and Forestry, New Jersey State Park Service.)

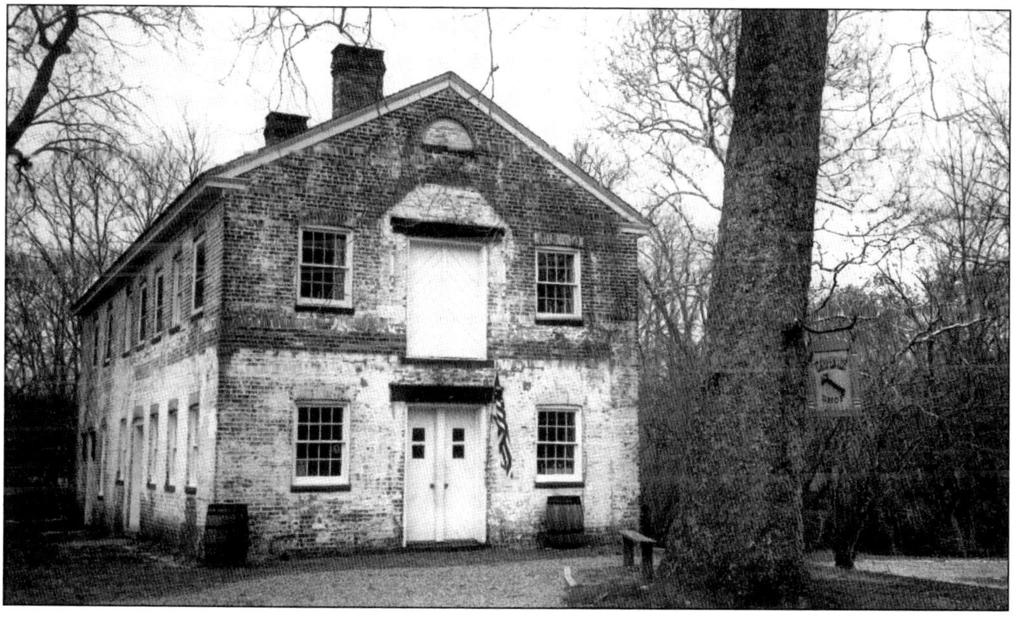

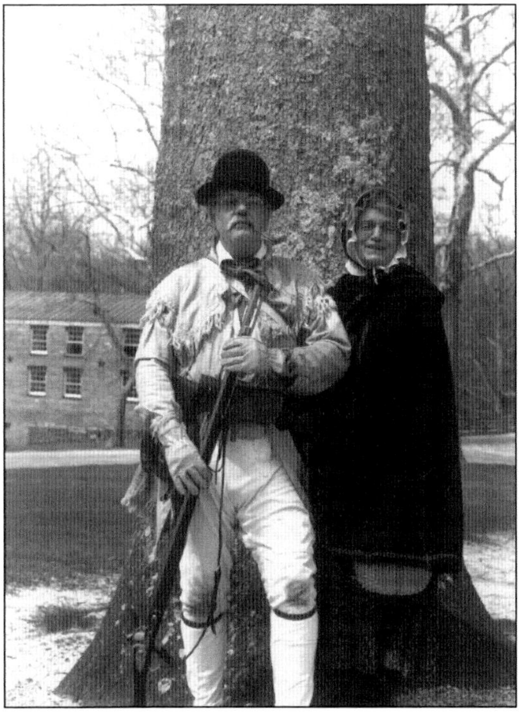

Pictured are historical interpreters Al and Diane Lingsch. Diane Lingsch once served as the coordinator of museum education and interpretation. Toward the fulfillment of its educational mission, Allaire Village Inc. relies on generous contributions and patronage from its retail stores and various fund-raising events.

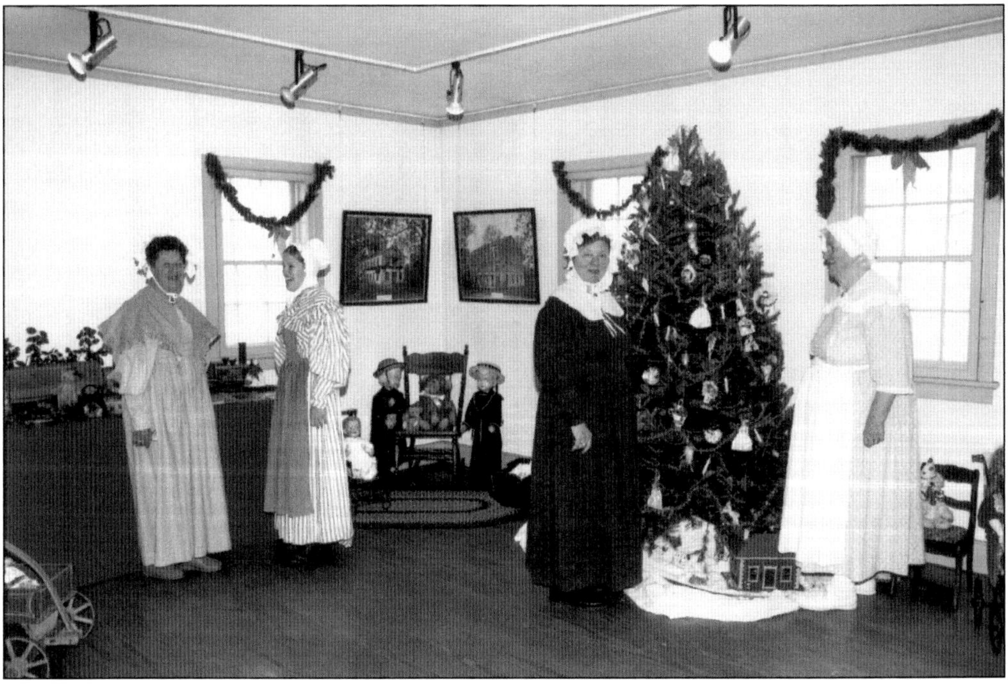

It is Christmastime for the Allaire Village Auxiliary at the Enameling Building. From left to right are Evelyn Kessler Morton, Laura Osborn, unidentified, and Helen Berringer. Berringer has been an active member for many years. Auxiliary members sell baked goods at various functions throughout the year, conduct the Stocking Stuffer Sale in November, and host many craft workshops throughout the year.

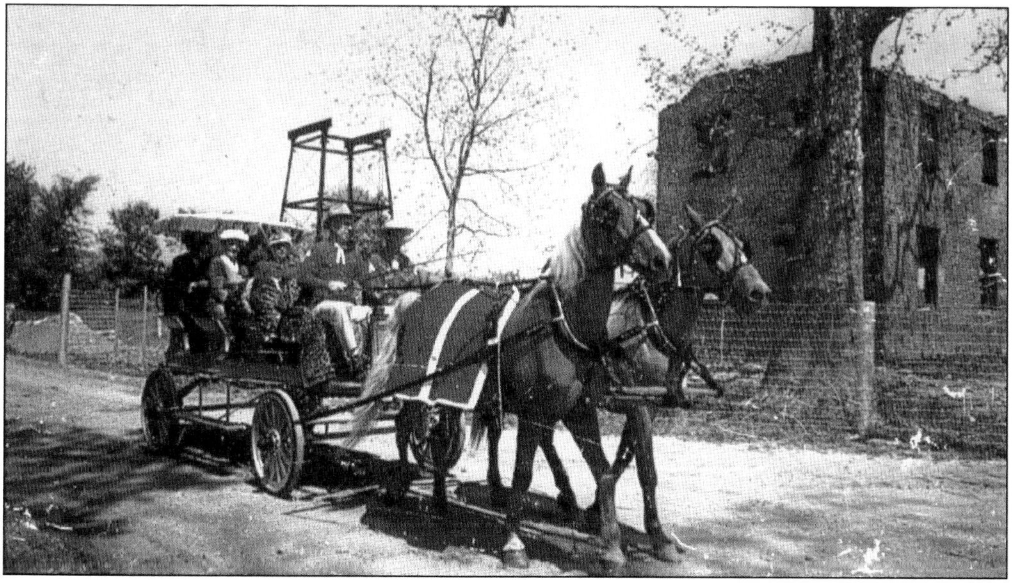

A surrey travels the roads at Allaire Village in the 1960s. The slaughterhouse (right) was one of the last structures to collapse at Allaire. During the Howell Works era, the slaughterhouse (built in 1835) was used for butchering livestock and provided meat for sale at the general store. It later served as a chicken coup and general farm building during Brisbane's ownership of Allaire. It collapsed *c.* 1970.

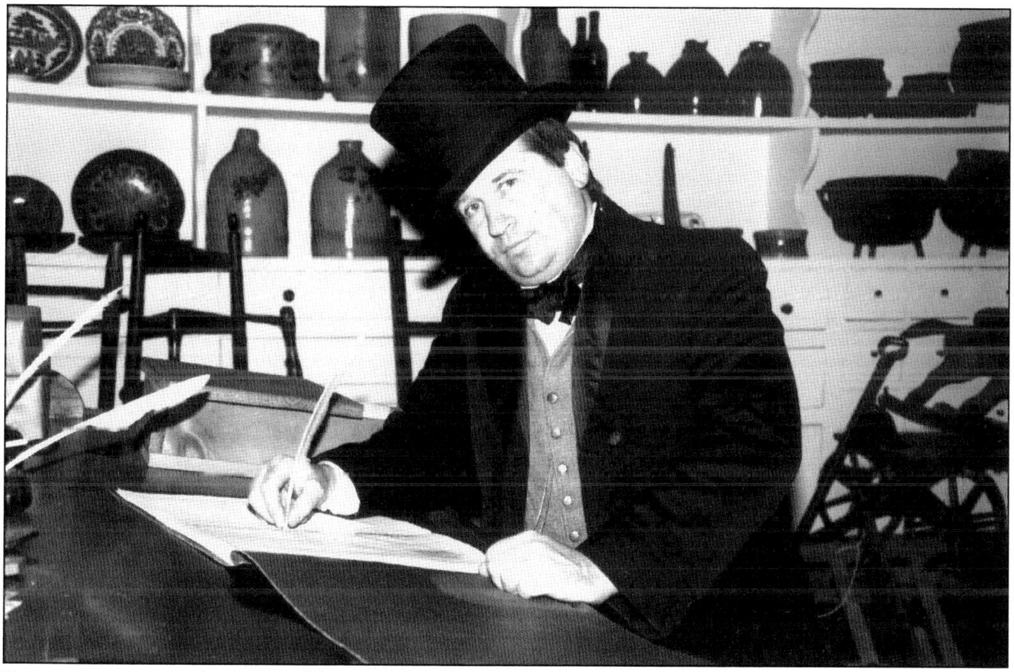

Former executive director Sibley J. Smith Jr. strikes a pose. Smith is dressed as a wealthy Howell Works resident.

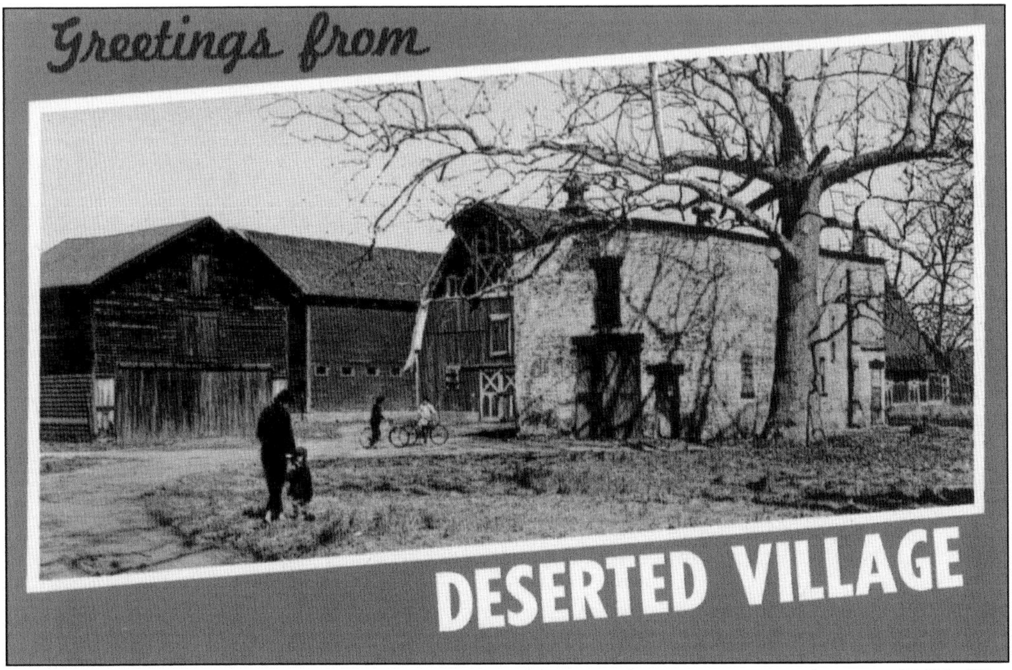

After Brisbane died in 1936, the barns fell quickly into disrepair, as seen here *c.* 1957. The stables and farm buildings were restored *c.* 1960 and housed horses and a riding stable. The Sears, Roebuck and Company barn, built in the early 1930s, was the center of this operation. In the early 1970s, the modern barns, including the Sears barn, were dismantled to restore an 1830s view in this section of the village. As in the Howell Works era, the carriage house, built in 1833, contains carriages, carts, wagons, and sleighs used by the works. A three-story apartment was added to the rear to provide accommodations for a full-time gardener. Draft animals, including oxen, mules, and horses, were stabled in the series of barns near the carriage house.

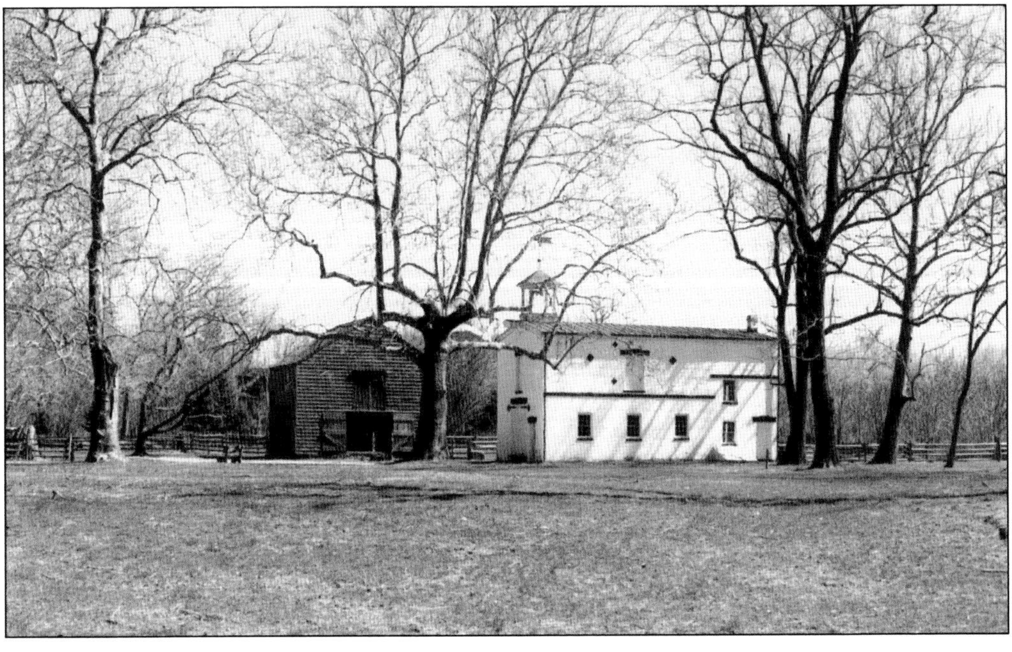

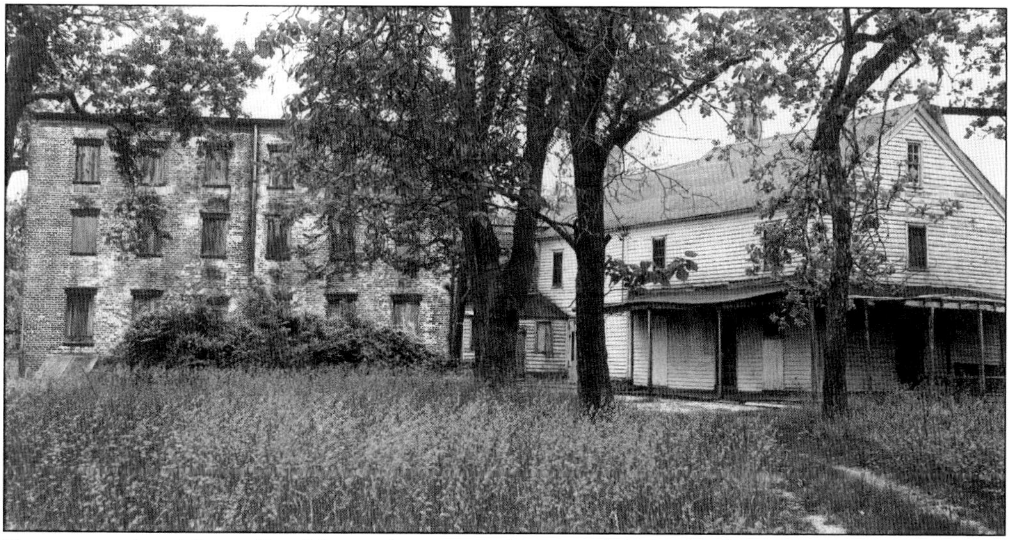

Known as the Allaire Big House (pictured above and below), this was James P. Allaire's residence when he visited the village in its early days. It later became his retirement residence. In the mid-1830s, amid a cholera epidemic in New York City, Allaire made arrangements to escape the sickness and moved his family into the Allaire Big House. Frances, Allaire's first wife, had been sick for many years and died here in 1836. The adjacent three-story dormitory, added in 1835, housed single workers on the upper floors and contained a large dining room on the first floor. During the 20th century, the Allaire Big House served as a residence for Arthur Brisbane's caretakers. The Service family was the last to occupy the home. In 1955, as seen above, the dormitory and the Allaire Big House were unoccupied. A hurricane in 1962 did serious damage to the dormitory, and it soon crumbled. The Allaire Big House was not restored or opened to the public until 1997, as seen below. The dormitory has not been rebuilt.

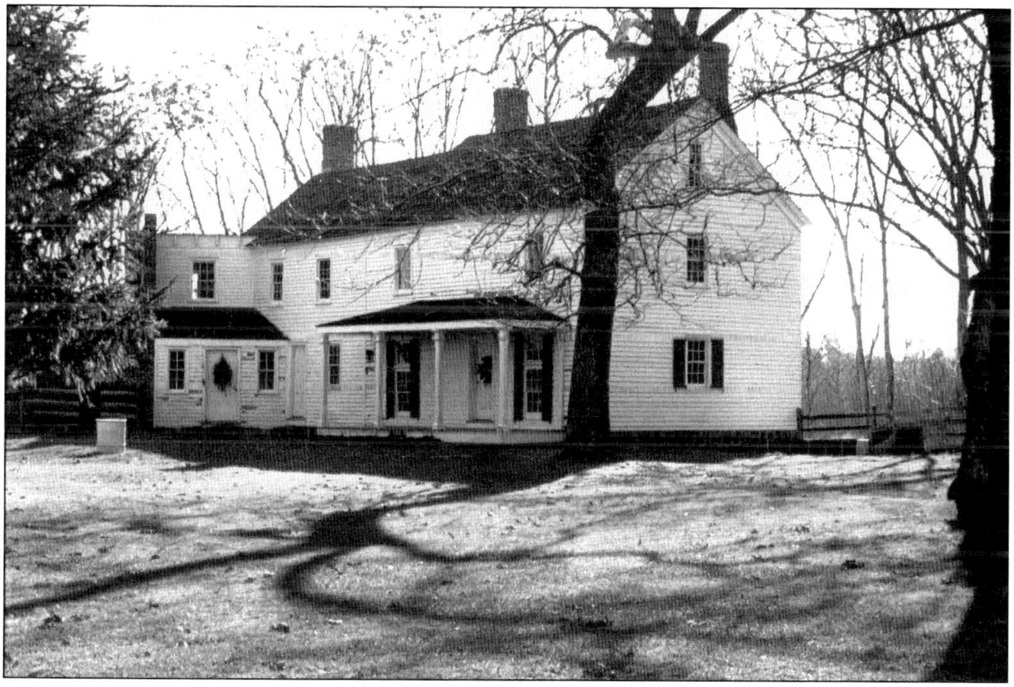

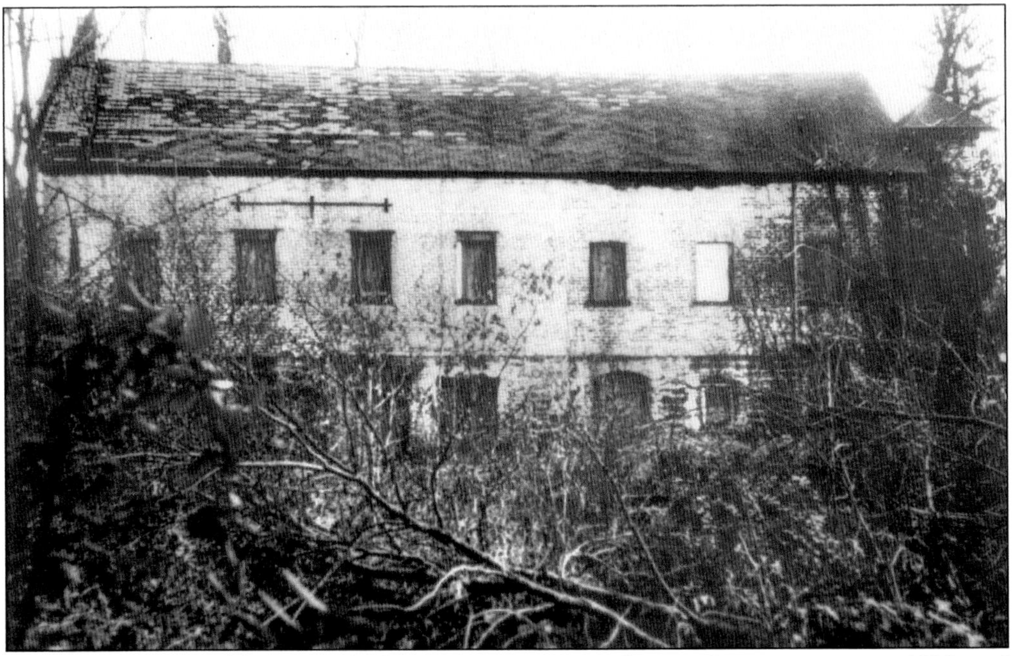

The Enameling Building was built in two sections—the northern section in 1828 and the southern section in 1834. The southern section was added when iron production was increasing. It also contained a small furnace used to bake an enamel finish onto hollowware. The enameling process used a variety of clays and was largely experimental. It is unclear as to whether it was ever perfected. By 1837, the enameling operation was shut down, as iron production shifted back to pig iron. The Enameling Building served as a private residence from c. 1850 to 1950. The building quickly fell into disrepair. It is shown above in an abandoned state next to a dried-up millpond in 1955. The photograph below shows a restored Enameling Building next to the millpond filled with water once again. Today, the building hosts various exhibits and special events.

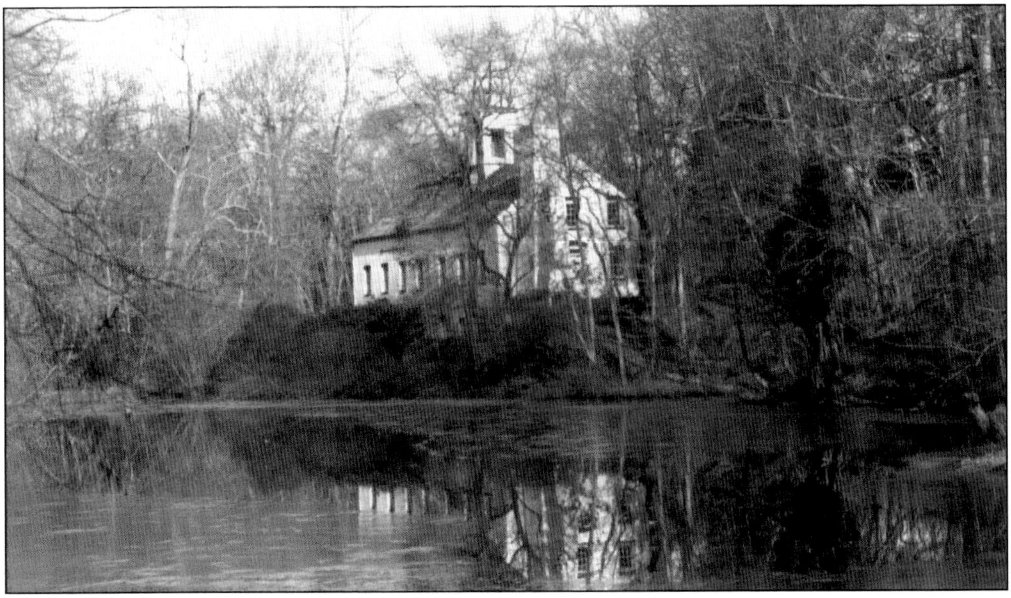

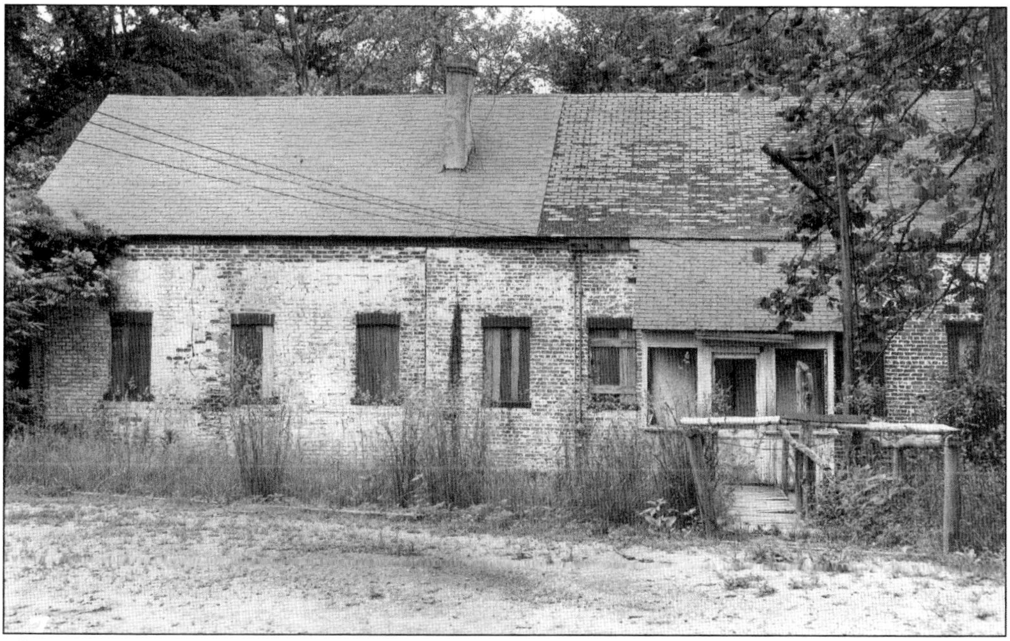

The Macauleys, caretakers to Arthur Brisbane's Allaire estate, received life rights to the Enameling Building, as seen here. They later gave up the rights and moved to New York State by the time this photograph was taken in 1955. When the Brisbane family donated 1,200 acres, which included Allaire Village, to the state in 1940, various families received life rights to the buildings they occupied. (Courtesy Division of Parks and Forestry, New Jersey State Park Service.)

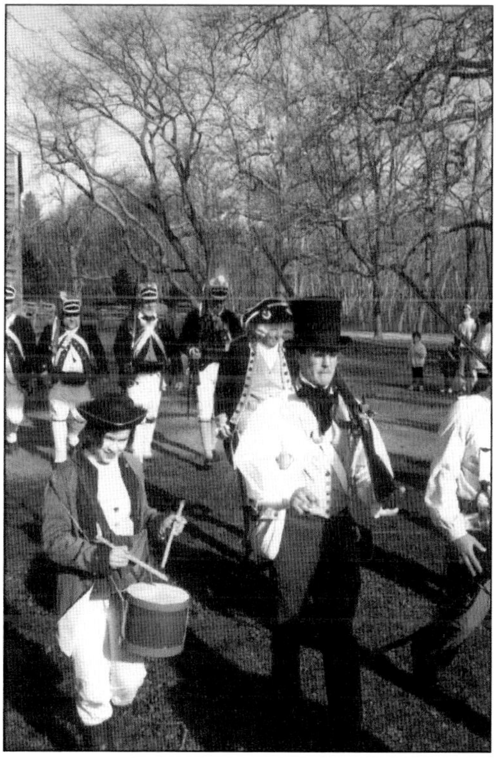

An 1830s Washington Birthday celebration is re-created each year at Allaire Village. Brian Collins, former coordinator of museum education and interpretation, is to the left of drummer Abbey Murphy. Other 1830s holiday events that are conducted at Allaire Village include St. Patrick's Day, the Fourth of July, Allhallows Eve, Thanksgiving, and Christmas. A Temperance rally is conducted in the summer.

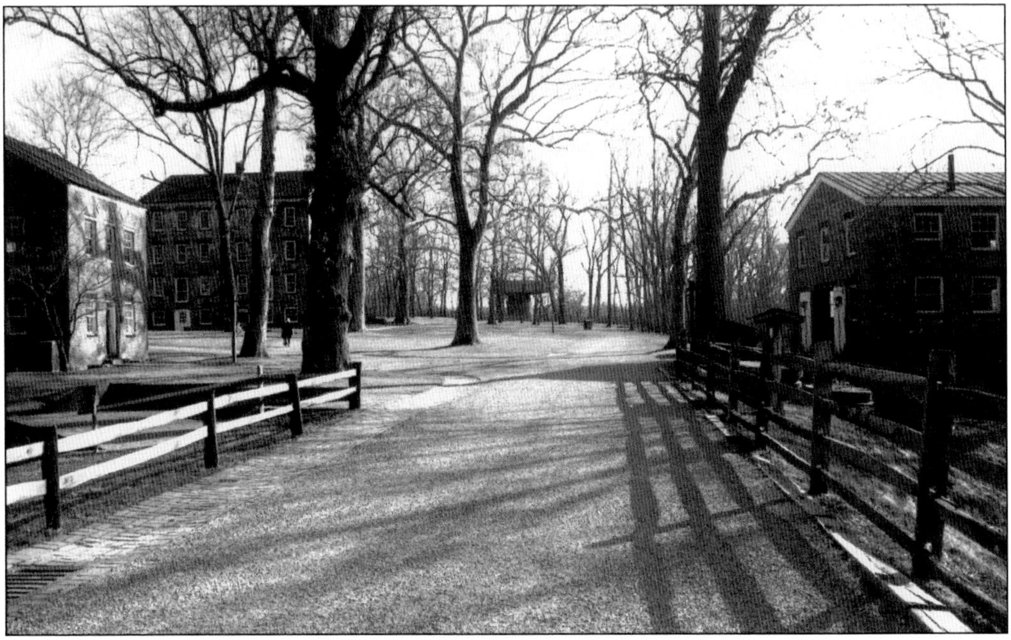

Pictured here, from left to right, are the bakery, the rear of the general store, the blast furnace, and the blacksmith shop. Many historic villages have been re-created or restored well beyond their original attributes. Allaire Village is unique in that the structures reside on their original foundations and contain most of their original fabric.

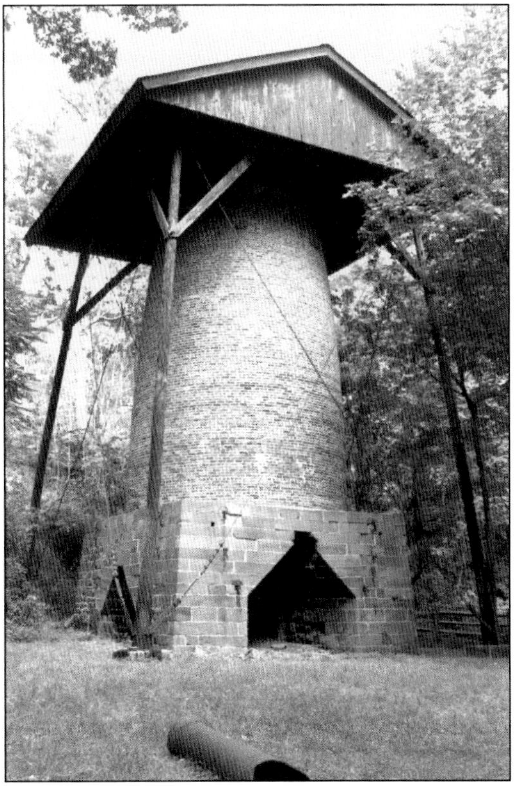

The blast furnace, as pictured here, received a protective roof in the 1960s. The ironworks buildings that once surrounded the blast furnace have not been rebuilt, largely due to the enormous amount of capital that would be needed. Where there was a whole network of furnaces that made use of the vast resources of bog iron, now only a few remain. Allaire Village is the most complete example of this early industry remaining in New Jersey. Long-range plans call for the rebuilding of those structures that have fallen down, such as the charcoal depot and ironworks buildings. However, restoration funds are limited.

Seven

THE OUTSKIRTS OF ALLAIRE

This chapter features familiar sites and businesses that have existed on the outskirts of Allaire Village. In the early 20th century, Monmouth County was reputed as giving the best farm produce, for it yielded more crops per acre than any farm in the United States. Many farms existed in central New Jersey during the 20th century, and Kessler Farms was one of the finest. Four Kessler brothers began Kessler Farms, now part of Allaire State Park and the Manasquan River Reservoir, in 1917 (Charles, John, Elias, and Jake Kessler) and farmed the 180 acres until 1986. The farm was located just west of the intersections of Atlantic Avenue and the Garden State Parkway. Considering its acreage, sales, and productivity, it was one of the largest and most successful produce farms in the state. Neighboring Kessler Farms was Meadow Brook Farm, owned and operated by Lloyd Thompson and his family from c. 1920 to 1960. For 43 years, Thompson's pasteurized milk and had an expansive milk route serving the immediate area, shore communities, Point Pleasant, and Bay Head. From 1951 to 1987, Hance Herbert Morton had a mason contracting business that operated from his Allaire home. Morton capitalized on the urbanization and the suburban growth that ensued after millions of World War II veterans returned home. He operated one of the largest non-union mason businesses in central New Jersey.

Looking for a site to keep his airplane in 1937, a young Ed Brown was led by Elvin Simmill, Wall Township attorney, to approach Phoebe Brisbane about buying her late husband's property that bordered Route 34 and Hurley Pond Road. Brown, only 20 years old and working for $40 a week at the Asbury Park A & P, met with William Frostick, superintendent of Arthur Brisbane's Allaire estate, and set up a meeting with Phoebe Brisbane. Brown took several aerial photographs of the property he was interested in renting. To Brown's surprise, Brisbane climbed into his 1931 Chevy and drove out to explore the property firsthand. Phoebe Brisbane used to ride horses in the area and knew it quite well. The "late Arthur," as she referred to him, stated this property was only good for two reasons—an airport or a racetrack. Ironically, both were developed as such. After the tour, Brown was instructed to meet with the family lawyers in New York City regarding a potential sale. Brown was permitted to rent a portion of the Brisbane property for $100 a year, a bargain, until the family came up with a sale value. In 1938, Brown began a five-year financing plan to purchase 450 acres. Today, the airport he developed there, known as Monmouth County Executive Airport, encompasses about 700 acres and is believed to be the largest privately owned airport in the country. Brown can be considered a maverick and pioneer in local aviation. He is a self-made millionaire who started with an idea, some pinewoods, and a World War I tank.

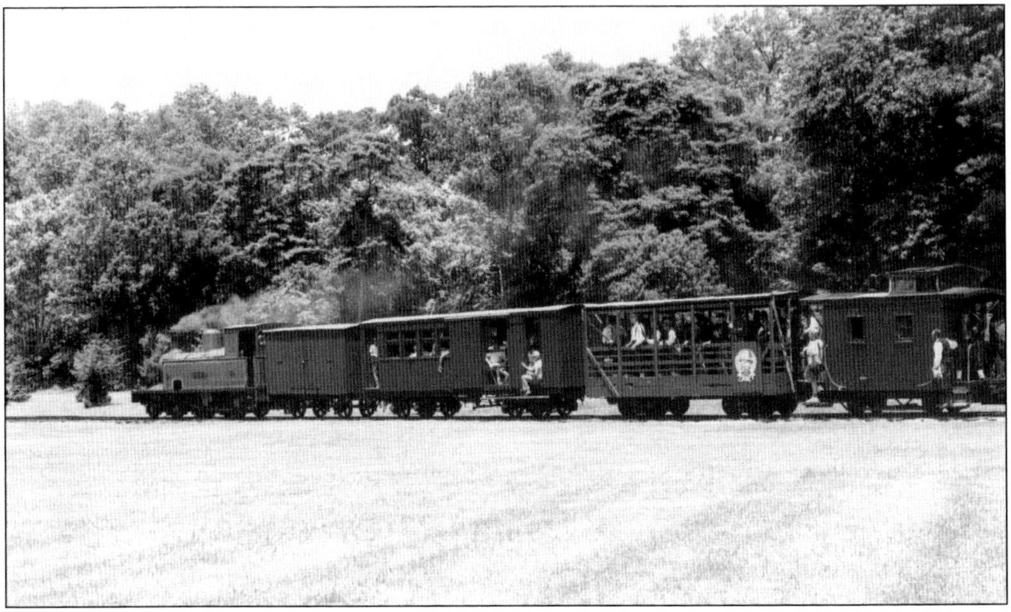

Built in Ireland in 1887, the *Lady Edith* is the oldest steam locomotive in the collection of the New Jersey Museum of Transportation. Also known as the Pine Creek Railroad, this organization operates a narrow-gauge railroad just outside Historic Allaire Village on the grounds of Allaire State Park. This photograph was taken during a Civil War battle reenactment and encampment once sponsored at Allaire.

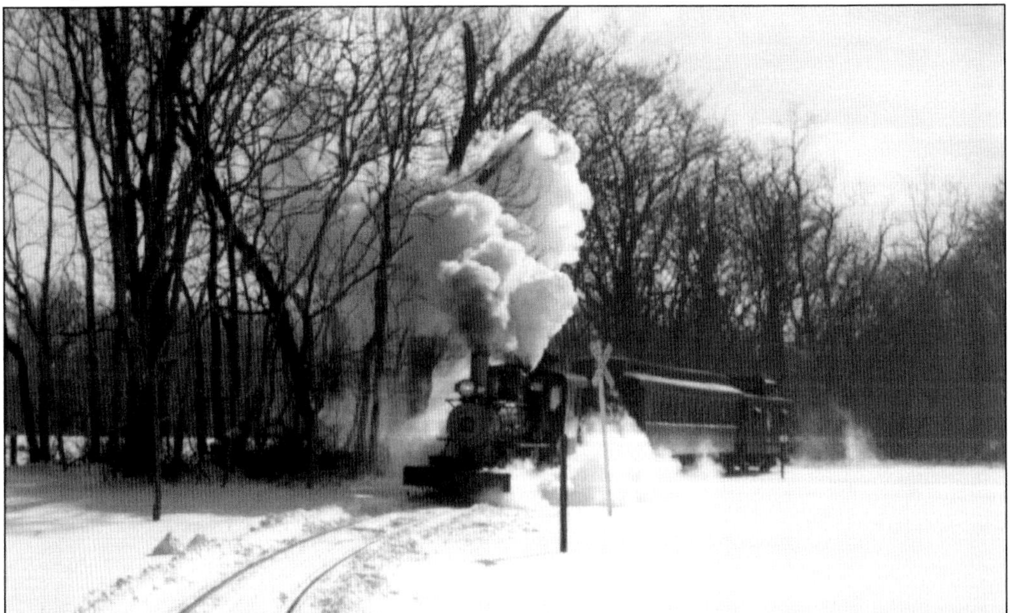

Former Surry, Sussex and Southampton Baldwin locomotive No. 26 (2-6-2), built in 1920 and acquired by the museum in 1972, rounds the curve at Allaire after a recent snowfall. The former Central Railroad of New Jersey caboose at the rear was originally a boxcar built in 1874. Transformed into a caboose in 1902, it is the oldest piece of equipment in the museum's collection. It is an eight-wheeled unit, the first of its kind.

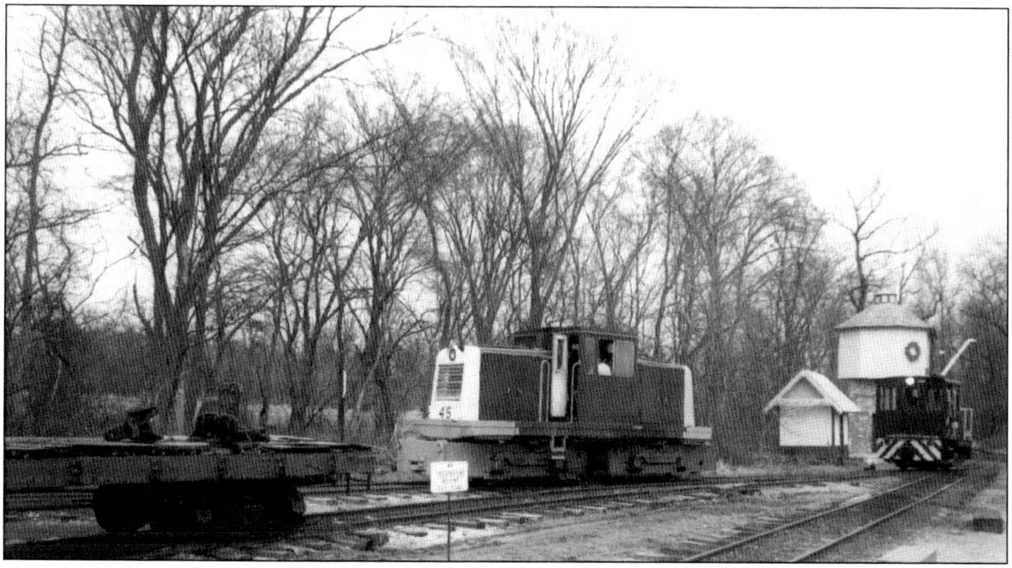

The New Jersey Museum of Transportation continues to acquire museum pieces, as seen here in 1992 with the arrival of No. 45 (left), a 50-ton diesel electric. The 25-ton diesel electric (right), acquired in 1978, is probably used the most in pulling museum passengers. The museum is boasted to be the oldest continuously operating steam preservation railway exhibit in the country. It began operation in 1952 near Marlboro and relocated to Allaire State Park in 1963.

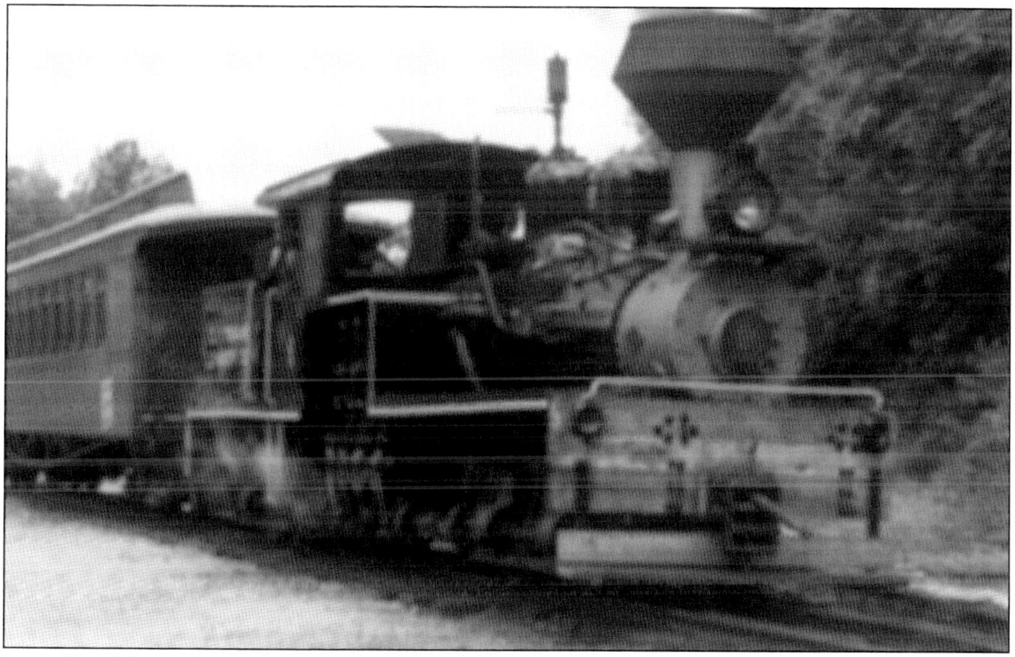

Lima *Shay* No. 9, formerly of the Ely Thomas Lumber Company, is pulling passengers at Allaire. The locomotive was built in 1927 and was acquired by the museum in 1955. The coach, built in 1902, can seat about 50 passengers and once ran on Canada's Newfoundland railways. In the winter, the coach can be heated with steam from the locomotive. Narrow-gauge locomotives, such as the *Shay*, once served the great mining, timber, and grazing areas of the country and helped to open America's frontier.

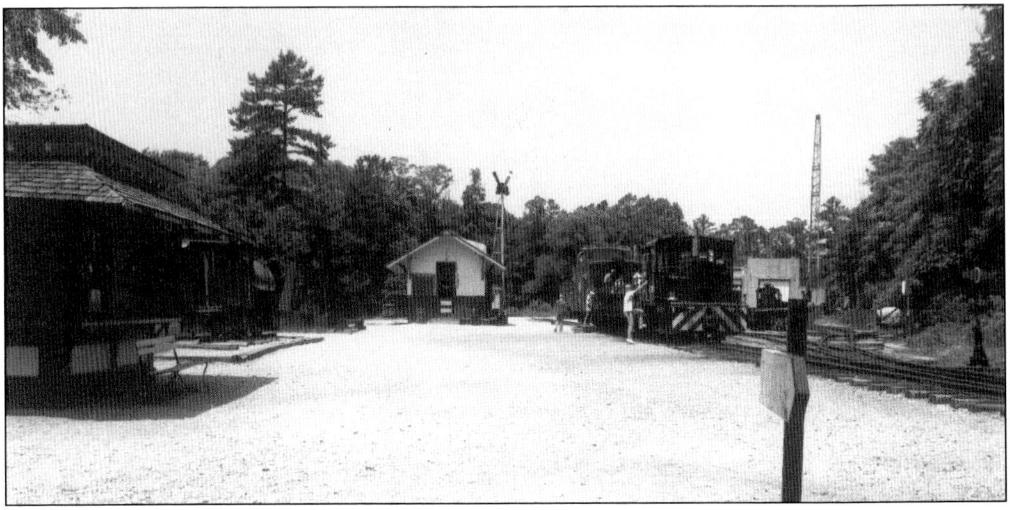

The New Jersey Museum of Transportation has a number of historical railroad structures on its property, including the Freehold and New York's Freneau Station (left of the train), which was built in 1906. A nonprofit educational organization, the New Jersey Museum of Transportation is supported exclusively by train fares, souvenir sales, and contributions. Volunteers, who donate more than 16,000 hours annually, staff the organization. Numerous events are offered throughout the year, including the Easter Express, Christmas Express, Halloween Express and Fall Foliage Runs, and Railroaders Day.

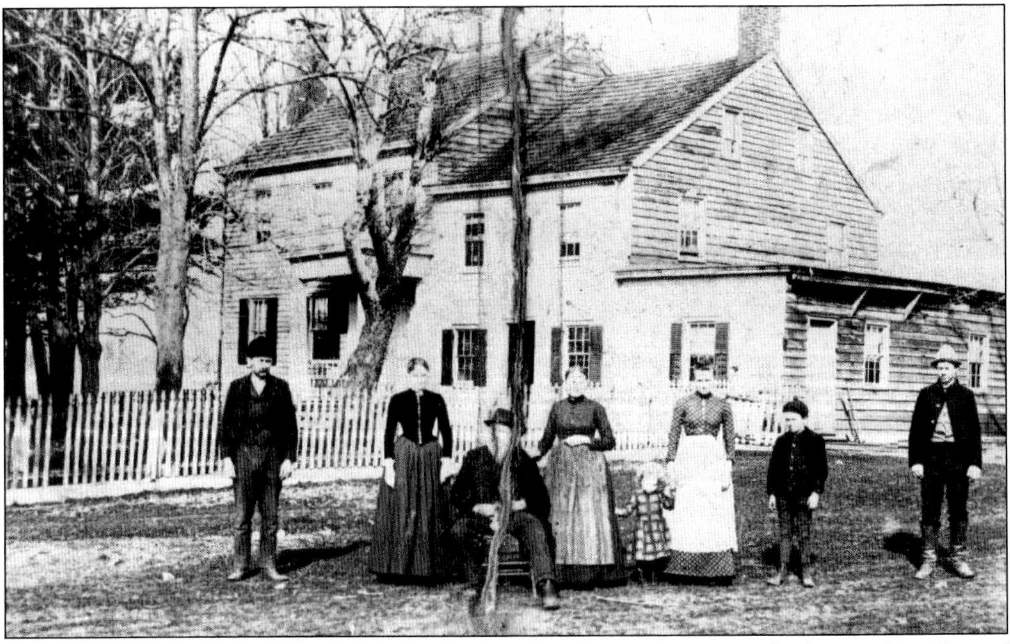

Members of the Gifford family are shown outside their farmhouse in the late 1800s. One of the earliest families in the area, the Giffords purchased a large amount of land east of Allaire Village in 1668. Anniah Gifford, chief surveyor for the Howell Works, made this his home. A Quaker, Anniah Gifford married Elizabeth Brewer (of Farmingdale), and their son John B. Gifford (sitting) served as state assemblyman and as Wall tax assessor.

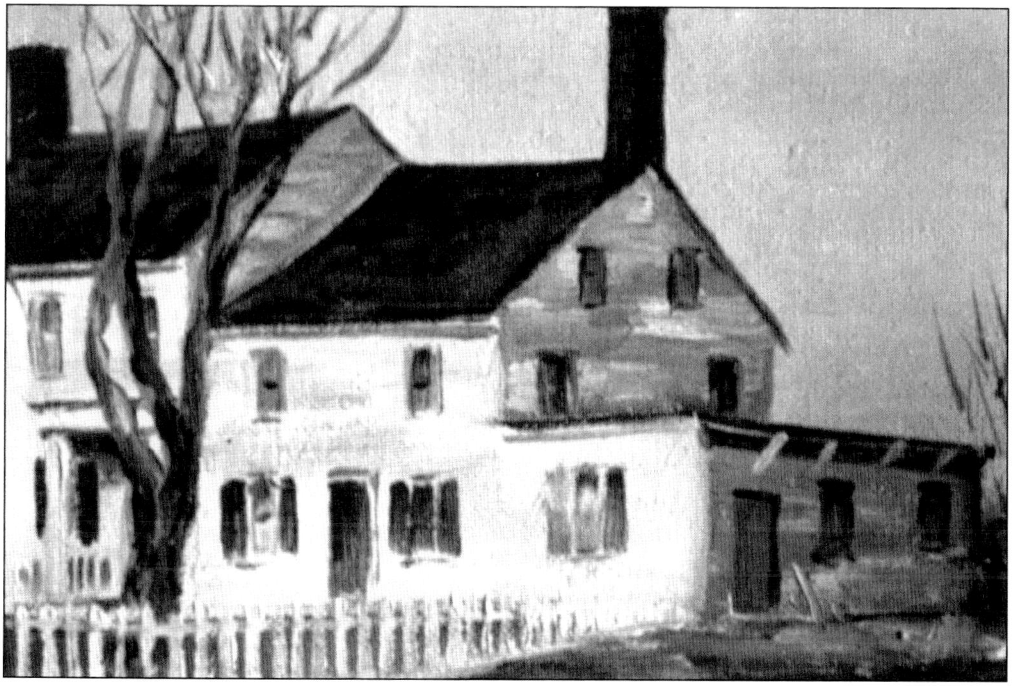

Anniah Gifford, surveyor to Monmouth and Ocean Counties, struck the dividing line between Wall and Howell Townships. Clay for the bricks needed to construct the buildings at Allaire Village was obtained from the Gifford farm. As many as 600,000 bricks were manufactured in a year. This farmhouse was located in the heart of what became Kessler Farms in 1917. Kessler relatives occupied the home up until it burned down in the early 1990s.

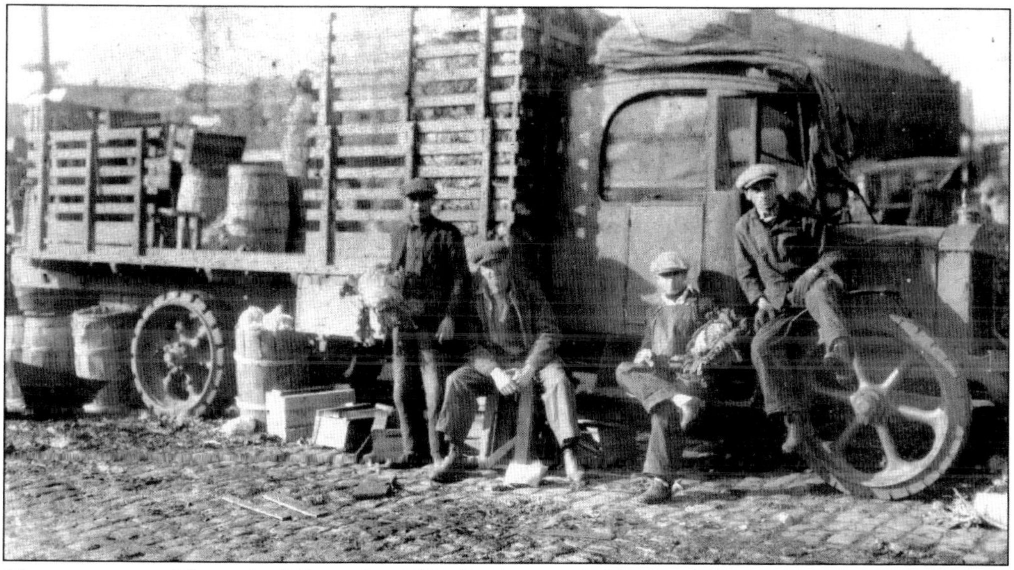

The man second from the left on this 1930 Backus truck filled with farm produce is Jake Kessler, cofounder of Kessler Farms. This picture was taken at the Newark farmers' market. Kessler Farms was responsible for growing all kinds of delicious vegetables, such as spinach, carrots, celery, cucumbers, turnips, kale, parsley, peppers, eggplant, corn, squash, and tomatoes. Several varieties of lettuce were grown, and the fields could yield about three crops per year.

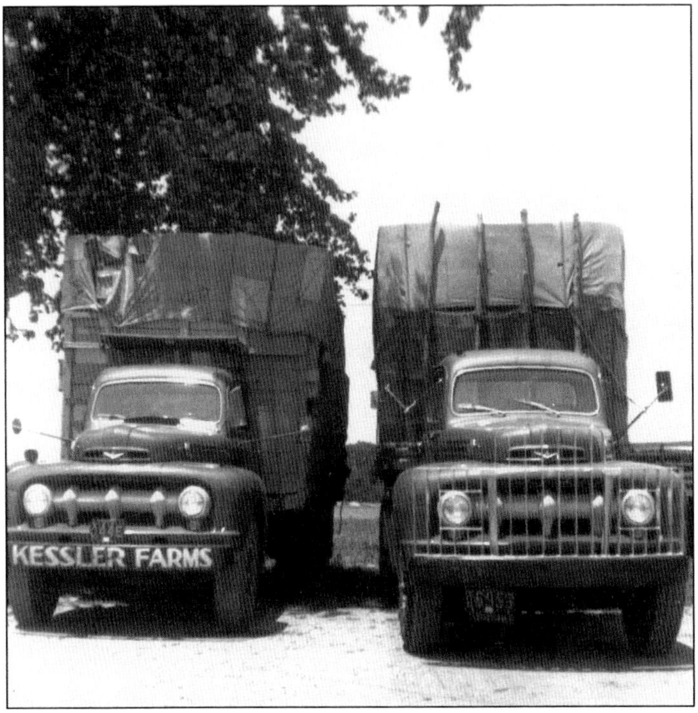

Kessler produce was distributed to all corners of New Jersey, including Vineland, Newark, Neptune, Bradley Beach, Trenton, and Asbury Park. It was here that brokers could buy Kessler produce and then disperse it to cities and regions throughout the United States. It was common for Kessler produce to reach Philadelphia, New York City, Chicago, Florida, and Canada. Produce was sold to A & P, the Campbell Soup Company, and even our very own Delicious Orchards.

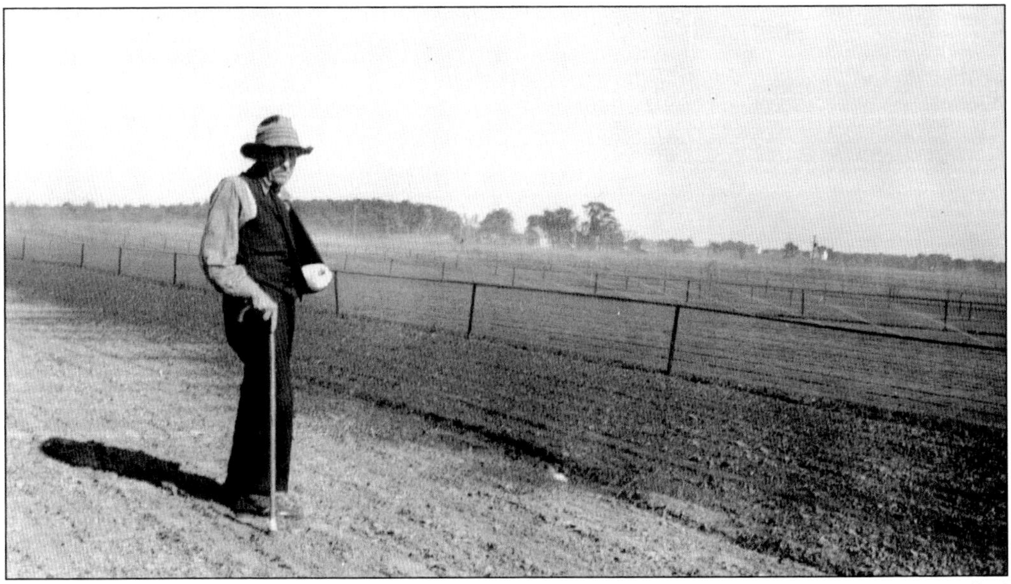

Charles Kessler Sr., father to the founders of Kessler Farms, observes the newly installed irrigation system in 1931. Kessler Farms had the first successful modern irrigation system in the county. Adopting the skinner system, Charles Kessler Jr. laid out the irrigation system, and most of it was complete by 1940. Brooks, swamps, and fields were expanded into a system of large freshwater ponds. Only one pond, of an irrigation system that once boasted five, remains fully active today. Several electric water pumps, installed in the 1930s, were still used when the farm closed in 1986.

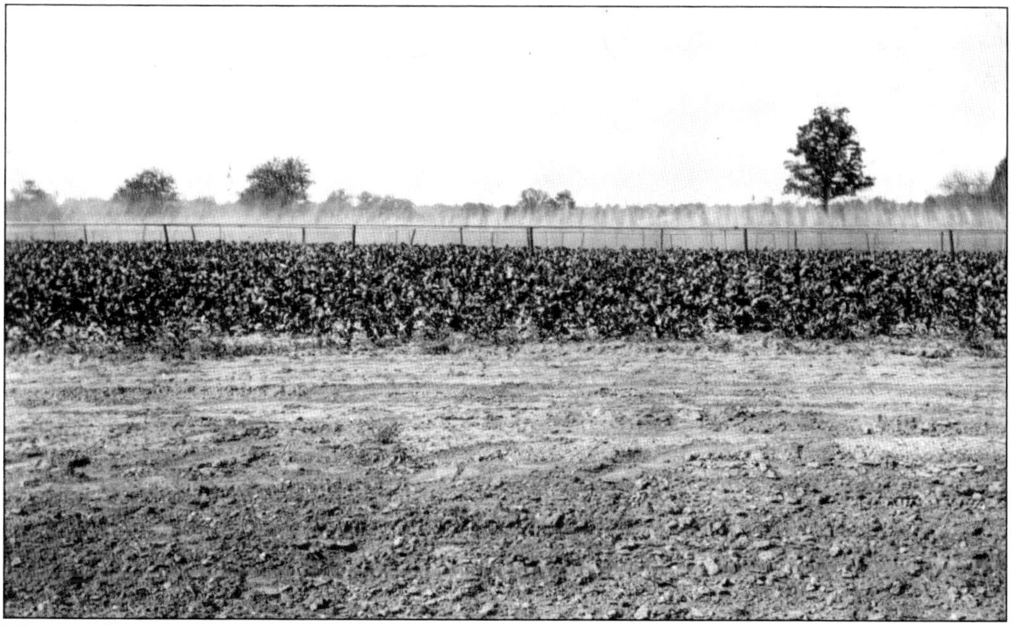

The Kessler Farms irrigation system and fields are shown in 1931. The farm faired pretty well through the 1930s despite the Great Depression and a fire that nearly destroyed the nearby homes of Elias and John Kessler. Although farm produce prices bottomed out during the Great Depression, the Kesslers worked hard, planned well, and found a variety of ways to earn money. They lost money at the Bradley Beach Bank when it closed in the crash of 1929 but had reserves at Famingdale Bank.

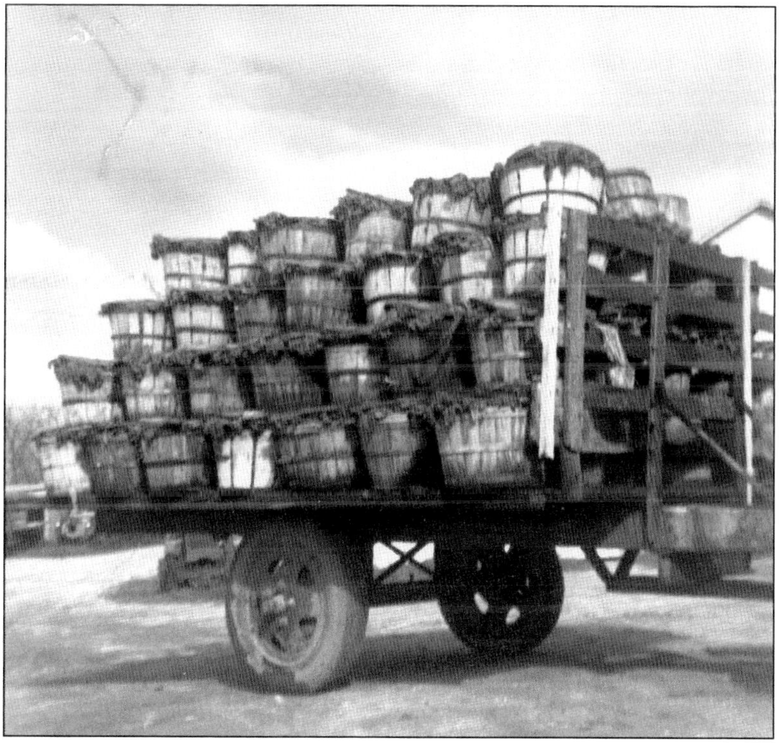

Of all the variety of produce grown, the greens were most popular at Kessler Farms, especially spinach, as seen piled up here. A truck full of greens left for market almost every day from May through October. New crops were grown annually, largely on a trial-and-error basis.

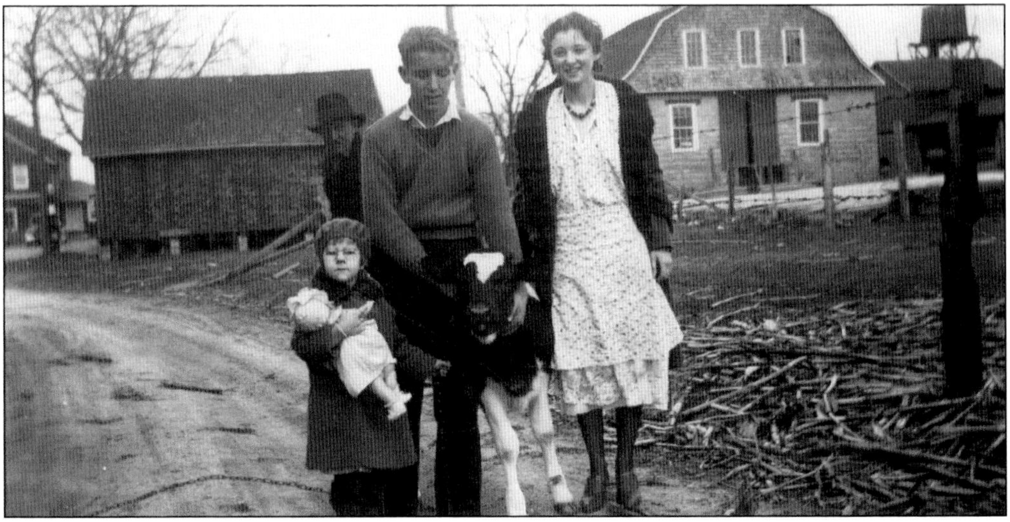

Shown with a calf in 1934 are, from left to right, Marie Kessler (who died in 1935), Charles Kessler Sr., Charles Kessler III, and Helen Kessler. Various types of farm animals were kept at the farm. Horses first served as beasts of burden, later replaced by tractors. Around the time of this photograph, the Civilian Conservation Corps (CCC) performed terracing projects on the farm. The big washhouse to the right still stands today.

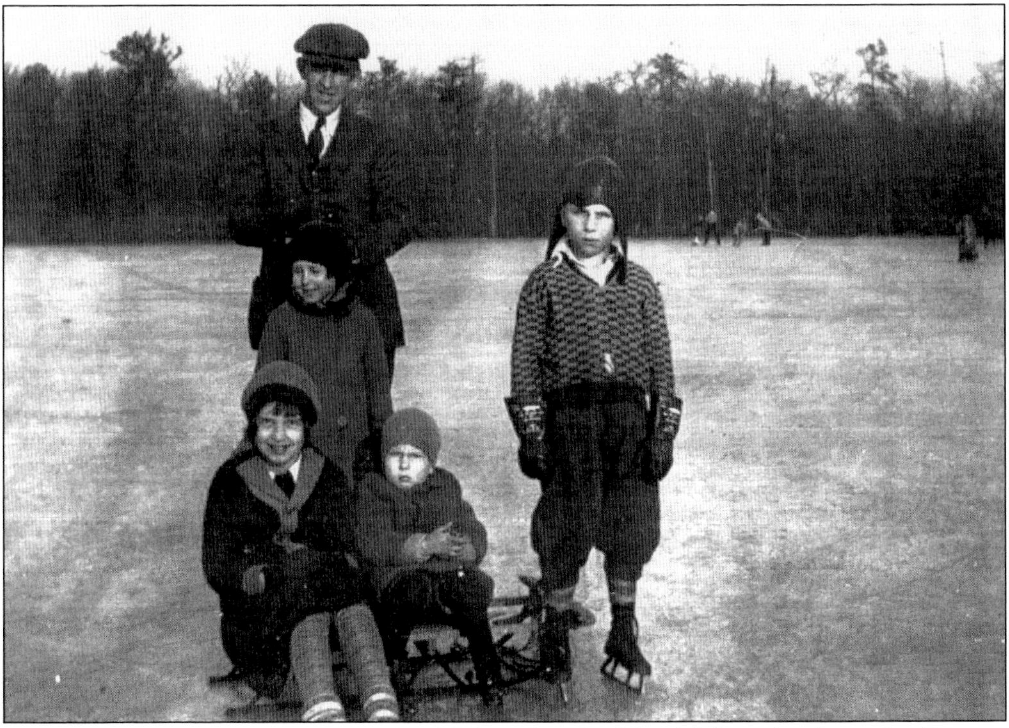

John Kessler (back), Evelyn Kessler (middle), Sid Gifford (middle), and Bill Kessler (bottom right) are shown in the early 1930s on Johnny B. Gifford Pond, now called Kessler Pond. During the winter months, farm work slowed to repairing farm buildings, painting, fixing equipment, or partaking in winter sports, such as ice-skating and sledding. The Kesslers also took to cutting ice from nearby ponds, clearing fields, or cutting trees that were supplied to local sawmills.

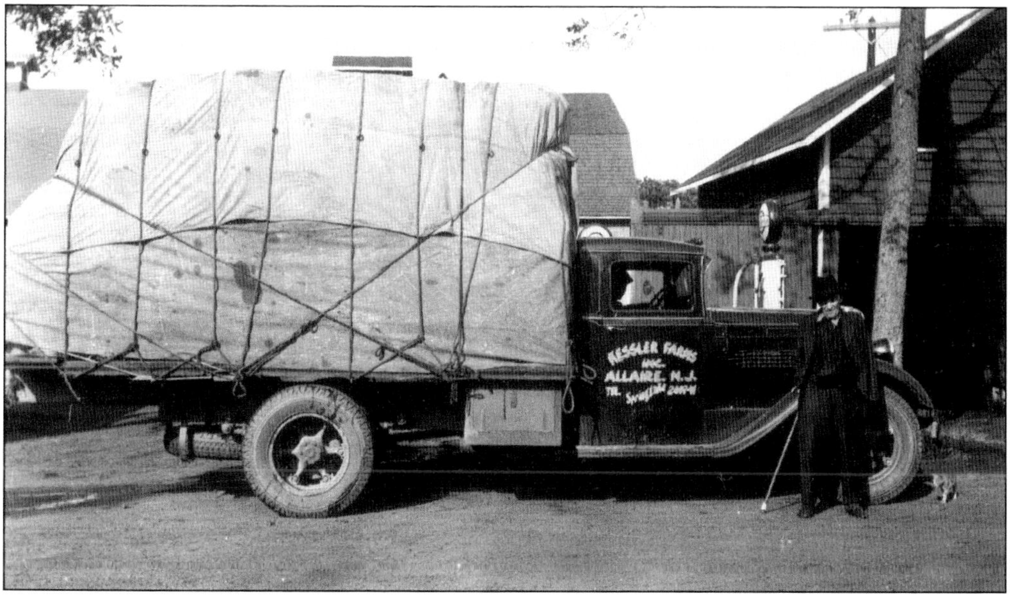

In this view, Jake Kessler is ready to deliver a truck full of farm produce. Charles Kessler Sr., Jake's father, stands outside. The Kesslers were of German descent and resided in the Long Island area before coming to Allaire in 1917.

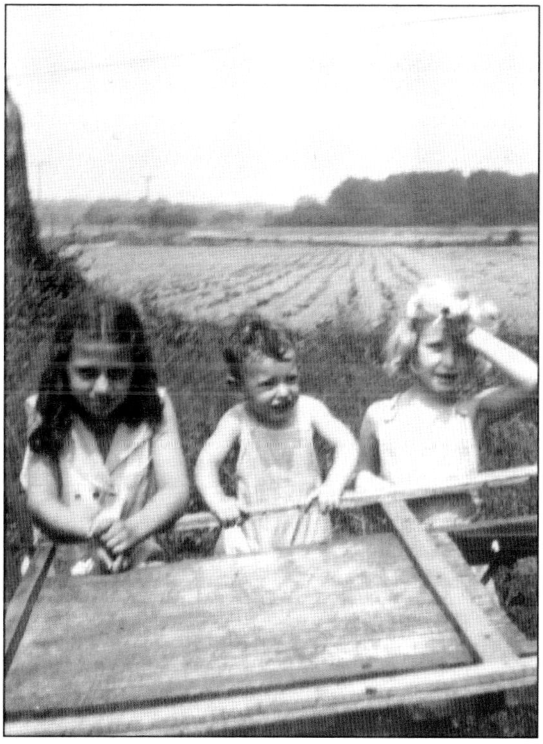

Alice Frawley (left), Bobby Kessler (center), and Alice Kessler are helping out on the farm *c.* 1940. Greens are growing in the background field. All kinds of migrant workers were employed at Kessler Farms. They were provided living quarters either in the large washhouse or in individual dwellings on the southeast edge of the farm.

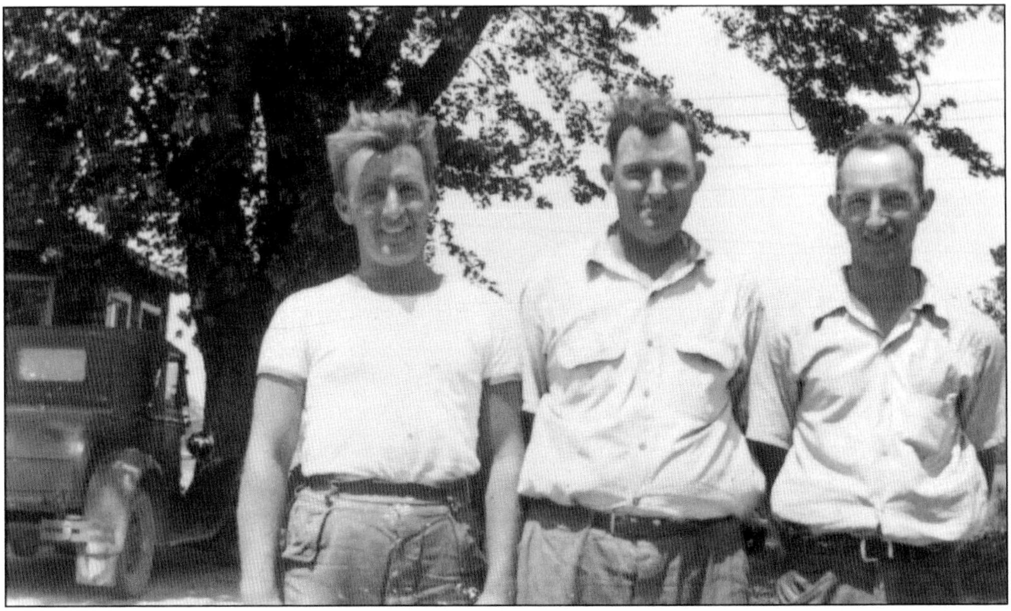

Seen here in 1940 are, from left to right, Felix Kessler (son), Charles Kessler Jr. (father and cofounder), and Charles Kessler III (son). Each of the Kessler families lived on the farm or adjacent to it. In 1950, Elias and John Kessler bought approximately 50 acres on the outskirts of the farm (land north of Atlantic and Allaire Roads). This property was later divided among descendants of the family, sold to third parties, or preserved for open space.

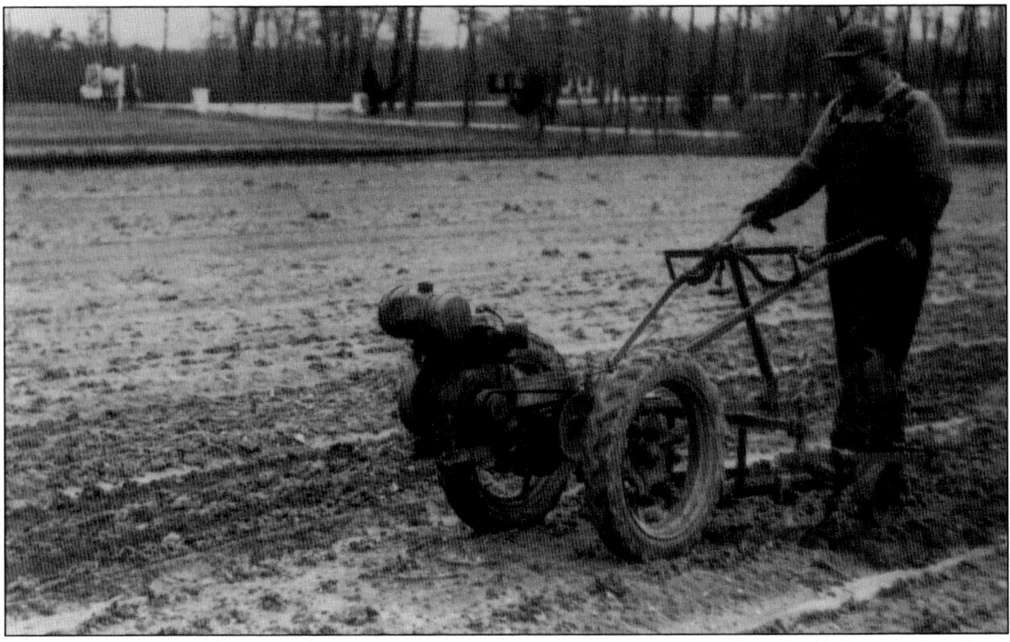

Lou Turner, a hired hand, cultivates spring spinach near Spring Meadow Golf Course. Produce was often begun in late winter at the greenhouse before being planted in the fields. The first greenhouse was bought in Neptune, erected in 1939, and included hot-water heat. In 1977, a second greenhouse was put into operation. For additional fields, the Kesslers even rented property near Allaire Village first from Arthur Brisbane and then from the state.

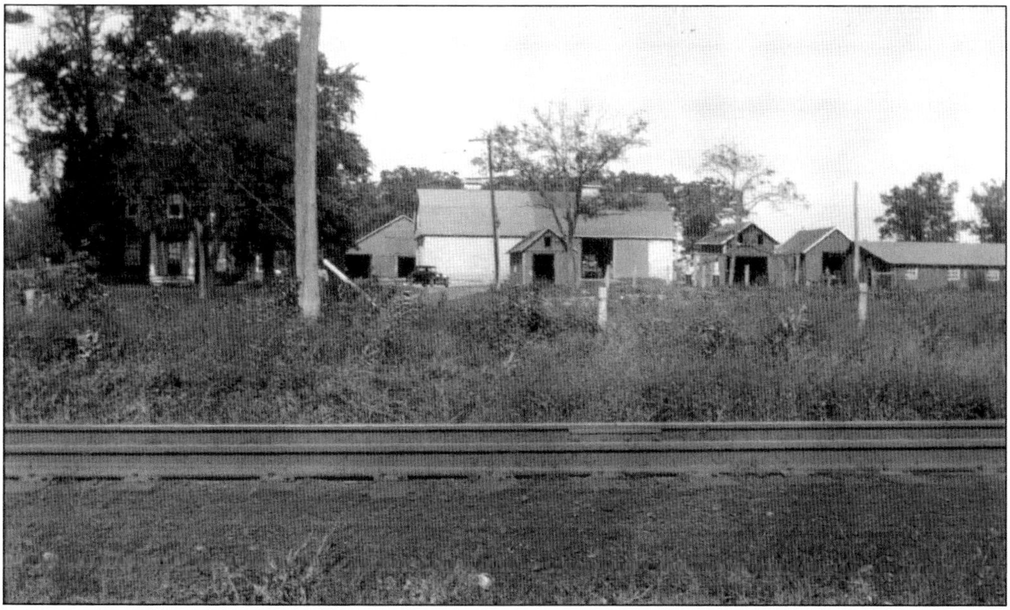

The Freehold and Jamesburg Agricultural Railroad ran almost directly through the center of Kessler Farms, as seen here in the 1930s. Although no produce was ever shipped via rail, fertilizer and supplies were delivered and picked up by the Kesslers at a rail siding in Allenwood. There were more than 15 farm buildings on the property. The land south of the railroad tracks (this photograph looks north) had the best farming soil.

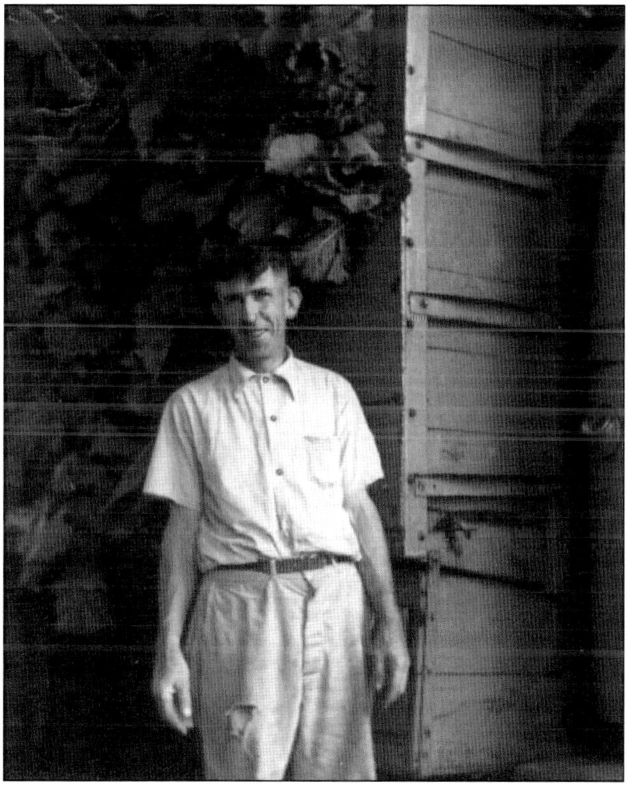

Cofounder John Kessler stands outside his truck filled with greens in 1953. Kessler Farms was a family operation. Jake delivered produce to the distant markets, leaving at midnight. Elias was in charge of seeding, spraying, and bookkeeping. Charles was in charge of the personnel. John delivered produce to the local markets, leaving at 4:00 a.m. daily. In one shipment, it was not uncommon for the Kessler Farms to deliver 800 crates of romaine lettuce to Vineland, 300 bushels of parsley to the Campbell Soup Company, and a truckload of cantaloupes to Troy, New York.

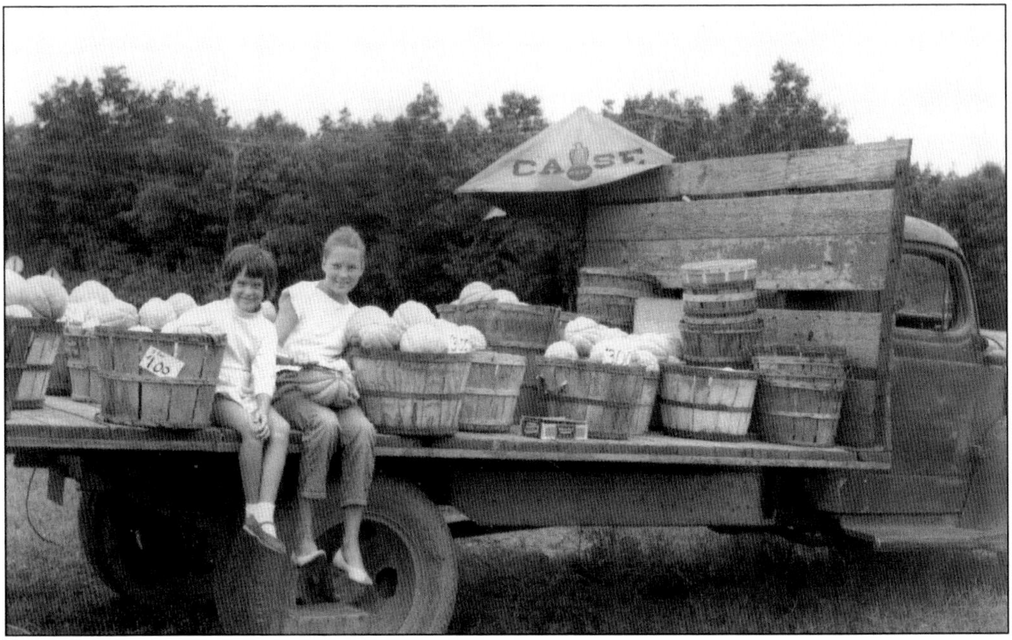

Shirley (left) and Linda Morton sell melons at a roadside stand in 1959 for their grandfather John Kessler. Occasionally, a roadside stand was set up to sell excess produce, but for the most part, whatever they grew was sold.

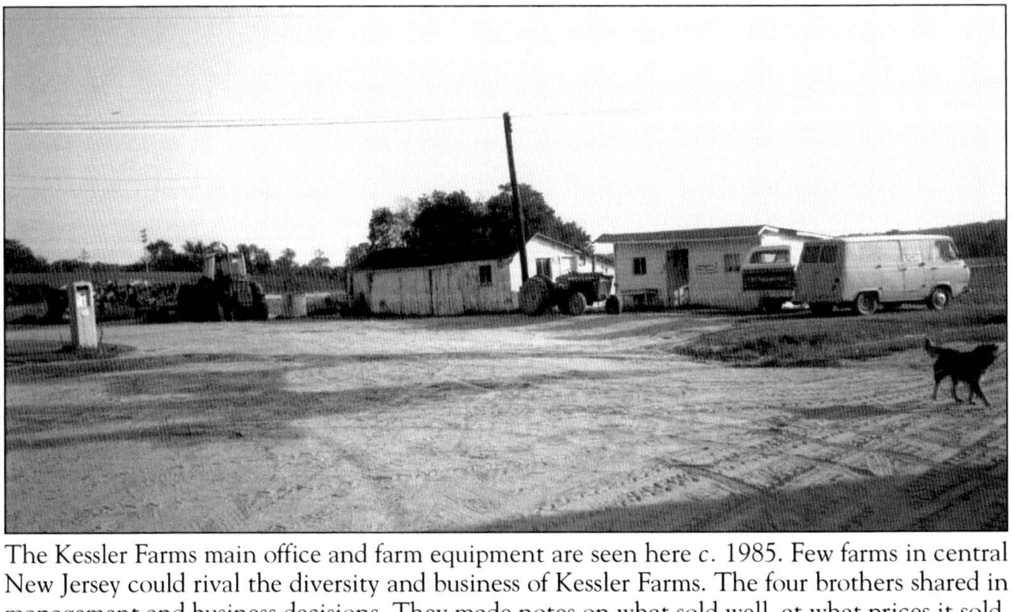

The Kessler Farms main office and farm equipment are seen here c. 1985. Few farms in central New Jersey could rival the diversity and business of Kessler Farms. The four brothers shared in management and business decisions. They made notes on what sold well, at what prices it sold, what they should grow for the following year, and what customers and contacts to retain.

John Kessler, cofounder of Kessler Farms, is pictured on his Ford tractor in 1952. The variety of crops grown at Kessler Farms was perhaps their secret to success—do not plant any more than you think you can sell. When Jersey lettuce gradually succumbed to California lettuce, Kessler Farms reduced the lettuce crop from 30 to 2 acres. The remaining 28 acres were quickly used for other existing crops or new experimental crops. The farm was very diversified.

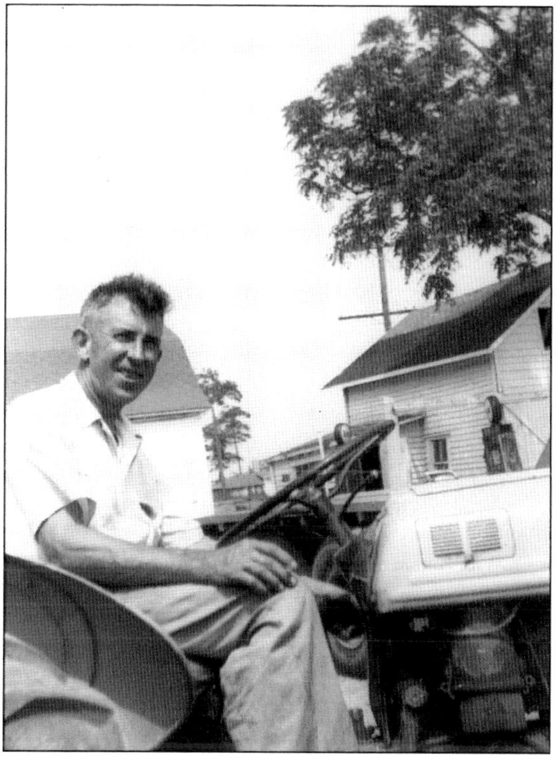

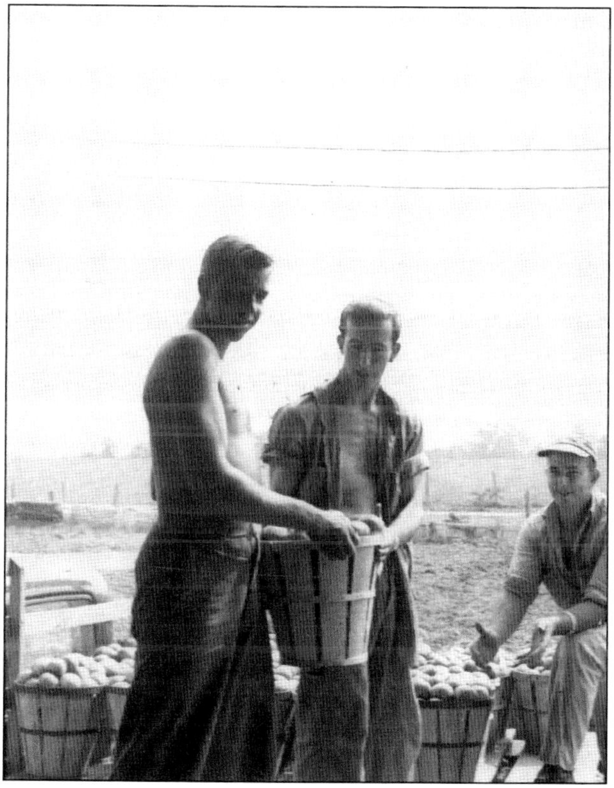

Three Kessler sons, Bill (left), Jerry (center), and Ed, load tomatoes for market in 1953. In 1974, the state's Green Acres Program purchased the farm for land preservation and reservoir development. From 1974 to 1986, these three Kessler sons rented the farm and operated it on a year-to-year lease until 1986. Ed was in charge of seeding and spraying. Jerry delivered produce to the distant markets. Bill oversaw the personnel and delivered produce to local markets.

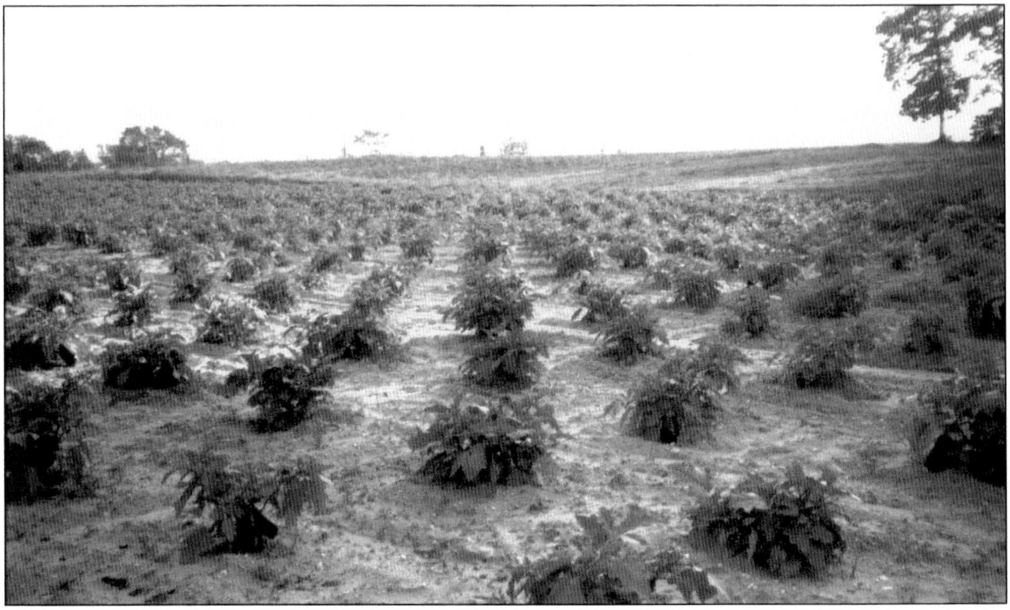

This photograph was taken in the final year of Kessler Farms' operation. The farm closed so the Manasquan River Reservoir could be built on a majority of the property in 1986. Although the state had plans for developing a model farm for the remainder, the project never materialized. Dean Kessler continued limited farming after 1986. Today, part of the original Kessler Farms property is rented to John Tobias of North Atlantic Farms.

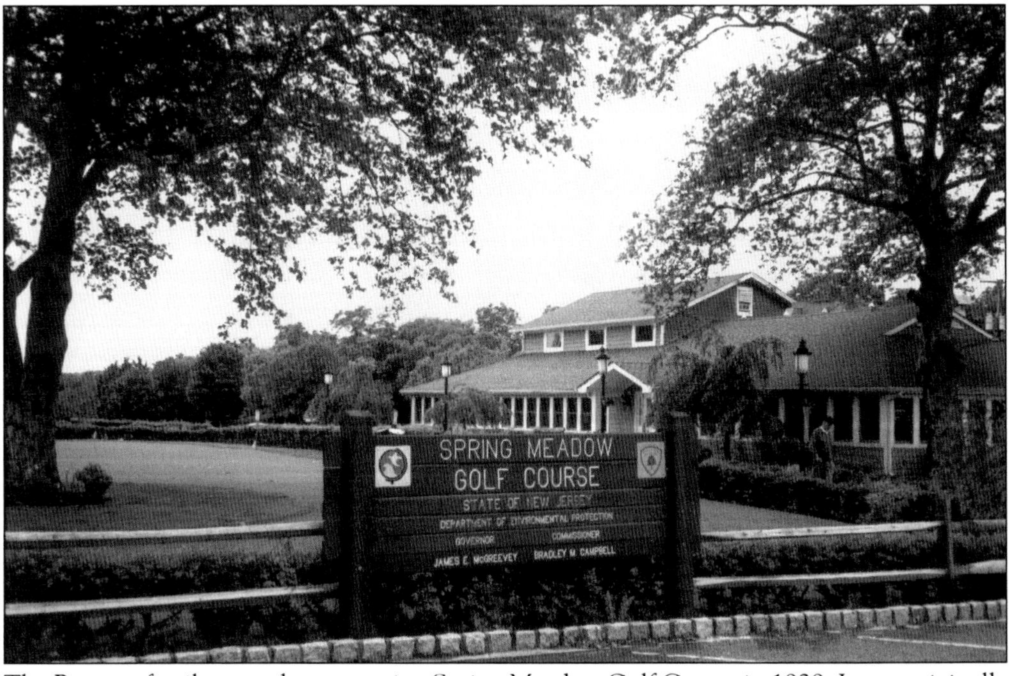

The Bennett family started constructing Spring Meadow Golf Course in 1929. It was originally a nine-hole course and then expanded south of the Manasquan River to include 18 holes. Like Kessler Farms, Spring Meadow was purchased and taken over by the state in the 1970s. Still in operation today, it is the only state-owned golf course in New Jersey.

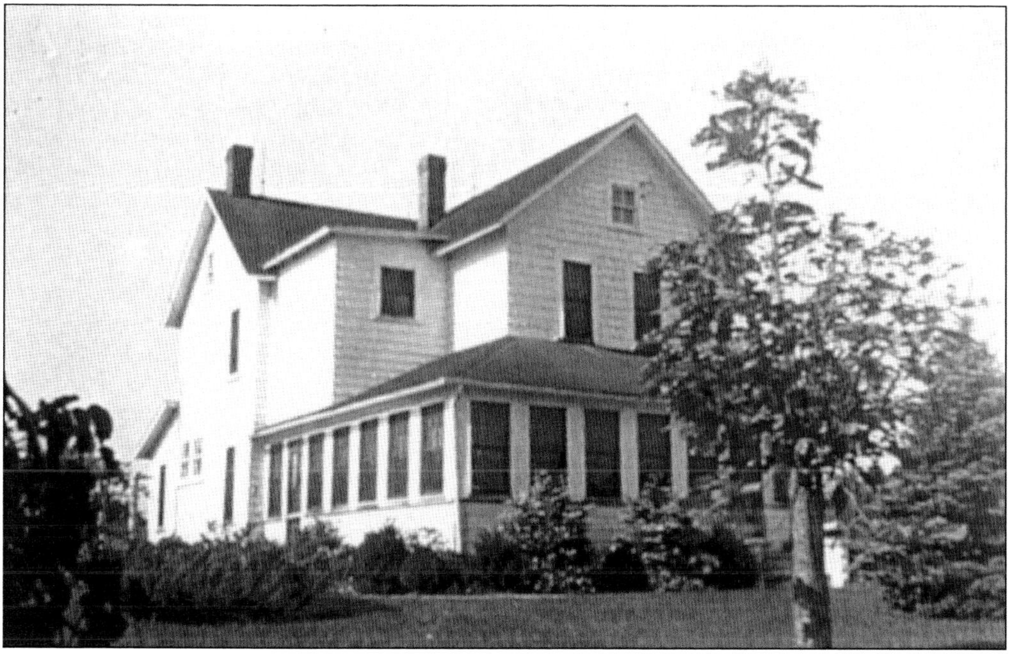

Pictured *c.* 1930, the Thompson family farmhouse at Allaire later burned down and was replaced by a modern country home. Next to Kessler Farms was Meadow Brook Farm, owned and operated by the Thompson family. Today, former Wall Township mayor Donald Corson owns part of the original Thompson farm.

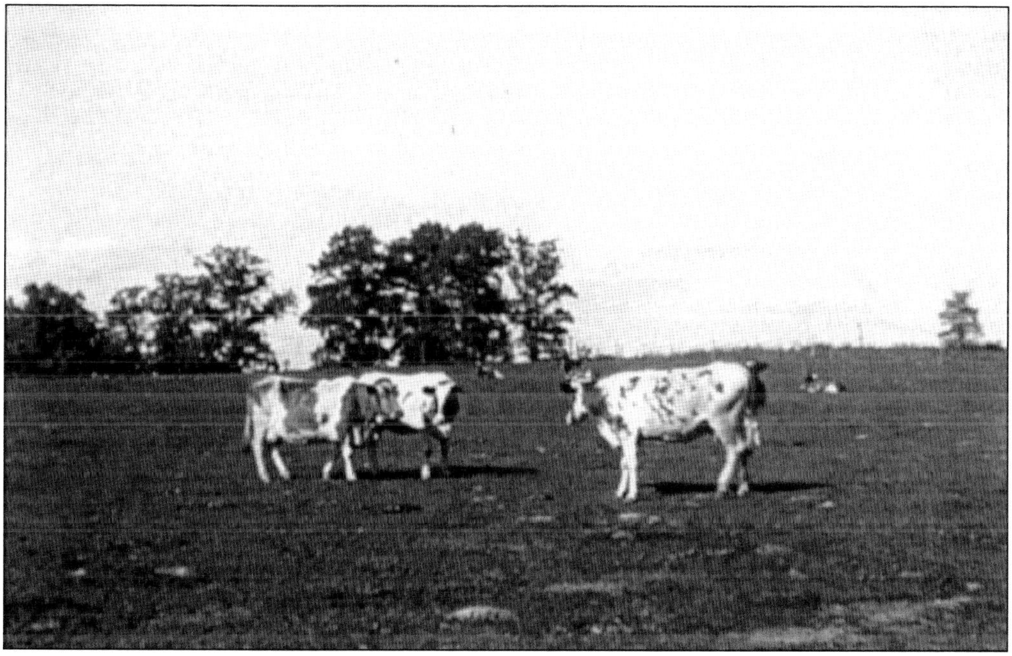

This view shows the Thompsons' Meadow Brook Farm at Allaire in the early 1900s. For 43 years (from the 1920s to the 1960s), the Thompsons' pasteurized milk and had an expansive milk route serving the immediate area, shore communities, Point Pleasant, and Bay Head. They had a herd of cows that included Jersey (solid brown) and Holstein cows.

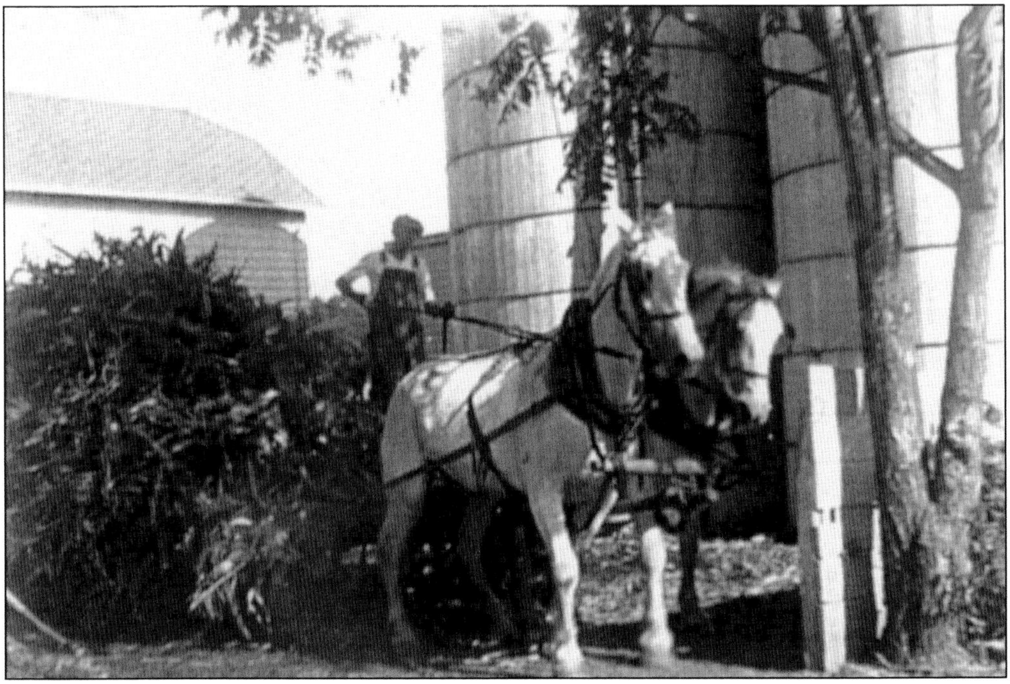

Lloyd Thomson (above) loads cornstalks to fill the silo (below). Thomson attended the school that was once located on the second floor of the Allaire Village Bakery. He was a graduate of Rider College. Lloyd and Harriet Thomson had four children—Marge Thompson L'Hommidieu, Louise Thompson King, George Thomson, and Gilbert Thomson.

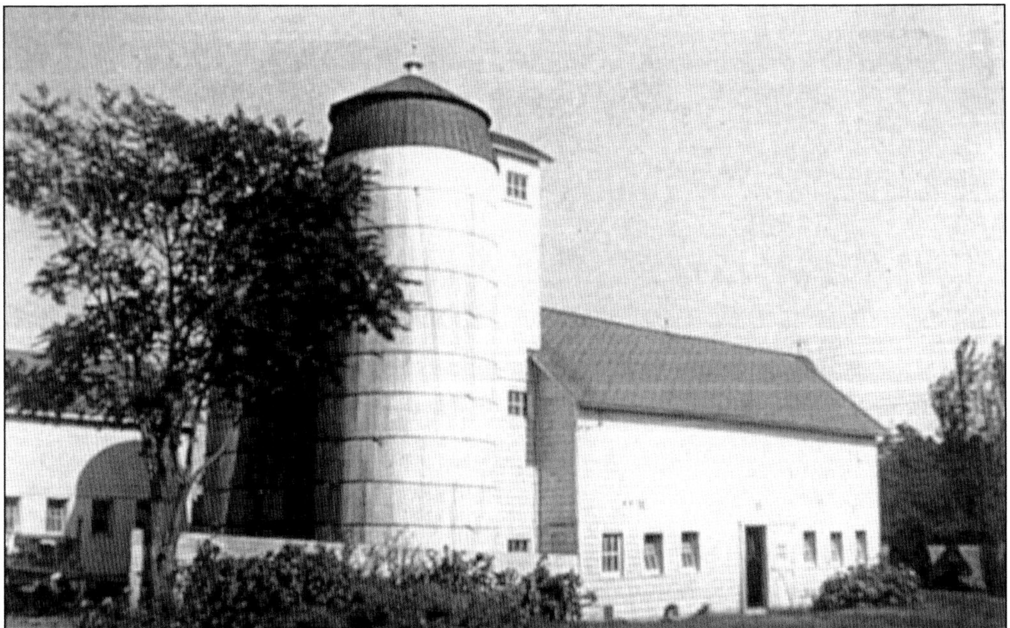

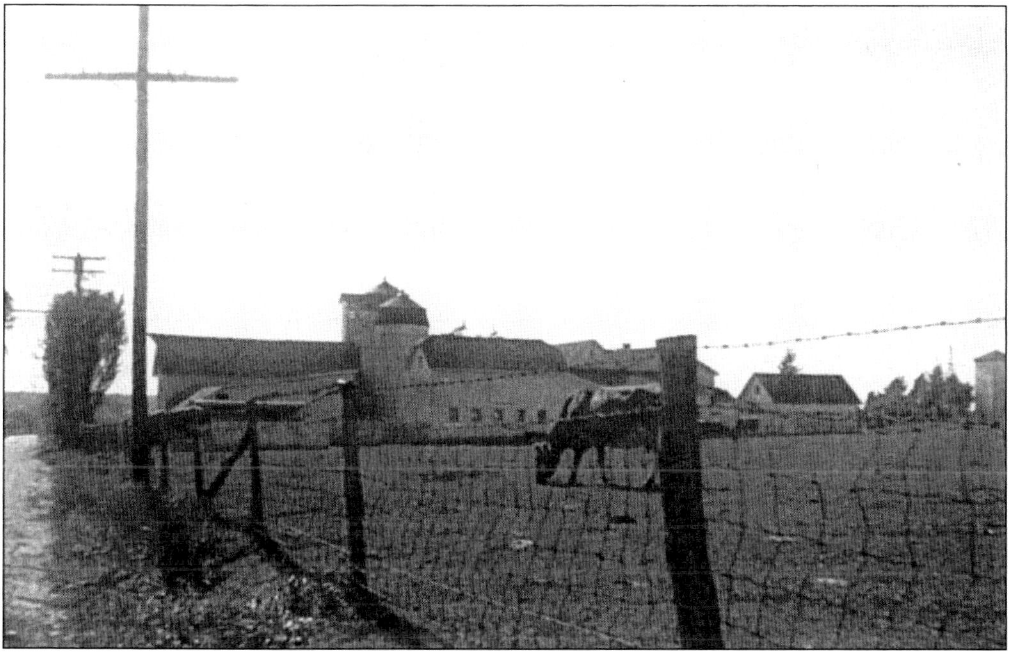

Taken *c.* 1930, this photograph looks down Hospital Road at the Thompson farm. Meadow Brook Farm stretched from Atlantic Avenue to the Manasquan River. Many of these farm buildings still stand today.

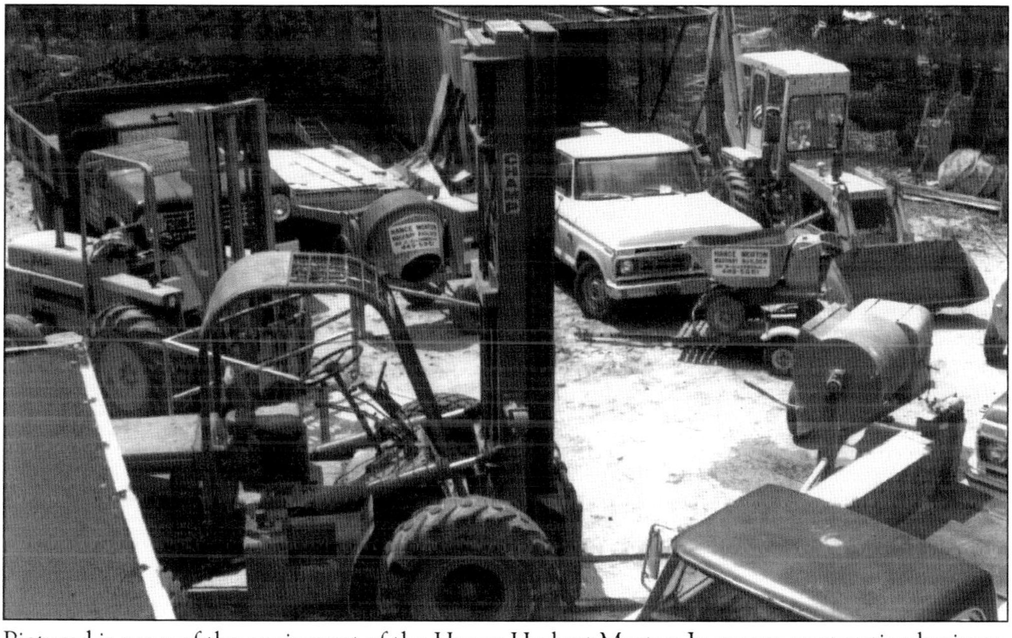

Pictured is some of the equipment of the Hance Herbert Morton Jr. mason contracting business. Started in 1951, the business was based out of Hance and Evelyn's Allaire home. Morton capitalized on the urbanization and the suburban growth that ensued after millions of World War II veterans returned home. He operated one of the largest non-union mason businesses around and built many homes, post offices, churches, commercial buildings, and town halls in central New Jersey.

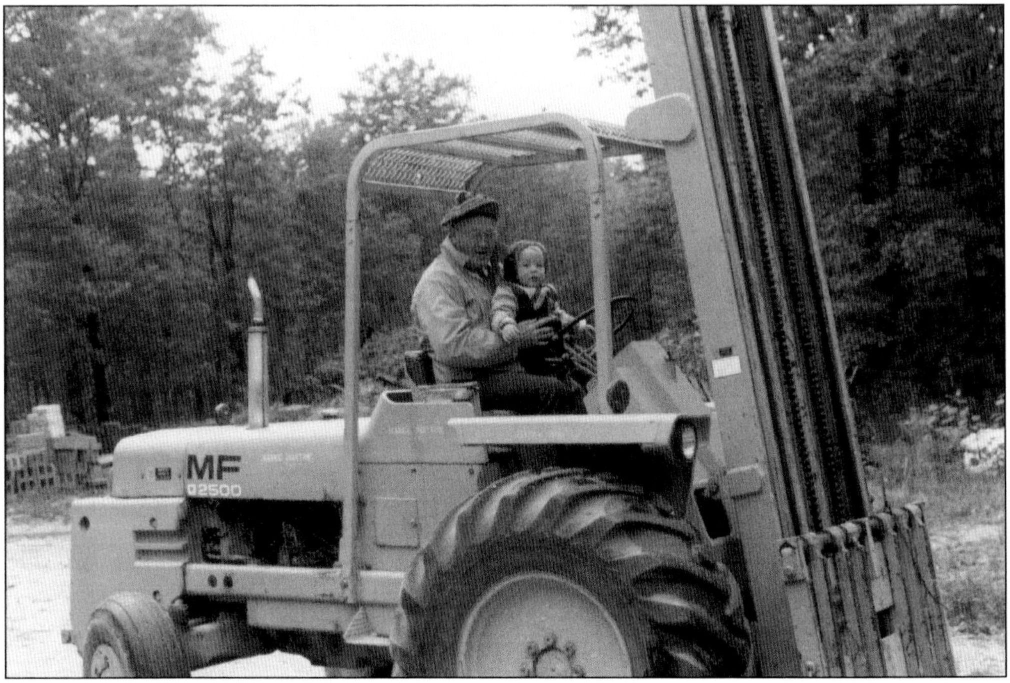

The author, Hance Morton Sitkus, and his grandfather Hance Herbert "Red" Morton Jr. are pictured on a forklift in 1979. Morton was born in Manasquan, and his ancestors have lived in the area since 1667. He was a Sea Bee in the Pacific during World War II. He retired in 1987 after 44 years as a mason contractor. Morton also served as Wall Township committeeman and was on the board of directors for Manasquan Savings Bank.

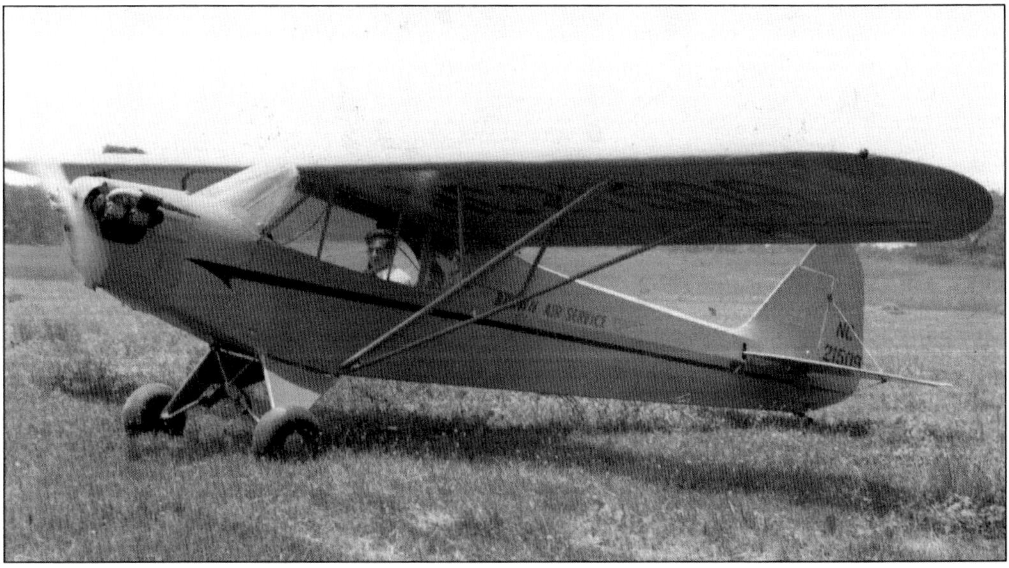

In 1937, Ed Brown bought his first airplane (pictured) after working out a payment plan with the seller, Morgan Barber of New England. The Cub plane was delivered to Brown in Belmar on Shark River. Born in 1917, Ed Brown was educated in Spring Lake and graduated from Rider College. While commuting home from college, Brown stopped off at Hightstown and paid $1 for a demonstration ride aboard an airplane. He was instantly hooked.

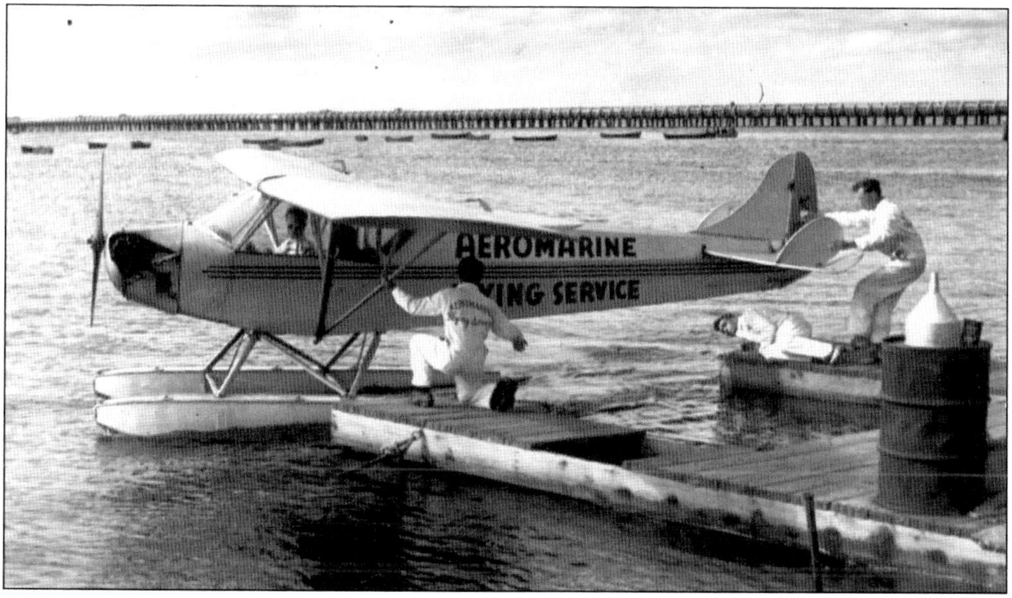

Ed Brown first kept his airplane on the water, as seen near the Seaside Heights Bridge. He also used Chapman's Boat Yard on the Manasquan River. Brown says that he learned how to fly by reading instructional books and by trial and error. Taking his A & P boss out for a trial run once, Brown took a couple of hours to land the plane safely on the Manasquan River. His boss thought he was just showing off when he kept bouncing off the water.

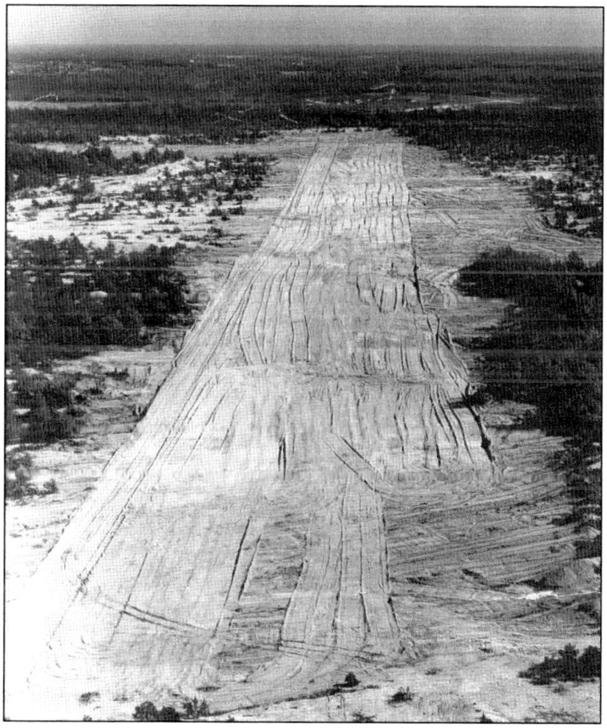

In 1937, Ed Brown began clearing the property he rented and later bought from the Brisbane family to construct the runway, as seen here in 1944. Prior to Brown's ownership, the Brisbanes had rented out the land to various gravel pit companies. After one company went bankrupt in 1929, Martha Chadwick and Elmer Geren (Monmouth County representative to Congress) formed the New Jersey Gravel Company and rented the property until it was sold to Brown. As arranged in the sale terms, New Jersey Gravel continued to obtain sand and gravel from Brown.

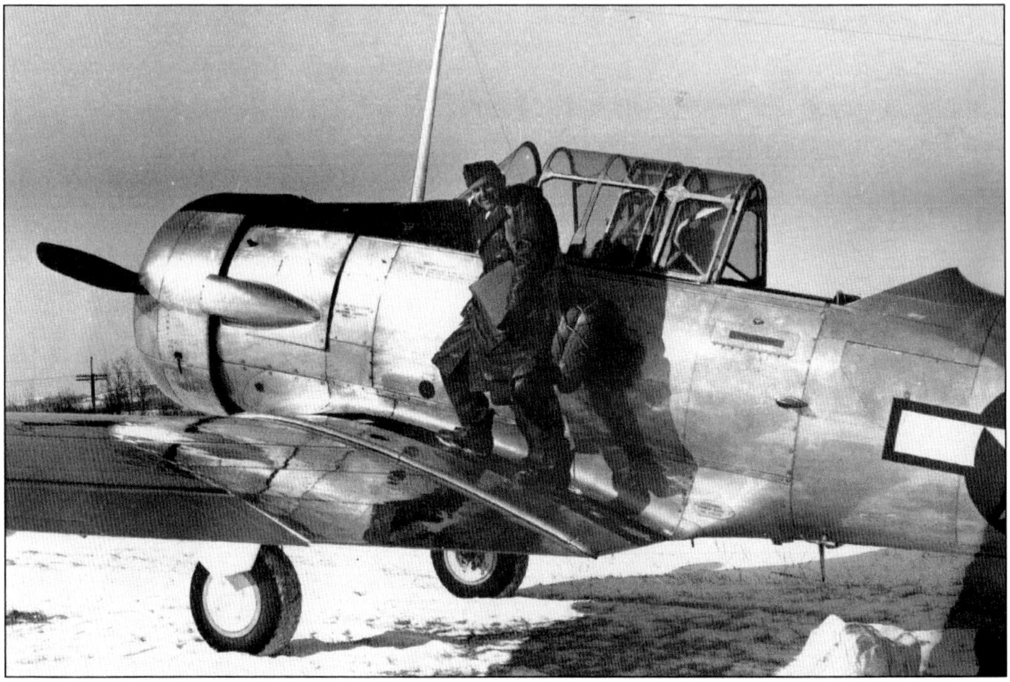

Ed Brown is pictured *c.* 1942 with his U.S. Navy plane. He was based out of Floyd Bennett Field Naval Station in Brooklyn, New York. While in the navy during World War II, Brown was engaged to take aerial photographs, principally along the Hudson River, of business enterprises that had won government war contracts or used government-loaned equipment. His aerial photographs were also used for geographical concerns. He came out of the navy in 1945 and devoted his life to developing an airport.

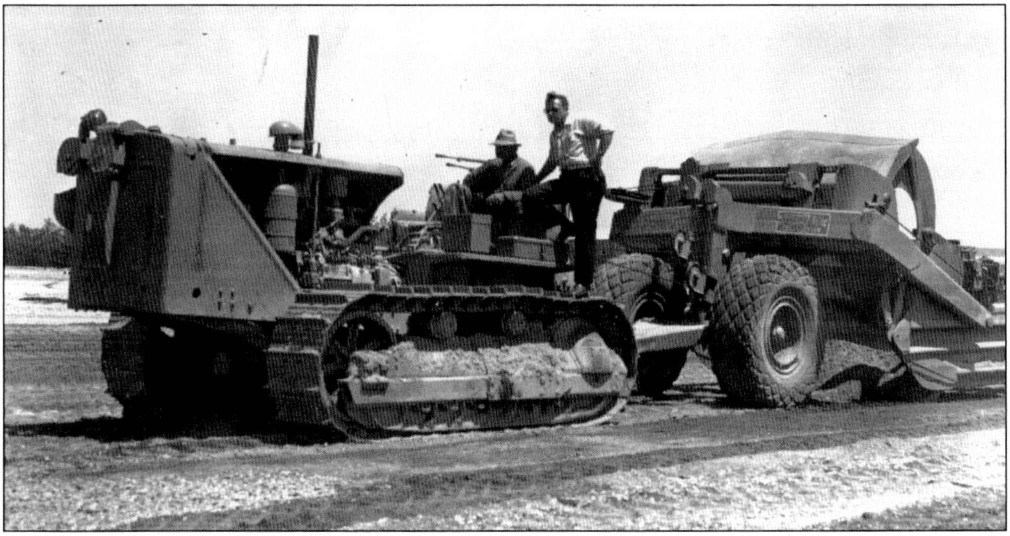

This earthmoving equipment was used to construct Allaire Airport. In the 1940s, Ed Brown bought surplus earthmoving equipment from the navy in Jacksonville, Florida. After Brown was unable to borrow equipment from Wall Township to help clear the runway, the Belmar mayor led him to the town's American Legion. The group let Brown use a World War I tank. A railroad rail was attached to the tank to help grade the runway.

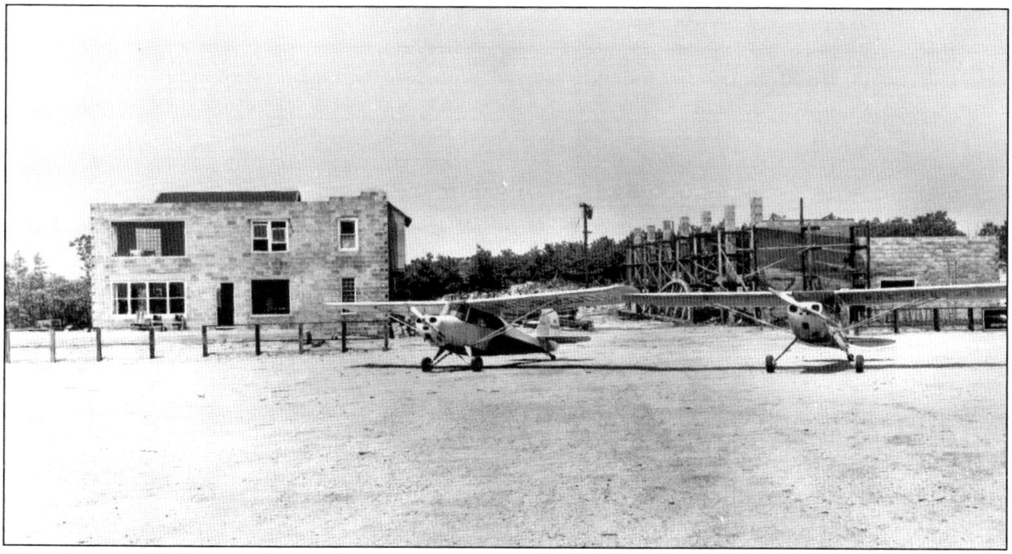

This August 1945 view shows the construction of building No. 1 at the airport. This building would serve as a flight school and have a second-floor apartment for Ed Brown. He has always lived on airport property and continues to do so today. The runway, originally 1,500 feet long, is now 7,400 feet. Today, there are 71 buildings at the airport.

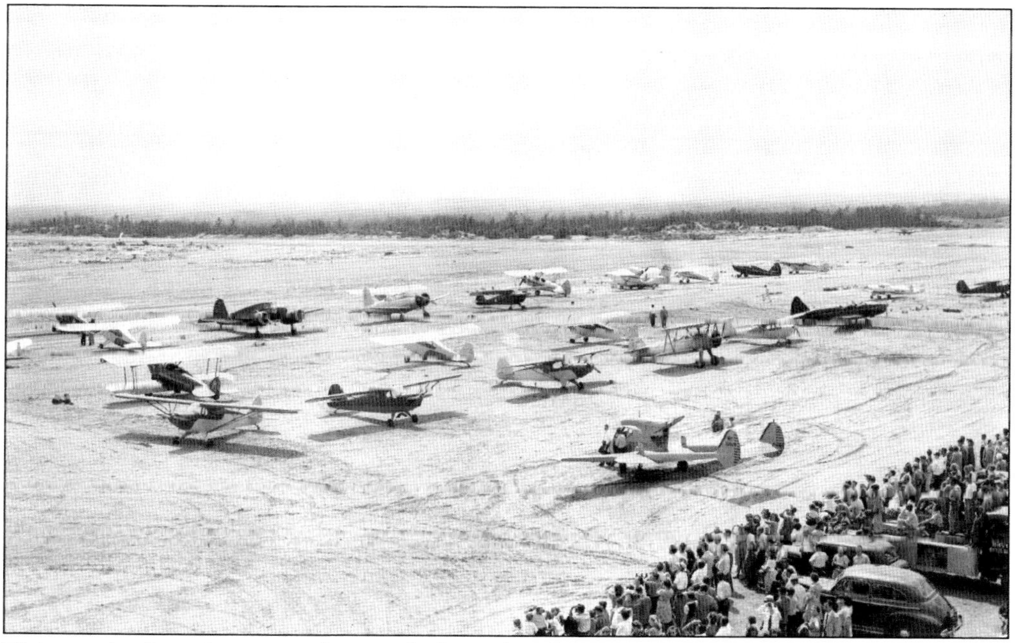

This was the first of many air shows to be hosted at the airport. Soon after this picture was taken in September 1945, Ed Brown began building private hangers. Today there are more than 100 hangers and 270 airplanes at the airport. In the 1970s, Brown launched the Monmouth Airline, transporting mostly business travelers to Washington, D.C., New York, Boston, and Florida. He later sold the airline.

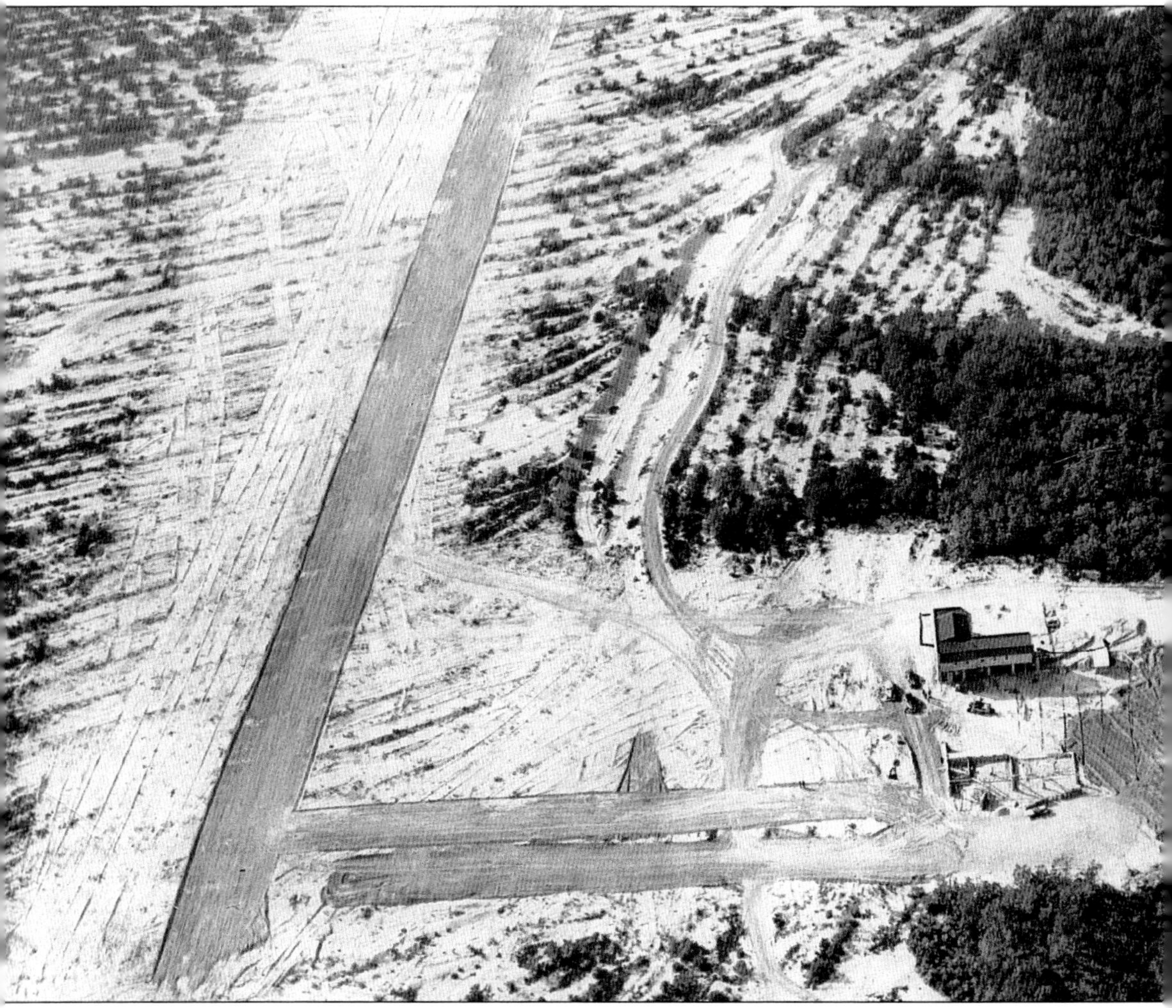

The airport officially opened in September 1945, shortly after this aerial photograph of the airport was taken. The airport has changed names many times over the years. It was first called Belmar Airport and then Monmouth Airport, Allaire Airport, and (today) Monmouth Executive Airport. Ed Brown even considered naming the airport after the Brisbane family for their kindness in selling him the land.

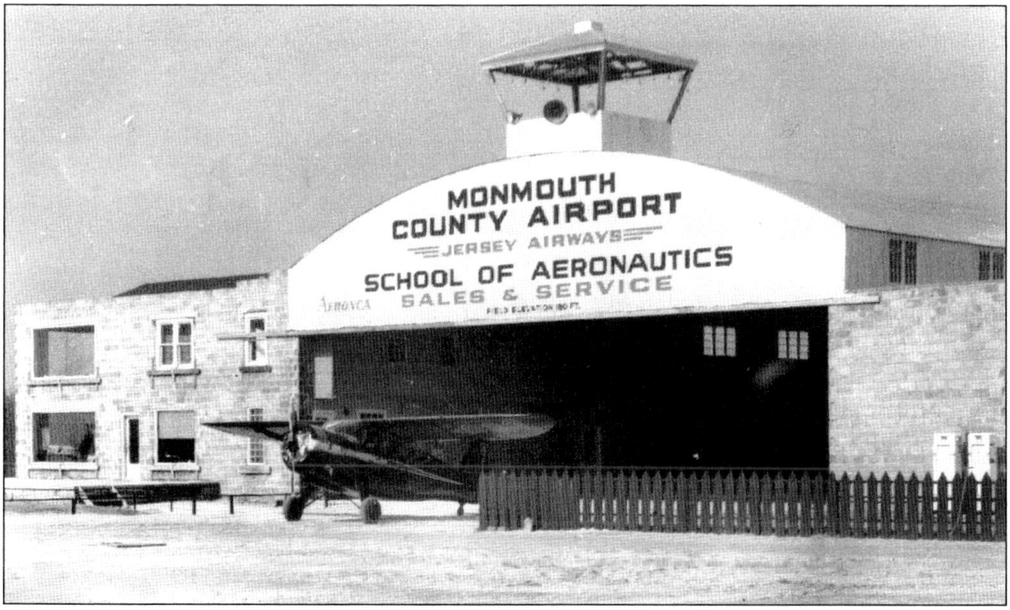

The purpose of Ed Brown's airport from the start was to host a flight school. Brown got his flight instructor's license in 1940 and first taught evening aviation classes at local colleges. Today, there are three flight schools and one helicopter training facility. Skydiving is also popular. Piper airplanes are sold on the property, selling largely to graduates. Brown taught the Piper grandchildren how to fly.

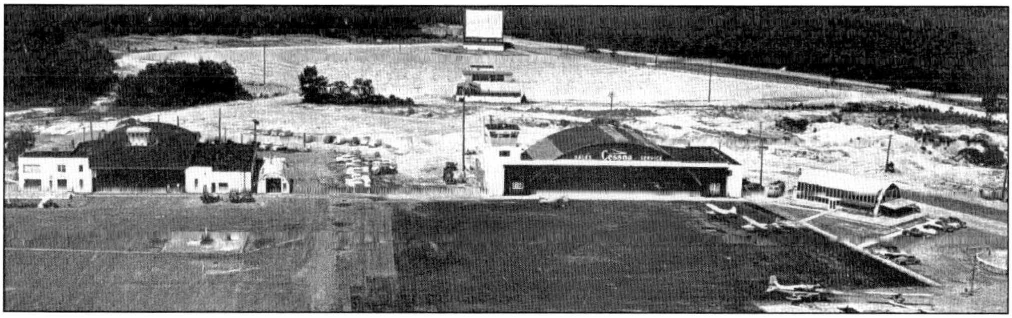

This aerial photograph shows the multiuse Allaire Airport. Brown used the airport in many ways over the years to make money. He opened a fly-in-drive-in movie theater in 1947, as seen in the background of this photograph. He opened two others in Manahawkin and Toms River. He also opened and operated for a few years a golf driving range and playground, known as Ed Brown's Playground, on airport property. Upon opening, the airport was a noted fuel stop. Columbia Aircraft runs the fueling business today, and there is self service and full service.

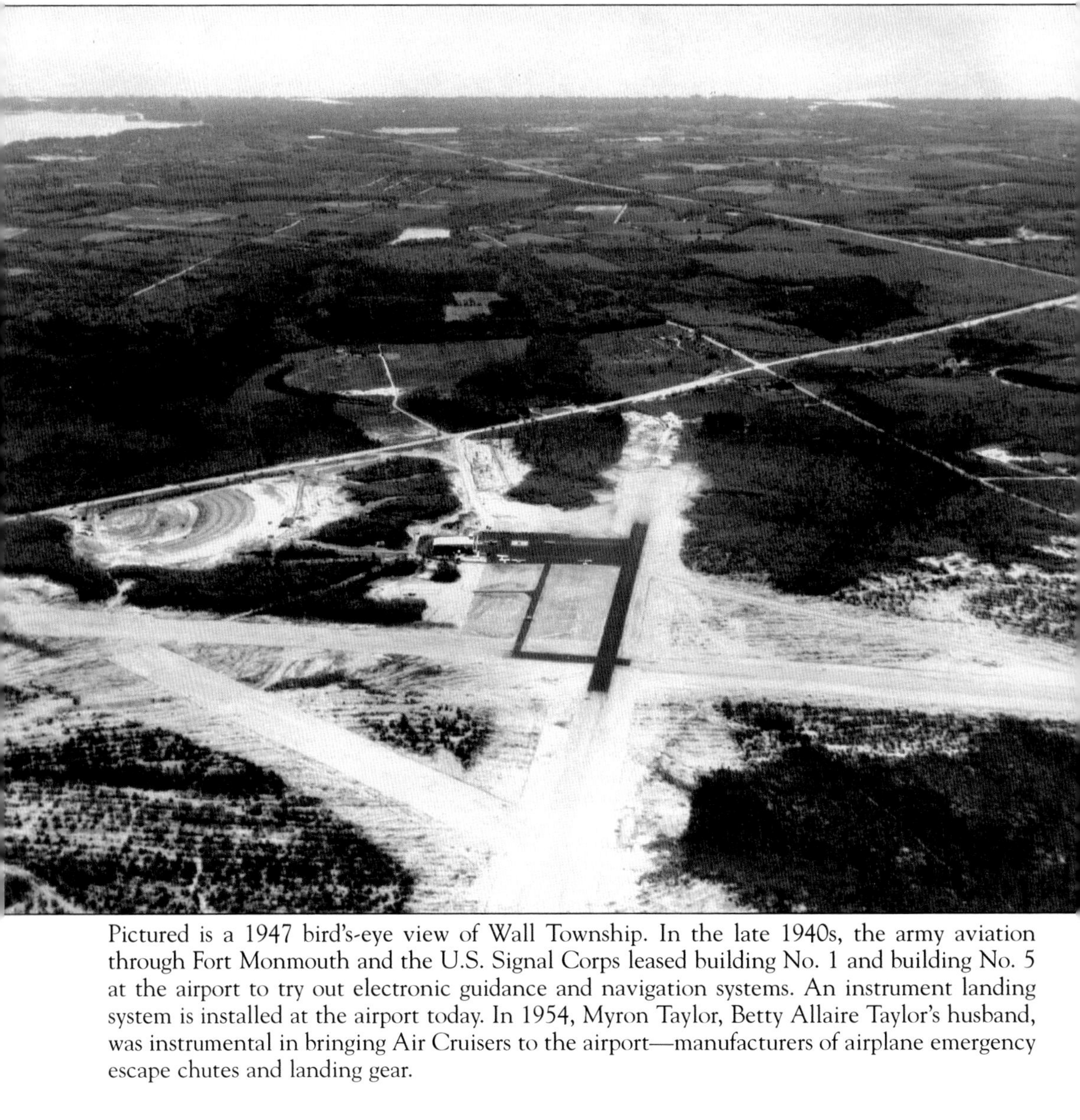

Pictured is a 1947 bird's-eye view of Wall Township. In the late 1940s, the army aviation through Fort Monmouth and the U.S. Signal Corps leased building No. 1 and building No. 5 at the airport to try out electronic guidance and navigation systems. An instrument landing system is installed at the airport today. In 1954, Myron Taylor, Betty Allaire Taylor's husband, was instrumental in bringing Air Cruisers to the airport—manufacturers of airplane emergency escape chutes and landing gear.

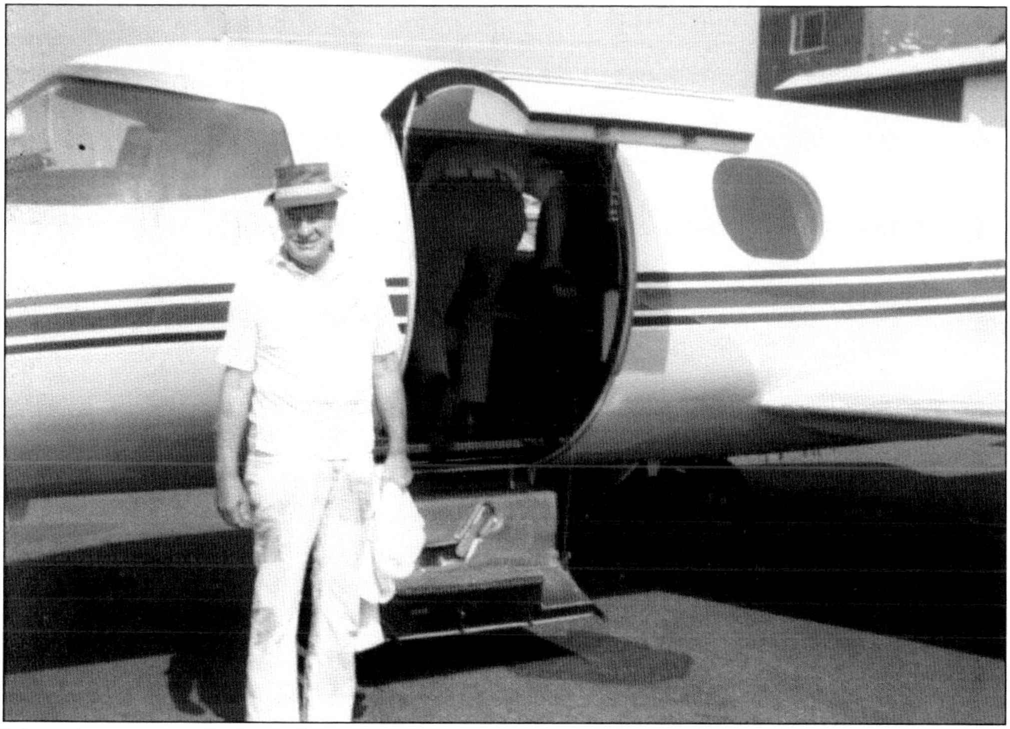

Many famous people have flown in and out of Allaire Airport, including Bob Hope, as seen here in the 1970s. Once, in the 1960s, Ed Brown recalls catching Hope as he fell out of the plane while trying to open the door. Others include performers at the PNC (Garden State) Arts Center, Bruce Springstein, Jimmy Buffet, Bob Dole, Richard Nixon, Gerald Ford, the Kennedys, Bon Jovi, many politicians, and even the prime minister of Malaysia.

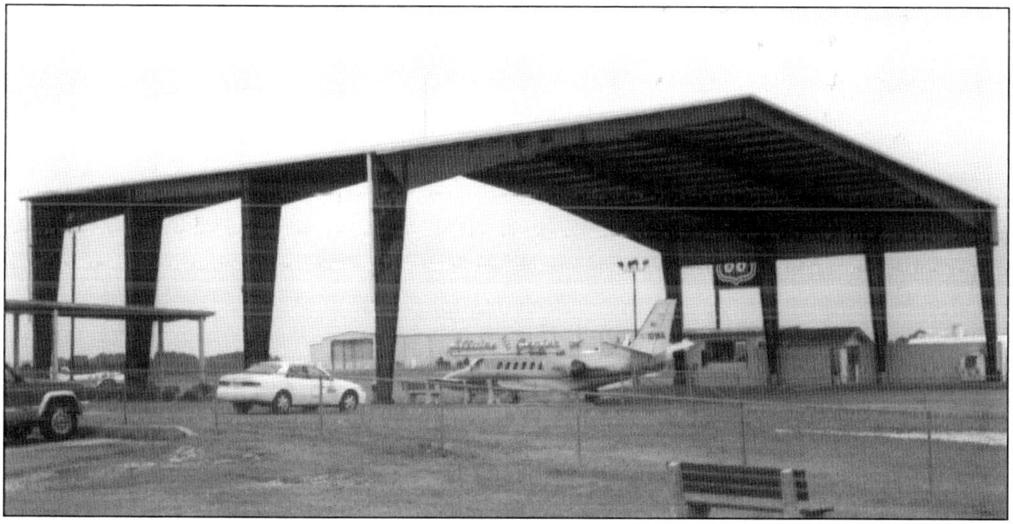

The Allaire Expo Center (background) was built in 1987 and is the largest building (44,000 square feet) at the airport. The center featured three aviation trade shows. Ross Perot gave campaign speeches from the center, broadcast on national television. Today, the Allaire Expo Center is used by Air Cruisers. The canopy, built in 1985, provides shelter for passengers. It was the first of its kind and later copied by other airports.

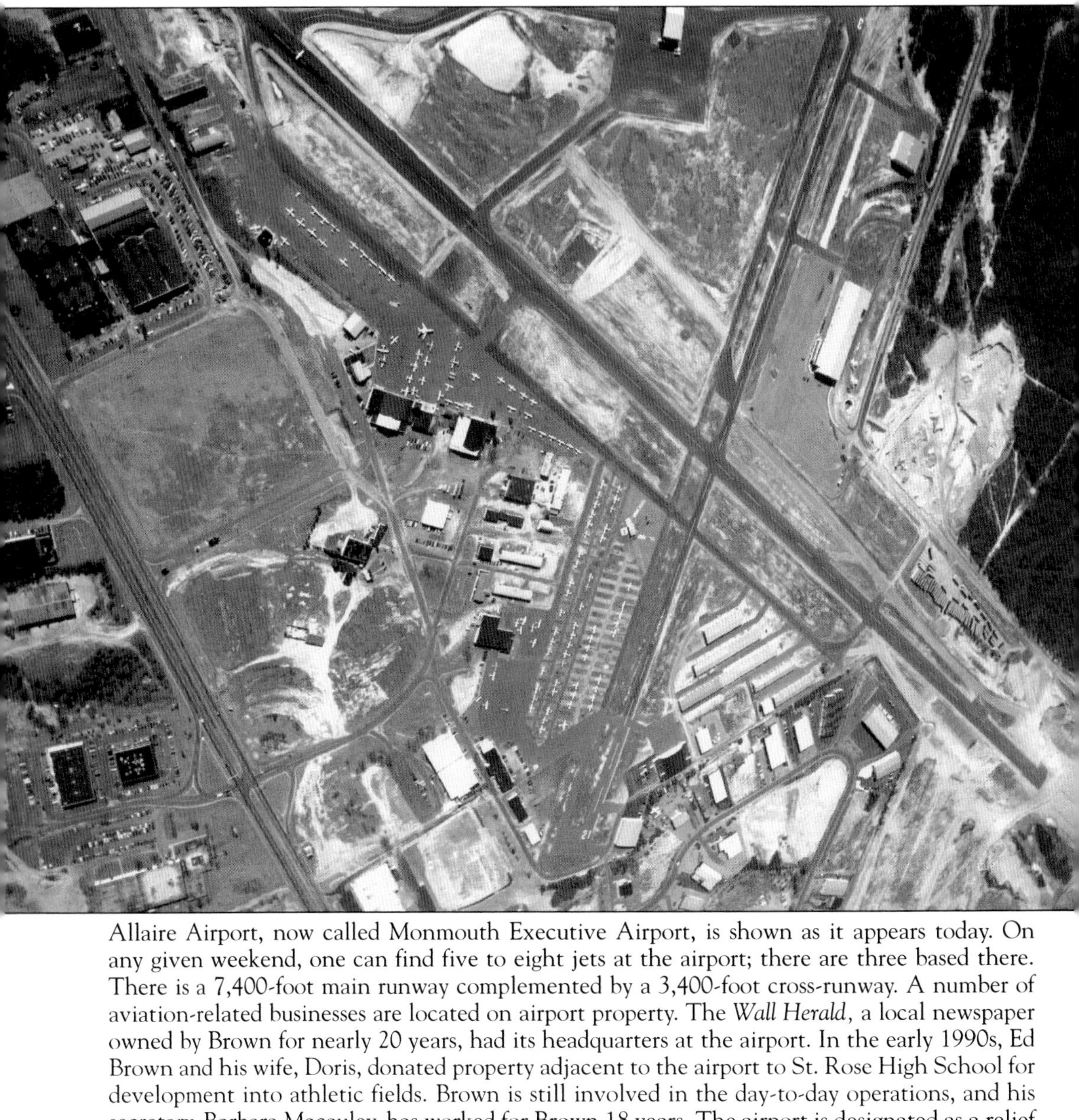

Allaire Airport, now called Monmouth Executive Airport, is shown as it appears today. On any given weekend, one can find five to eight jets at the airport; there are three based there. There is a 7,400-foot main runway complemented by a 3,400-foot cross-runway. A number of aviation-related businesses are located on airport property. The *Wall Herald*, a local newspaper owned by Brown for nearly 20 years, had its headquarters at the airport. In the early 1990s, Ed Brown and his wife, Doris, donated property adjacent to the airport to St. Rose High School for development into athletic fields. Brown is still involved in the day-to-day operations, and his secretary, Barbara Macauley, has worked for Brown 18 years. The airport is designated as a relief airport for the New York area. Currently, Monmouth County is considering purchasing it.